LATE MEDIEVAL ENGLAND

(1377–1485)

LATE MEDIEVAL ENGLAND (1377–1485)

A BIBLIOGRAPHY OF HISTORICAL SCHOLARSHIP

1990–1999

JOEL T. ROSENTHAL

Medieval Institute Publications

WESTERN MICHIGAN UNIVERSITY

Kalamazoo, Michigan, USA—2003

Library of Congress Cataloging-in-Publication Data

Rosenthal, Joel Thomas, 1934-
    Late medieval England (1377-1485) : a bibliography of
historical scholarship, 1990-1999 / Joel T. Rosenthal.
        p. cm.
Includes index.
    ISBN 1-58044-075-4 (alk. paper)
    1. Great Britain--History--Lancaster and York,
1399-1485--Bibliography. 2. Great Britain--History--Richard II,
1377-1399--Bibliography. 3. England--Civilization--1066-1485--
Bibliography. 4. Middle Ages--Bibliography. I. Title.
    Z2017.R69 2003
    [DA245]
    016.94703'8--dc21
                                                    2003009262

ISBN 1-58044-075-4

Cover design by Linda K. Judy

Printed in the United States of America

CONTENTS

INTRODUCTION

Much of what wisdom I have to offer about this kind of project was expended when I compiled and published a comparable volume, about a decade ago, on the scholarship produced between 1975 and 1989 on Ricardian, Lancastrian, and Yorkist England. As in my earlier volume, I have once again given the Celtic areas of the Islands short shrift. This is not as logical or as defensible as it once might have been, and if I ever offer a third volume of this sort I will keep my own strictures about "the new British history" in mind.

That said, the chronological boundaries of 1377 and 1485 do not seem as contentious as they once did. Largely due to the scholarly work of Geoffrey Elton and J. R. Lander, we worried, not too many years ago, about the gulf—or was it the absence of a gulf?—between the England of the Yorkist dynasty and that of the early Tudors. This aspect of the perennial issue of historical periodization no longer seems to have a very strong pull on our consciousness; we now feel relatively free to cross the divide of 1485 pretty casually, and in either direction, if and when we so choose. It is usually pretty easy to decide whether work that focuses on fourteenth-century England gives sufficient attention to the world of post-1377 to merit inclusion here. At the same time, I have tried to take a firm line about *not* covering work that deals with events after Henry VII's accession—though there are numerous exceptions and instances of editorial fudging.

When I covered the impressive corpus of work done between 1975 and 1989, I was struck by the spate of scholarly production, aware as I was that my coverage was far from complete. In this volume I have included almost the same number of entries (1910 items in the volume published in 1994; 1889 here: a few missed

vii

numbers, a few duplicates) and now it is for a mere decade of work, rather than fifteen years. Though I like to think I have become a better bibliographer, in the sense that I have missed fewer items that should have been included, the large number of entries for the 1990s perhaps owes more to the dedicated labor of hundreds of scholars around the world than it does to my enhanced note-taking prowess. A steady stream of colleagues, young and old, male and female, are ready, willing, and eager to publish their scholarly findings. So much for the decline of academia, the fading appeal of the Middle Ages, and the dreaded dilemma of finding an outlet for one's work.

The traditional gulf or gap between History and the various forms of literary research and analysis has obviously been the subject of a good deal of discussion—or controversy—in recent years. In compiling this bibliography I have tried to avoid items that focused primarily or extensively on what we would call creative writing, though academic historians certainly read historical sources with more sensitivity to rhetoric and the framing of authorial discourse (and of reception) than we once did. At least at this level of interdisciplinarity it is hard to think of the closing of the gap between history and literature as anything other than "a good thing," and for the most part the historical discipline and its most closely related "sister" disciplines have escaped the worst ravages of the culture wars. The comparative lengths of the chapters and numbers of items therein, as they appear below—at least as I have organized the material in the search for clarity and convenience—hardly gives much support to those who warn us of the imminent demise of the more traditional lines of historical endeavor and inquiry. Political history, in its various guises, continues to flourish, and there probably is more military history being written today for the general scholarly audience than was the case in 1975. Social history, women's history, family history, demography, and other forms of "the new social" history hold their own, as do inquiries into education, intellectual history, the Church both as an institution and as a body of living doctrine, and virtually any and all forms of work in the arts.

So I seem to be saying, in the cumbersome way that academics move forward, that the sub-fields of academic history are not so different from what they were a few decades ago. Conservative voices in academia love to lament the supposed eclipse of older focal points of scholarly interest, just as they love to condemn what they see as threatening trends, such as feminism and gender studies, that detract from "the canon." But this agenda of denunciation and Cassandra-like breast-beating is political rather than intellectual, and it is in no significant way supported by a sober analysis or assessment of what historians are working on, how they frame their findings, or how they talk to each other. Many rooms in the mansion, and no one has to sleep in all of them.

When I compiled my previous bibliography I said that I had begun my labors with the idea of covering "everything." I soon came to realize that in mere quantitative terms this is not a meaningful statement. Nor, given the problems of disciplinary boundaries, of late publication, of missing volumes (and no library ever has everything), and of obscure references (some by me to myself), are there any hard-and-fast substantive or conceptual boundaries to the history of late medieval England. I end this current work with full awareness that I could continue to add items almost indefinitely—except that there must come a time to bring things to an end. I apologize to authors who have been omitted, as I do to those who have suffered from my errors and, particularly, from infelicitous attempts at one-line summations that have gone astray. It is not easy to catch the substance of serious work—often the product of many years of thought and research—in a mere line or two, though I have usually been willing to try. The major exception to my efforts at one-liners pertains to entries on Julian of Norwich. After cobbling together one short statement after another about someone whose mystical writings are invariably a closed book to my secular and skeptical mind, I decided that those who use this volume might be best served if I just gave the reference and publication information on England's favorite recluse or anchorite.

Many libraries have extended their hospitality and resources as I worked my way toward closure. My three main databases (beyond what I myself had bought and shelved over the years) were the collections of my home library (The Melville Library, State University of New York at Stony Brook), those of the Institute of Historical Research of the University of London, and those of the reference and research division of the New York Public Library. Numerous other libraries were generous about offering access to their collections (and giving advice on how to use them): The Regenstein Library of the University of Chicago, The British Library, Columbia University, the American Numismatic Society, and various branches of the University of London: The Senate House Library, the Institute of Education, and the library of the Warburg Institute.

I usually owe some sort of debt, by the time I have finished a project, to such friends as Carolyn Barron, Carole Rawcliffe, Barrie Dobson, and Ralph Griffiths. This project is no exception. Specific advice from Phyllis Roberts and Michael Jones (University of Nottingham) steered me to some materials when I sought their guidance, and they helped me avoid errors both of commission and of omission. The staff of Medieval Institute Publications (MIP) at Western Michigan University encouraged me to pursue this enterprise, from early days through the fine tuning of editorial supervision and production. Tom Seiler, Candy Porath, Julie Scrivener, and Pat Hollahan, with the blessings of Paul Szarmach, have made it all possible, and others at MIP who have lent a hand to the editorial and the production side of publishing—both for this volume and for many others in which I have been a party—deserve any and all thanks an author can extend. Once again I have had the good fortune to have Juleen Eichinger as editor for this text. That alone raises it about two notches in accuracy and consistency. And last but hardly least: my wife is always supportive and helpful concerning my research. But this time she decided that this bibliography was to be the battlefield on which I would finally be called upon to wage the epic struggle for converting from the use of WordPerfect to that of WORD. Whether she was my opponent across a bleak and unfriendly no-man's-land, or my kindly squadron leader in the dark days of hanging indents and automatic italics is still not clear. But she says she has put up with so many things over the years that a little more marital recalcitrance and a good bit of computer ignorance are hard to take all that seriously. I dedicate this volume to her and her tutelage.

ABBREVIATIONS

AgHR	*Agricultural History Review*
AJLH	*American Journal of Legal History*
Antiq J	*Antiquaries Journal*
Arch Ael	*Archaeologia Aeliana*
Arch Cant	*Archaeologia Cantiana*
Arch J	*Archaeological Journal*
BJRUL	*Bulletin of the John Rylands University Library*
BNJ	*British Numismatic Journal*
Cornwall	*Proceedings of the Royal Institute of Cornwall*
Cumberland	*Transactions of the Cumberland and Westmorland Antiquarian and Archaeological Society*
D & C NQ	*Devon and Cornwall Notes and Queries*
Devon	*Transactions of the Devonshire Association*
Dorset	*Dorset Natural History and Archaeological Society*
DR	*Downside Review*
EcHR	*Economic History Society*
EETS	*Early English Text Society*
EHR	*English Historical Review*
Essex	*Transactions of the Essex Archaeological Society*
Hampshire	*Proceedings of the Hampshire Field Club*
HMSO	Her Majesty's Stationery Office
HR	*Historical Review*
JBAA	*Journal of the British Archaeological Association*
JBS	*Journal of British Studies*
J Eccl H	*Journal of Ecclesiastical History*
JIH	*Journal of Interdisciplinary History*

JLH	*Journal of Legal History*
JM & EMS	*Journal of Medieval and Early Modern Studies*
JM & RS	*Journal of Medieval and Renaissance Studies*
JMH	*Journal of Medieval History*
JSA	*Journal of the Society of Archivists*
Leeds	*Leeds Studies in English*
Leicester	*Transactions of the Leicestershire Archaeological and Historical Society*
LHR	*Law and History Review*
Lincoln	*Lincolnshire History and Archaeology*
London & Middlesex	*Transactions of the London and Middlesex Archaeological Society*
MBS	*Proceedings of the Monumental Brass Society*
Med Pros	*Medieval Prosopography*
Midland	*Midland History*
MQ	*Mystics Quarterly*
Norfolk	*Norfolk Archaeology*
Northants	*Northamptonshire Past and Present*
Northern	*Northern History*
Nottingham	*Nottingham Medieval Studies*
Oxon	*Oxoniensia*
PBA	*Proceedings of the British Academy*
PRO	Public Record Office
RCHM	Royal Commission on Historical Manuscripts
Southern	*Southern History*
Suffolk	*Proceedings of the Suffolk Institute of Archaeology*
Sussex	*Sussex Archaeological Collections*
TRHS	*Transactions of the Royal Historical Society*
Wiltshire	*Wiltshire Archaeological and Natural History Magazine*
Worcestershire	*Transactions of the Worcestershire Archaeological Society*
YAJ	*Yorkshire Archaeological Journal*

I. EDITED VOLUMES AND COLLECTED PAPERS.[1]

1.   Aers, David, and Lynn Staley, eds. *The Powers of the Holy: Religion, Politics, and Gender in Late Medieval English Culture.* University Park, Penn., 1996. [Items 1171, 1172, 1415.]

2.   Archer, Rowena E., ed. *Crown, Government and People in the Fifteenth Century.* Stroud, 1995. [A 1992 Conference at Manchester College, Oxford, with introduction, pp. xiii–xix; items 210, 247, 257, 349, 369, 381, 784, 991, 1024.]

3.   Archer, Rowena E., and Simon Walker, eds. *Rulers and Ruled in Late Medieval England: Essays Presented to Gerald Harriss.* London, 1995. [With an appreciation and bibliography of Harriss, pp. vii–xxiv; items 180, 328, 351, 444, 480, 502, 585, 591, 645, 737, 819, 1205.]

4.   Aston, Margaret. *Faith and Fire: Popular and Unpopular Religion.* London and Rio Grande, Ohio, 1993. [Ten

---

[1] Volumes of collected papers are listed here if three or more of the volume's items are appropriate entries for this bibliography (as in item 1). If there are but two items, that which appears first in this volume carries the full reference and the other item is cross-referenced (as for items 921 and 925). Volumes of papers by a single author who worked on England, 1377–1485, are listed here if the volume was published in the 1990s, even if the papers in the volume first appeared before the 1990s (as in item 46). In a few cases, papers in an edited volume are too short to be given individual listings. In such cases the authors are listed under the volume's main entry, wherever that appears (as in item 12).

of Aston's papers, published 1979–90, looking at
Wycliffe, the Northern Renaissance, Iconoclasm, and
Huizinga; well illustrated, as in their original form.]

5.   Aston, Margaret, and Colin F. Richmond, eds. *Lollardy
       and the Gentry in the Later Middle Ages*. Stroud, 1997.
       [Items 1294, 1305, 1315, 1338, 1340, 1348, 1412, 1437,
       1445.]

6.   Atherton, Ian, Eric Fernie, Christopher Harper-Bill, and
       Hassell Smith, eds. *Norwich Cathedral: Church, City
       and Diocese, 1096–1996*. London and Rio Grande, Ohio,
       1996. [Items 1071, 1235, 1279, 1614, 1688, 1697, 1795,
       1825, 1849, 1886.]

7.   Barron, Caroline M., and Anne F. Sutton, eds. *Medieval
       London Widows, 1300–1500*. London and Rio Grande,
       Ohio, 1994. [Barron's introduction, "Widows' World in
       Later Medieval London," pp. xiii–xxxiv; items 828, 835,
       842, 851, 895, 910, 916, 927, 928, 937, 951.]

8.   Barron, Caroline M., and Nigel Saul, eds. *England and
       the Low Countries in the Late Middle Ages*. Stroud, 1995
       (paperback ed. 1998). [Valuable introduction by Barron
       on Anglo-Low countries relations, 1327–1477, pp. 1–25;
       items 473, 687, 709, 820, 1625, 1747, 1749, 1817.]

9.   Bassett, Steven, ed. *Death in Towns: Urban Responses to
       the Dying and the Dead, 100–1600*. Leicester and New
       York, 1992. [Covering a wide range of topics; relevant
       here are items 755, 995, 1005, 1011, 1527.]

10.   Bates, David, and Anne Curry, eds. *England and Nor-
       mandy in the Middle Ages*. Stroud, 1994. [A 1992
       Reading conference. Items 179, 226, 1031, 1775.]

11.   Beadle, Richard, and A. J. Piper, eds. *New Science Out of
       Old Books: Studies in Manuscripts and Early Printed
       Books in Honour of A. I. Doyle*. Aldershot and Brookfield,
       Vt., 1995. [Items 1245, 1303, 1405, 1793.]

12. Bertram, Jerome, ed. *Monumental Brasses as Art and History*. Stroud, 1996. [Foreword by Nigel Saul and short papers by Kay Staniland on costume, Claude Blair on interpretation, John Goodall on heraldry, Cecil Humphery-Smith on genealogy, and Bertram on historiography, iconography, inscriptions, and indents. Longer papers, items 1764, 1767, 1783. A valuable survey and assessment of current scholarly views.]

13. Biller, Peter, and R. Barrie Dobson, eds. *The Medieval Church: Universities, Heresy and the Religious Life: Essays in Honour of Gordon Leff*. Studies in Church History, Subsidia 11 (1999). [An appreciation of Leff by Gerald Aylmer, pp. 1–4, and a Leff bibliography, 1956–98, pp. 325–42, by Simon Ditchfield; items 1177, 1204, 1234, 1306, 1431, 1875.]

14. Blair, John, and Brian Golding, eds. *The Cloister and the World: Essays in Medieval History in Honour of Barbara Harvey*. Oxford, 1996. [An appreciation of Harvey by Jennifer Loach, pp. 1–3, and a bibliography, p. 4; items 433, 965 1198, 1528, 1875.]

15. Blake, Norman, ed. *The Cambridge History of the English Language: Volume II, 1066–1476*. Cambridge, 1992. [Blake's introduction, pp. 1–22, and "The Literary Language," pp. 500–42; items 633, 654.]

16. Bowers, Roger. *English Church Polyphony: Singers and Sources from the 14th to the 17th Century*. Aldershot, 1999. [Ten of Bowers's papers, five published in the 1990s.]

17. Brand, Paul. *The Making of the Common Law*. London and Rio Grande, Ohio, 1992. [Twenty of Brand's papers, from 1975 onwards: three published anew, plus Brand's introduction. His 1987 "Courtroom and Schoolroom: The Education of Lawyers in England prior to 1400" is reprinted (from *Historical Research*).]

18.   Britnell, Richard H., ed. *Daily Life in the Late Middle Ages*. Stroud, 1998. [With many illustrations. Introduction, pp. 1–3; items 771, 802, 944, 972, 976, 992, 1165A, 1336, 1604.]

19.   Britnell, Richard H., and Anthony J. Pollard, eds. *The McFarlane Legacy: Studies in Late Medieval Politics and Society*. Stroud and New York, 1995. [Introduction on McFarlane's influence, pp. xi–xviii; items 216, 296, 310, 313, 465, 481, 518, 912.]

20.   Britnell, Richard H., and John Hatcher, eds. *Progress and Problems in Medieval England: Essays in Honour of Edward Miller*. Cambridge, 1996. [An appreciation of Miller by George Holmes, pp. xiii–xiv, and a bibliography, pp. 308–17; items 531, 699, 704, 808, 1114, 1149, 1841, 1869.]

21.   Brown, Jacqueline, and William P. Stoneman, eds. *A Distant Voice: Medieval Studies in Honor of Leonard E. Boyle, O.P.* Notre Dame, Ind., 1997. [Bibliography of Boyle's writing, pp. 642–57; items 1386, 1554, 1613A.]

22.   Carley, James P., and Colin G. C. Tite, eds. *Books and Collectors, 1200–1700: Essays Presented to Andrew Watson*. London, 1997. [Eric Stanley on Watson at age seventy, pp. ix–xv, and a Watson bibliography, pp. 473–76; items 1493A, 1640, 1742.]

23.   Carlin, Martha, and Joel T. Rosenthal, eds. *Food and Eating in Medieval Europe*. London and Rio Grande, Ohio, 1998. [Items 642, 676, 931, 1003.]

24.   Catto, Jeremy I., and Ralph Evans, eds. *The History of the University of Oxford: Volume II: Late Medieval Oxford*. Oxford, 1992. [With maps, ground plans, and a list of properties outside the halls in 1444. Items 509, 1202, 1203, 1212, 1231, 1462, 1481, 1484, 1506, 1507, 1510, 1525, 1584, 1585, 1593, 1618, 1711, 1713.]

25. Chrimes, Stanley B., Charles D. Ross, and Ralph A. Griffiths, eds. *Fifteenth Century England, 1399–1509. Studies in Politics and Society.* Stroud, 1995. [A reissue of the seminal 1972 volume, the first of all the fifteenth-century conferences, with a foreword to the second edition by Griffiths, pp. ix–xiii. Original papers are by A. L. Brown, B. P. Wolffe, Ross, Chrimes, T. B. Pugh, R. L. Storey, and Griffiths.]

26. Clayton, Dorothy J., Richard G. Davies, and Peter McNiven, eds. *Trade, Devotion and Governance: Papers in Later Medieval History.* Stroud, 1994. [A 1989 Manchester conference, in the Fifteenth Century series. Items 148, 338, 378, 490, 593, 619, 635, 1043, 1101, 1215.]

27. Collinson, Patrick, Nigel Ramsay, and Margaret Sparks, eds. *History of Canterbury Cathedral.* Oxford, 1995. [Appendix of medieval estate holdings, pp. 566–70; items 1232, 1599, 1660, 1822.]

28. Curry, Anne, and Michael Hughes, eds. *Arms, Armies and Fortifications in the Hundred Years War.* Woodbridge, 1994. [An Oxford conference, 1991, illustrated by thirty-eight plates. Items 194, 225, 266, 307, 333, 359, 392, 445, 474, 1734.]

29. Denton, Jeffrey, ed., *Orders and Hierarchies in Late Medieval and Renaissance Europe.* Toronto, 1999. [Items 712, 1095, 1656, 1828.]

30. DeWindt, Edwin Brezette, ed. *The Salt of Common Life: Individuality and Choice in the Medieval Town, Countryside, and Church: Essays Presented to J. Ambrose Raftis.* Kalamazoo, Mich., 1995. [Introduction and tribute to Raftis, pp. xi–xvii; items 631, 721, 905, 1106, 1139, 1840, 1857.]

31. Dobson, Richard Barrie. *Church and Society in the Medieval North of England.* London and Rio Grande,

Ohio, 1996. [Thirteen Dobson papers, four from the
1990s; #4 is item 42, pp. 124–54; item 1229, pp. 311–32,
was first published in *Church and City: Essays in
Honour of Christopher Brooke*, ed. David Abulafia,
Michael Franklin, and Miri Rubin, Cambridge, 1992;
another paper is in item 99, pp. 201–18.]

32.   Duffy, Michael, Stephen Fisher, Basil Greenhill, David
J. Starkey, and Joyce Youings, eds. *The New Maritime
History of Devon, from the Earliest Times to the Late
Eighteenth Century*. 2 vols. Exeter, 1992. [In vol. 1,
items 622, 651, 674, 1022.]

33.   Dunn, Diane E. S., ed. *Courts, Counties and the Capital
in the Later Middle Ages*. Stroud and New York, 1996.
[A fifteenth-century conference at Chester, 1994. Items
217, 568, 601, 604, 605, 606, 1464, 1611.]

34.   Fallows, David. *Songs and Musicians in the Fifteenth
Century*. Aldershot, 1996. [Fourteen of Fallows's papers,
published 1976–94, including "English Song Repertories
in the Mid-15th Century" (1976–77), a review of Julia
Boffey, *Manuscripts of English Courtly Love Lyrics in
the Later Middle Ages* (1987), and "The *contenance
anglais*: English Influence on Continental Composers of
the Fifteenth Century" (1987).]

35.   Fernie, Eric C., and Paul Crossley, eds. *Medieval Archi-
tecture and Its Intellectual Content: Studies in Honour of
Peter Kidson*. London and Ronceverte, W. Va., 1990.
[Items 498, 1737, 1750.]

36.   Franklin, M. J., and Christopher Harper-Bill, eds.
*Medieval Ecclesiastical Studies in Honour of Dorothy M.
Owen*. Woodbridge, 1995. [Appreciations of Dorothy
Owen, pp. xiii–xxi, by Joan Varley, David S. Chambers,
and Christopher Brooke; a bibliography compiled by
Arthur Owen, pp. 299–307; items 1085, 1334, 1344,
1417, 1430.]

37.   Gillespie, James L., ed. *The Age of Richard II.* Stroud and New York, 1997. [Many of the papers were first presented at the International Congress on Medieval Studies at Western Michigan University. Items 144, 214, 264, 270, 271, 364, 373, 437, 499, 1563, 1630.]

38.   Gillingham, John, ed. *Richard III: A Medieval Kingship.* New York and London, 1993. [Introduction on Richard's enduring appeal, pp. 1–19, in this well illustrated "History Today" publication. Items 289, 303, 318, 327, 342, 419, 455.]

39.   Glasscoe, Marion, ed. *The Medieval Mystical Tradition in England: Exeter Symposium, V.* Cambridge, 1992. [A 1992 conference. Items 838, 1208, 1218, 1259, 1367, 1380, 1448.]

40.   ———, ed. *The Medieval Mystical Tradition: England, Ireland, and Wales: Exeter Symposium VI.* Cambridge, 1999. [Papers of a July 1999 conference. Items 896, 953, 1258.]

41.   Goldberg, P. J. P., ed. *Woman is a Worthy Wight: Women in English Society, c. 1200–1500.* Stroud, 1992. [A 1988 conference at Cambridge. Items 681, 822, 841, 860, 861, 868, 922.]

42.   Goodman, Anthony, and Anthony Tuck, eds. *War and Border Societies in the Middle Ages.* London and New York, 1992. [A 1988 conference on the 600th anniversary of the Battle of Otterburn, with an introductory essay on medieval frontiers by Goodman, pp. 1–29; items 288, 470, 807, 1067, 1230.]

43.   Goodman, Anthony, and James L. Gillespie, eds. *Richard II: The Art of Kingship.* Oxford, 1999. [Goodman's introduction, pp. 1–13, is a summary of the reign rather than a run-through of the papers; items 171, 197, 282, 285, 439, 467, 761, 966, 1221, 1499, 1790.]

44.   Gordon, Dillian, Lisa Monnas, and Caroline Elam, eds.,
        with an introduction by Caroline M. Barron. *The Royal
        Images of Richard II and the Wilton Diptych.* London,
        1997. [Lavish volume with twenty-three color plates on
        many aspects of the diptych and related topics. Items
        191, 352, 435, 795, 1509, 1575, 1646, 1655, 1667, 1703,
        1725, 1741, 1755, 1757, 1787, 1789, 1813, 1823.]

45.   Greatrex, Joan, ed. *The Vocation of Service to God and
        Neighbor: Essays on the Interests, Involvement and
        Problems of Religious Communities and Their Members
        in Medieval Society.* Turnhout, 1998. [Selected pro-
        ceedings from the International Medieval Congress,
        University of Leeds, July 1997. Items 1263, 1290, 1482.]

46.   Griffiths, Ralph A. *King and Country: England and
        Wales in the Fifteenth Century.* London and Rio Grande,
        Ohio, 1991. [Twenty-one of Griffiths's papers from
        1964–90: political topics, mostly on Wales and Welsh
        leaders, and with a focus on the 1450s. Item 291
        republished here.]

47.   ———. *Conquerors and Conquered in Medieval Wales.*
        Stroud, 1994. [Nineteen papers collected here from
        1963–90; several on Owain Glyndwr and many on Welsh
        urban development.]

48.   Hanawalt, Barbara A., ed. *Chaucer's England: Litera-
        ture in Historical Context.* The University of Minnesota's
        "Medieval Studies at Minnesota," 4. Minneapolis, 1992.
        [Introduction on the "intersection of history and litera-
        ture," pp. xi–xxii; items 195, 451, 523, 685, 757, 791, 963,
        1077, 1103, 1121, 1466.]

49.   Hanawalt, Barbara A., and Kathryn L. Reyerson, eds.
        City and Spectacle in Medieval Europe. Minneapolis,
        1994. [Items 959, 973, 983, 1035.]

50.   Hanawalt, Barbara A., and David Wallace, eds. *Bodies and Discipline: Intersections of Literature and History in Fifteenth-Century England.* Minneapolis and London, 1996. [1993 conference at the University of Minnesota. Items 570, 701, 855, 873, 889, 1211.]

51.   ———. *Medieval Crime and Social Control.* Minneapolis and London, 1999. [Items 1010, 1130, 1552.]

52.   Harper-Bill, Christopher, ed. *Religious Belief and Ecclesiastical Careers in Late Medieval England.* Woodbridge, 1991. [1989 Strawberry Hill Conference. Items 776, 974, 1282, 1324, 1423.]

53.   Hellinga, Lotte, and Joseph B. Trapp, eds. *Cambridge History of the Book in Britain: Volume III, 1400–1557.* Cambridge, 1999. [Comprehensive treatment, with editors' introduction, pp. 1–30; items 507, 551, 576, 616, 713, 1247, 1461, 1463, 1465, 1469, 1512, 1513, 1514, 1538, 1542, 1546, 1555, 1569, 1590, 1621, 1631, 1632, 1647, 1751.]

54.   Hicks, Michael, ed. *Profit, Piety, and the Professions in Later Medieval England.* Gloucester, 1990. [A fifteenth-century conference at Winchester, 1987. Introduction, pp. x–xxii; and items 294, 449, 510, 521, 524, 594, 809, 859, 1196.]

55.   ———. *Richard III and His Rivals: Magnates and Their Motives in the Wars of the Roses.* London and Rio Grande, Ohio, 1991. [Twenty-three of Hicks's papers from the 1970s and 1980s: Cardinal Beaufort, the Hungerfords, Lord Hastings, Richard III, and more of the usual suspects.]

56.   Holt, Richard, and Gervase Rosser, eds. *The English Medieval Town: A Reader in English Urban History, 1200–1500.* London and New York, 1990. [Papers originally published prior to 1990; introduction, pp. 1–18,

is a survey of current work. Papers by R. H. Hilton, G. H. Martin, E. M. Carus-Wilson, D. J. Keene, E. M. Veale, R. Holt, C. M. Barron, M. Kowaleski, G. Rosser, C. P. Adams, and R. B. Dobson.]

57.   Horrox, Rosemary, ed. *Fifteenth-Century Attitudes: Perceptions of Society in Late Medieval England.* Cambridge, 1994. [Introduction, pp. 1–12, offers an overview; items 309, 592, 624, 705, 745, 789, 864, 1046, 1086, 1392, 1467, 1544.]

58.   Keen, Maurice. *Nobles, Knights, and Men-at-Arms in the Middle Ages.* London and Rio Grande, Ohio, 1996. [Fourteen of Keen's papers, first published 1962–93.]

59.   Kermode, Jennifer, ed. *Enterprise and Individuals in Fifteenth-Century England.* Stroud, 1991. [Liverpool Conference, 1988. Items 595, 596, 649, 665, 788, 1152, 1157.]

60.   Matheson, Lister M., ed. *Popular and Practical Science of Medieval England.* Medieval Texts and Studies, 11. East Lansing, Mich., 1994. [Essays on and edited versions of the texts in this well-illustrated volume with a glossary. Items 731, 1459, 1474, 1492, 1534, 1548, 1560A, 1570, 1578, 1597, 1627, 1636.]

61.   McEntire, Sandra, ed. *Margery Kempe: A Book of Essays.* New York and London, 1992. [Introduction and historiographical survey of work on Margery, pp. ix–xvii; items 824, 827, 837, 848, 878, 897, 900, 903, 915, 933, 949. Reviewed by Roger Ellis, *MQ* 19 (1993), 182–85.]

62.   ———, ed. *Julian of Norwich: A Book of Essays.* New York and London, 1998. [Wide-ranging collection. Items 1179, 1184, 1273, 1319, 1341, 1343, 1382, 1384, 1403, 1439, 1451.]

63.   Meale, Carol M., ed. *Women and Literature in Britain,*
        1150–1500. Cambridge, 1993; 2nd ed., 1996. [Intro-
        duction has extensive chronological table of women's
        activity; items 917, 1468, 1568, 1607.]

64.   Michalove, Sharon D., and A. Compton Reeves, eds.
        Estrangement, Enterprise, and Education in Fifteenth-
        Century England. Stroud, 1998. [University of Illinois
        conference, 1995. Items 293, 383, 423, 543, 574, 1391,
        1572.]

65.   Miller, Edward, ed. *Agrarian History of England and*
        Wales, III: 1348–1500. Cambridge, 1991. [The entire
        project is under the editorship of Joan Thirsk. Miller's
        introduction to this volume, pp. 1–33, covers "land and
        people" and each entry follows a basic format, covering
        "occupation of the land," then "farming practices," and
        finally "tenant farming and tenant farmers." Items 1090,
        1094, 1096, 1109, 1112, 1113, 1115, 1117, 1123, 1127,
        1129, 1131, 1134, 1135, 1144, 1146, 1164, and a review
        listed below as item 1097.]

66.   Minnis, Alastair J., ed. *Late-Medieval Religious Texts*
        and Their Transmission: Essays in Honour of A. I. Doyle.
        Cambridge, 1994. [A York conference, 1991, with intro-
        ductory address by Doyle, pp. 1–7; items 1250, 1300,
        1389, 1435, 1500.]

67.   Minnis, Alastair J., Charlotte C. Morse, and Thorlac
        Turville-Petre, eds. *Essays on Ricardian Literature in*
        Honour of J. A. Burrow. Oxford, 1997. [Items 540, 1475,
        1574, 1608.]

68.   Morgan, Philip, and A. D. M. Phillips, eds. *Staffordshire*
        Histories: Essays in Honour of Michael Greenslade.
        Staffordshire Record Society, 4th series, 19 (1999), and
        the Centre for Local History, University of Keele. [Items
        804, 1021, 1354.]

69. Munro, John H. *Bullion Flows and Monetary Policies in England and the Low Countries.* Aldershot, 1992. [Eight of Munro's papers, 1970–88; five are on England and the Low Countries, covering bullion flows, deflation, banking, and related issues.]

70. ———. *Textiles, Towns and Trade: Essays in the Economic History of Late-Medieval England and the Low Counties.* Aldershot, 1994. [Some of Munro's collected papers with introduction, pp. vii–xiv; since 1990, only "The International Law Merchant and the Evolution of Negotiable Credit in Late-Medieval England and the Low Countries" (pp. 49–80), and one from 1991 on European banking practices.]

71. Owen, Dorothy, ed. *A History of Lincoln Minster.* Cambridge, 1994. [Items 1191, 1376, 1661.]

72. Page, Christopher. *Music and Instruments of the Middle Ages.* Aldershot, 1997. [Twenty of Page's papers, 1973–93; relevant is "String-Instrument-Making in Medieval England and some Oxford Harpmakers, 1380–1466" (1978).]

73. Parkes, Malcolm B. *Scribes, Scripts and Readers: Studies in the Communication, Presentation and Dissemination of Medieval Tasks.* London and Rio Grande, Ohio, 1991. [Sixteen papers by Parkes, from 1958 on, especially "A 15th-Century Scribe: Henry Mere" (1961); "Literacy of the Laity" (1973); and "Book Provision and the Libraries of the Medieval University of Oxford" (1987–88).]

74. Parsons, John Carmi, and Bonnie Wheeler, eds. *Medieval Mothering.* New York and London, 1996. [Items 872, 920, 1350, 1414.]

75. Phillips, Helen, ed. *Langland, the Mystics, and the Medieval English Religious Tradition: Essays in Honour*

of S. S. Hussey. Cambridge, 1990. [Items 849, 1180, 1192, 1260, 1494.]

76. Pollard, Anthony J., ed. *The Wars of the Roses.* Basingstoke, 1995. [Introduction on "Society, Politics and the Wars of the Roses," pp. 1–19; items 135, 231, 244, 329, 615, 638, 1220, 1776.]

77. ———, ed. *The North of England in the Age of Richard III.* Stroud, 1996. [A volume in the Fifteenth Century series. Introduction, pp. ix–xx; items 240, 290, 406, 549, 753, 1068, 1308.]

78. Pollard, William F., and Robert Boenig, eds. *Mysticism and Spirituality in Medieval England.* Cambridge, 1997. [Items 843, 1194, 1243, 1267, 1321.]

79. Razi, Zvi, and Richard M. Smith, eds. *Medieval Society and the Manorial Court.* Oxford, 1996. [Introduction, pp. 1–35: historiographical survey of manorial studies and the use of court rolls, from Maitland and Vinogradoff onward; items 520, 1088, 1093, 1104, 1151, 1155. Reviewed in item 126.]

80. Rogers, Nicholas, ed. *England in the Fourteenth Century: Proceedings of the 1991 Harlaxton Symposium.* Harlaxton Medieval Studies, III. Stamford, 1993. [Items 1061, 1160, 1223, 1758.]

81. ———, ed. *England in the Fifteenth Century: Proceedings of the 1992 Harlaxton Symposium.* Harlaxton Medieval Studies, IV. Stamford, 1994. [Items 346, 496, 565, 715, 736, 801, 1289, 1393, 1434, 1564, 1620, 1645, 1748, 1750, 1782.]

82. Rousseau, Constance M., and Joel T. Rosenthal, eds. *Women, Marriage, and Family in Medieval Christendom: Essays in Memory of Michael M. Sheehan, CSB.* Studies in Medieval Culture, 37. Kalamazoo, Mich.,

1998. [A "personal profile" of Sheehan by Walter H. Principe, pp. 1–10, and "The Interdisciplinary Context of a Career" by J. Ambrose Raftis, pp. 11–16; items 875, 906, 908.]

83. Saul, Nigel, ed. *England in Europe, 1066–1453*. New York, 1994. [General essays. Items 284, 431, 472.]

84. ———, ed. *The Oxford Illustrated History of Medieval England*. Oxford, 1997. [A handsome general volume, with useful overviews. Items 280, 667, 1328, 1595, 1670A.]

85. Sheehan, Michael M., CSB. *Marriage, Family, and Law in Medieval Europe*. Toronto, 1996. [Sixteen of Sheehan's papers, 1961–92, edited by James K. Farge. [Farge's foreword, pp. vii–xi; introduction by Joel T. Rosenthal, pp. xiii–xxviii; bibliography by Mary C. English, pp. 324–30. "The Formation and Stability of Marriage in Fourteenth-Century England: The Evidence of an Ely Register" (1971) is included.]

86. Sherborne, James. *War, Politics, and Culture in Four-teenth-Century England*. Edited by Anthony Tuck. London and Rio Grande, Ohio, 1994. [Introduction and appreciation of Sherborne, by Tuck (pp. ix–xvi); eleven papers reprinted, including item 442.]

87. Shiels, W. J., and Diana Wood, eds. *Women in the Church: Papers Read at the 1989 Summer Meeting and the 1990 Winter Meeting of the Ecclesiastical History Society*. Studies in Church History, 27. Oxford and Cambridge, Mass., 1990. [Items 1176, 1239, 1363.]

88. Slater, T. R., and Gervase Rosser, eds. *The Church in the Medieval Town*. Aldershot, 1998. [Items 1000, 1015, 1055, 1070.]

89.   Smith, David M., ed. *The Church in Medieval York: Records Edited in Honour of Professor Barrie Dobson.* Borthwick Texts and Calendars, University of York 24 (1999). [Items 569, 1288, 1297, 1357, 1419.]

90.   Smith, Lesley, and Jane H. M. Taylor, eds. *Women, The Book, and the Godly: Selected Proceedings of the St Hilda's Conference, 1993, Volume II.* Cambridge, 1995. [Items 867, 1617, 1623.]

91.   Strickland, Matthew, ed. *Armies, Chivalry and Warfare in Medieval Britain and France: Proceedings of the 1995 Harlaxton Symposium.* Harlaxton Medieval Studies, VII. Stamford, 1998. [Items 227, 286, 1460.]

92.   Taylor, John, and Wendy Childs, eds. *Politics and Crisis in Fourteenth-Century England.* Gloucester, 1990. [1986 Leeds conference. Items 189, 341, 442, 464.]

93.   Thompson, Benjamin, ed. *Monasteries and Society in Medieval Britain: Proceedings of the 1994 Harlaxton Symposium.* Harlaxton Medieval Studies, VI. Stamford, 1999. [Editor's introduction, pp. 1–33, "Monasteries and Medieval Society"; items 1200, 1233, 1398, 1470, 1530, 1784.]

94.   Virgoe, Roger. *East Anglian Society and the Political Community of Late Medieval England: Selected Papers of Roger Virgoe.* Edited by Caroline M. Barron, Carole Rawcliffe, and Joel T. Rosenthal. East Anglian Studies, University of East Anglia, Norwich, 1997. [Sixteen of Virgoe's papers, 1959–95, with a personal memoir by Harry Cobb, pp. 9–12; introduction by Joel T. Rosenthal, pp. 13–19; and bibliography, pp. 361–63. Items republished in this volume are 475, 609, 610, 809.]

95.   Walker, Sue Sheridan, ed. *Wife and Widow in Medieval England.* Ann Arbor, Mich., 1993. [Items 529, 871, 876, 919.]

96.   Wallace, David, ed. *The Cambridge History of Medieval English Literature.* Cambridge, 1999. [A chronology of events and of literary production, 1350–1500, pp. 866–76; items 109, 454, 728, 1029, 1083, 1317, 1452, 1553.]

97.   Watts, John L., ed. *The End of the Middle Ages? England in the Fifteenth and Sixteenth Centuries.* Stroud, 1998. [Papers from a 1998 conference at Aberystwyth, with a debate on traditional periodization, pp. 1–22, and conclusion, pp. 263–70; items 177, 232, 268, 298, 424, 640.]

98.   Wood, Diana, ed. *Life and Thought in the Northern Church, c. 1100–c.1700: Essays in Honour of Claire Cross.* Studies in Church History, Subsidia, 12 (1999). [A tribute by Barrie Dobson, pp. 1–9; a Cross bibliography by Christine M. Newman, pp. 563–74; items 1008, 1307, 1409, 1432, 1456.]

99.   Wood, Ian, and G. A. Loud, eds. *Church and Chronicle in the Middle Ages: Essays Presented to John Taylor.* London, 1991. [Tribute by Barrie Dobson, pp. xi–xx; a Taylor bibliography, xxi–xxiii; items 119, 384, 894, 1254.]

II. Bibliographies, Review Articles, Reference Studies, Etc.[2]

100. Albano, Robert A. *Middle English Historiography*. New York, 1993. [Brut, Higden, etc.: history as literature, and vice versa.]

101. *Agricultural History Review* [An annual listing with brief reviews of the year's work, compiled in the 1990s by Raine Morgan, plus a "list of books and pamphlets" by V. J. Morris and D. J. Orton.]

102. Ainsworth, Peter J. *Jean Froissart and the Fabric of History: Truth, Myth and Fiction in the Chroniques*. Oxford, 1990. [Mostly on the *Chroniques* as literature.]

103. Ashbee, Andrew, and David Lasocki, assisted by Peter Holman and Fiona Kisby. *A Biographical Dictionary of English Court Musicians, 1485–1714*. 2 vols. Aldershot, 1998. [Little early stuff; though there was a court sackbuttist by 1482.]

104. Barron, Caroline M. "Twenty Years of Writing on London History: London in the Later Middle Ages." *London Journal* 20/2 (1995), 22–33. [A survey of

---

[2] General historiography, or items focusing on more than one primary source or scholarly work, are included in this chapter (as item 142). Items dealing with a single source that was edited during the 1990s (such as item 278) or those reviewing a single monograph are usually listed under that item (as per item 427). However, do not expect total consistency.

scholarly work and then a bibliography of 179 items, by categories, from Sylvia Thrupp and Ruth Bird through current work.]

105.   ———. "London in the Later Middle Ages." In *Capital Histories: A Bibliographical Study of London*. Edited by Patricia L. Garside. Aldershot, 1998. Pp. 29–40. [A survey of scholarly work and nine pages of bibliography.]

106.   Becket, J., ed. *The Thoroton Society: A Commemoration of Its First Hundred Years*. Thoroton Society, Nottingham, 1997. [Short papers on Robert Thoroton and Nottinghamshire historiography by Becket, Adrian Henstock, and Neville Hospins.]

107.   Berg, Maxine. "The First Women Economic Historians." *EcHR* 45 (1992), 308–29. [Eileen Power, The Fabians, The London School of Economics, Oxbridge; covering most of the waterfront.]

108.   ———. *A Woman in History: Eileen Power, 1889–1940*. Cambridge, 1996. [An appreciative biography and professional assessment of a great historian, with a select bibliography, pp. 266–70.]

109.   Boffey, Julia. "Middle English Lives." In item 96. Pp. 610–34. [What we can do by way of biography: Margery Kempe, the Pastons, saints, and insights from poetry.]

110.   Boyd, Kelly, ed. *Encyclopedia of Historians and Historical Writing*. 2 vols. Chicago and London, 1999. [Not much on late medieval England; entries have "further reading" suggestions.]

111.   Brooke, Christopher. "Dom David Knowles and His Vocation." *DR* 110 (1992), 209–25. [Intellectual biography; reconciling academic scholarship and the monastic calling.]

112. Cannon, John. *Oxford Companion to British History.* Oxford and New York, 1997. [A reference volume; items alphabetized.]

113. Carpenter, Christine. "Empiricism and Ideas in Medieval Studies." *JBS* 33 (1994), 99–103. [A review article, with a call for some "skinnerism" and a look at items 283, 312, 346 *et al.*]

114. Castleden, Rodney. *Harrap's Book of British Dates.* London, 1991.

115. Creaton, Heather, ed. *Bibliography of Printed Works on London History to 1939.* Centre for Metropolitan History, Institute of Historical Research, University of London, and the Library Association, 1994. [Very inclusive; a vast work of reference.]

116. Crosby, Alan G. *"A Society with No Equal": The Chetham Society, 1843–1993.* Chetham Society, 3rd series, 37 (1993). [A narrative, officials of the Society, a list of publications, pp. 63–82.]

117. Currie, Christopher R. J., and Christopher P. Lewis, eds. *English County Histories: A Guide: A Tribute to C. R. Elrington.* Stroud, 1994. [A survey of county histories (though without Rutland), looking at scholarly work on each county.]

118. Dils, Joan, ed. *An Historical Atlas of Berkshire.* Berkshire Record Society, 1998. [Maps by Heather Browning. Maps 11–20 cover late medieval Berkshire: markets, chantries, deserted villages, etc., with a short essay accompanying each map. Material by Grenville Astill, Jeremy Sims, Anne Curry, Brian Kemp, Andrew D. Brown, Brian O'Callaghan, Josephine Cormier, Margaret York, and John Brooks.]

119. Dobson, Richard Barrie. "Contrasting Chronicles: Historical Writing at York and Durham at the Close of

the Middle Ages." In item 99. Pp. 201–18. [Contracting
intellectual horizons after 1399, except for Wessington.]

120.   Dockray, Keith. "James Gairdner: A Colossus of
         Victorian Historians of the Wars of the Roses, Richard
         III, and Henry VII." *Ricardian* 11/144 (March 1999),
         426–45. [He was sympathetic to Richard, though, alas, a
         bit soft on Henry Tudor.]

121.   Doyle, Anthony Ian. "Neil Ripley Ker." *PBA* 80 (1993),
         349–59. [The obituary notice and tribute.]

122.   *Economic History Review.* [The November issue carries
         the "Annual List of Publications" of the previous year;
         the February issue has the "Review of Periodical Litera-
         ture," done recently by Chris Dyer and Richard Britnell.]

123.   Eldredge, Lucius G. *The Index of Middle English Prose:
         Handlist IX: A Handlist of Manuscripts Containing
         Middle English Prose in the Ashmole Collection,
         Bodleian Library, Oxford.* Cambridge, 1992. [Also see
         items 131, 145, 150, 154, 159, 169. All these volumes
         survey collections of manuscripts rich in historical,
         medical, alchemical, astrological, and religious material
         (including a good deal about Wycliffe and Lollardy).]

124.   English, Barbara, and Joseph John N. Palmer. "The
         Making of the RHS Annual Bibliography." *History and
         Computing* 4 (1992), 110–14. [On a course to put us all
         out of business, sooner or later; see item 166.]

125.   *English Historical Review.* [Annual notices of periodical
         and occasional publications appear in each year's July
         issue.]

126.   Faith, Rosamund. "Peasants, Manors, and Courts in the
         Middle Ages." *JBS* 37 (1998), 330–36. [A review article
         covering items 79 and 1116, plus work by J. Ambrose
         Raftis.]

127.　Gaines, Barry. *Sir Thomas Malory: An Anecdotal Bibli-ography of Editions, 1485–1985.* New York, 1990. [From Caxton on, listing over 219 editions and related volumes.]

128.　Gransden, Antonia. "The Chronicles of Medieval England and Scotland, part 1." *JMH* 16 (1990), 129–50. [A brief survey; the motives behind writing, government use of propaganda, and the decline of historiographical standards.]

129.　Gray, Douglas. "Norman Davis." *PBA* 80 (1993), 261–73. [The obituary note for the editor of the *Paston Letters and Papers* (among his many contributions).]

130.　Hammond, Peter W., ed. *The Complete Peerage, Volume xiv: Addenda and Corrigenda.* London, 1998. [Peer by peer, with corrections to the entries and the appendices of volumes 1–12; attributions are given for corrections.]

131.　Hanna, Ralph III. *The Index of Middle English Prose: Handlist XII: Smaller Bodleian Collections: English Miscellaneous, English Poetry, English Theology, Finch, Latin Theology, Lyell, Radcliffe Trust.* Cambridge, 1997. [A small group of manuscripts with the usual miscellany of subjects; see item 123.]

132.　Harriss, Gerald, ed., with a memoir by Karl Leyser. *K. B. McFarlane's Letters to Friends, 1940–1966.* Magdalen College, Oxford, 1997. [Especially valuable for McFarlane's reflections on wartime Oxford and the return to peacetime.]

133.　———. "John Smith Roskell (1913–1998): Historian of the Medieval Parliament." *Parliamentary History* 17 (1998), 293–96. [An obituary appreciation of the supervisor of the four volumes of the History of Parliament, 1388–1422; see items 156, 427.]

134.   Hicks, Michael A. *Who's Who in Late Medieval England (1272–1485)*. Chicago and London, 1991. [Volume 3 in a series: mostly covering the major players.]

135.   ———. "The Sources." In item 76. Pp. 20–40. [A survey of records, chronicles, modern editors, and Tudor propaganda.]

136.   Hinton, David A. "'Closing' and the Later Middle Ages." *Medieval Archaeology* 43 (1999), 172–82. [Closure theory, the role of taxes, and an awareness of social stratification as seen by an archaeologist.]

137.   Horrox, Rosemary. "The State of Research." *JMH* 18 (1992), 391–403. [Local and national politics, bastard feudalism and the gentry, royal affinities; fourteen books surveyed.]

138.   Humphreys, Maggie, and Robert Evans. *Dictionary of Composers for the Church in Great Britain and Ireland.* London and Herndon, Virginia, 1997. [Late medieval just sneaks in, and there is no chronological listing of musicians.]

139.   Hunt, Arnold. "E. Gordon Duff and the Bibliography of English Incunabula." *Cambridge Bibliographical Society* 9/5 (1990), 409–33. [Typographical materials and Duff's problems in preparing his work for publication.]

140.   Institute of Historical Research, University of London. *Historical Research for Higher Degrees in the United Kingdom: Theses Completed.* [Compiled annually, and done for the 1990s by Joyce Horn and then by Jane Winters (with help from Annie Payne).]

141.   *International Medieval Bibliography.* [Published twice per year by the University of Leeds's International Medieval Institute. By topics, with a variety of indices. Edited in the 1990s by Simon Forde and then Alan V. Murray.]

142. Karras, Ruth M. "Recent Work on Medieval English Society." *JBS* 35 (1996), 398–402. [A review article, looking at items 683, 696, 1059, plus work by Sue Sheridan Walker; generally complimentary but some lament for the absence of theory.]

143. Leyser, Henrietta. "Medieval Women and the Woman Medievalist." *JBS* 37 (1998), 441–46. [Review article of items 108, 890, 1335, plus work by Roberta Gilchrist.]

144. Martin, Geoffrey H. "Narrative Sources for the Reign of Richard II." In item 37. Pp. 51–69. [Survey of the sources and their editing.]

145. Marx, William. *The Index of Middle English Prose, Handlist XV: Manuscripts in the National Library of Wales (Llyfrgell Genedlaethol Cymru) Aberystwyth.* Cambridge, 1999. [Prophetic material, medicine, Chaucer on the astrolabe; see item 123.]

146. Matheson, Lister M. *The Prose "Brut": The Development of a Middle English Chronicle.* Medieval and Renaissance Texts and Studies, 180. Tempe, Ariz., 1998. [A full description and discussion of each manuscript, their variations and relationships, plus a quick look at the earliest printed version.]

147. McKendrick, Scot. *"La Grande Histoire Cesar* and the Manuscripts of Edward IV." *English Manuscript Studies* 2 (1990), 109–38. [Royal Ms 17 Fii: texts from the Continent, perhaps coming to England with Louis of Gruuthuse.]

148. McLaren, Mary-Rose. "The Aims and Interests of the London Chroniclers in the Fifteenth Century." In item 26. Pp. 158–76. [Why the London chronicles were written, and a comparison of their treatment of Richard duke of York and Henry VI.]

149. *Medieval Feminist Forum.* [Formerly *Medieval Feminist Newsletter.* A bibliography on women's history (compiled by Chris Africa) and sometimes on "women and medicine" (by Monica Green) are regular features.]

150. Mooney, Linne R. *Manuscripts in the Library of Trinity College, Cambridge.* Woodbridge and Rochester, N.Y., 1995. [See item 123 for the format and general coverage of volumes in this series.]

151. Murph, Roxanne. *The Wars of the Roses in Fiction: An Annotated Bibliography.* Westport, Conn., and London, 1995. [Reaching almost six hundred volumes.]

152. Neve, Susan, and Stephen Ellis, eds. *An Historical Atlas of East Yorkshire.* University of Hull, 1996. [Medieval maps scattered through the volume: Hull, Beverley, markets, regular houses, and much more.]

153. Newman, Christine M. "Printed Calendars and Historical Research." *Archives* 22/95 (October 1996), 136–41. [A review article on recent publications, especially Feet of Fines, and mostly treated in a complimentary fashion.

154. Ogilvie-Thomson, S. J. *A Handlist of Manuscripts Containing Middle English Prose in Oxford College Libraries.* Cambridge and Rochester, N.Y., 1991. [See item 123.]

155. Owen, Arthur E. B. "Henry Bradshaw and his Correspondents." *Cambridge Bibliographical Society* xi/4 (1999), 480–96.

156. Palmer, Alan, and Veronica Palmer. *The Chronology of British History.* London and Sydney, 1992. [Year by year, with maps, lists of notable figures, etc.]

157. Panton, Kenneth J., and Keith A. Cowlard. *Historical Dictionary: United Kingdom, Volume I: England and the*

United Kingdom. Lanham, Md., and London, 1997. [Number 17 in the European Historical Dictionaries series.]

158. Philpott, Mark. "Bibliography of the Writings of F. W. Maitland. In *The History of English Law: Centenary Essays on "Pollock and Maitland."* Edited by John Hudson. *PBA* 89 (1996). Pp. 261–78. [Covers collected volumes and editions up to 1995.]

159. Pickering, Oliver S., and Veronica M. Omara. *Manuscripts in Lambeth Palace Library, Including Those Formerly in Sion College Library.* Woodbridge and Rochester, N.Y., 1999. [See item 123.]

160. Preston, Jean F., and Laetitia Yeandle. *English Handwriting, 1400–1650: An Introductory Manual.* Binghamton, N.Y., 1992.

161. Principe, Walter H. "An Obituary Notice of Michael M. Sheehan." *Mediaeval Studies* 55 (1993), vii–xi. [A Sheehan bibliography, compiled by Mary C. English and James K. Farge, pp. xi–xvi; see item 85.]

162. Rawcliffe, Carole, and Linda Clark. "A Personal Memoir of the Making of *The House of Commons, 1386–1422.*" *Parliamentary History* 17 (1998), 297–300. [A tribute to Roskell; see items 133 and 427.]

163. Rexroth, Frank, ed. *Research on British History in the Federal Republic of Germany, 1983–88.* German Historical Institute, London, 1990. [For books, pp. 22–30, and for articles, pp. 83–90. Work done in 1989–94 is covered in a comparable volume of 1996, ed. Ulrike Jordan, pp. 24–33 and 156–60; for 1995–97 ed. Andreas Fahrmeir (in 1998), pp. 27–33 and 140–46.]

164. Riddy, Felicity. "John Hardyng's Chronicle and the Wars of the Roses." *Arthurian Literature* 12 (1993), 91–108.

[The political context of Hardyng's second version and
the Yorkist claim as it was presented in the 1450s.]

165.   Rosenthal, Joel T. *Late Medieval England (1377–1485):
        A Bibliography of Historical Scholarship, 1975–1989.*
        Kalamazoo, Mich., 1994. [Never leave home without it.]

166.   Royal Historical Society. *Annual Bibliography of British
        and Irish History.* Oxford. [Annual volume: Barbara
        English and J. J. N. Palmer, general editors, and
        Andrew Ayton and David M. Palliser covering England,
        1066–1500, with Katherine F. Beedham contributing in
        1993 and Austin Gee taking over in 1995. Each volume
        focuses on work of the previous year; see item 124.]

167.   Sharpe, Richard. *A Handlist of the Latin Writers of
        Great Britain and Ireland before 1540.* Turnhout, 1997.
        [A publication of the *Journal of Medieval Latin.* Alpha-
        betical listing, with dates, works, manuscripts, editions,
        etc.; no master chronological list.]

168.   Stoker, David. "'Innumerable Letters of Good Conse-
        quence in History': The Discovery and First Publication
        of the Paston Letters." *The Library*, 6th series, 17/2
        (1995), 107–55. [The most complete account of the tale of
        the discovery of the letters and their publication.]

169.   Taavitsainen, Irma. *Manuscripts in Scandinavian
        Collections.* Cambridge and Rochester, N.Y., 1994. [See
        item 123.]

170.   Taylor, John. "The Origins of the Anonimalle Chronicle."
        Northern 31 (1995), 45–64. [Assembled at St Mary Abbey,
        York, probably from components like the French *Brut.*]

171.   ———. "Richard II in the Chronicles." In item 43.
        Pp. 15–35. [Rich sources but with a mixed message.]

172.   Usilton, Larry W. *The Kings of Medieval England,
        c. 560–1485: A Survey and Research Guide.* Pasadena,

Calif., 1996. [A guide to publications; not comprehensive, but with commentary.]

173. Wade-Martins, Peter, ed., Jane Everett, assistant ed., and maps by Phillip Judge. *An Historical Atlas of Norfolk*. Norwich, 1993. [Maps 19–40 (pp. 48–91) cover this period: markets, trade, town planning, deserted villages, the swathe cut by the peasants in 1381.]

174. Waldron, Ronald, and Henry Hargreaves. "The Aberdeen Ms. of Trevissa's Translation of the *Polychronicon* (AUL Ms. 2): A Workshop Crisis and Its Resolution." *Scriptorium* 46 (1992), 276–82. [An elegant manuscript and a missing quire.]

175. Wood, Anthony. *The Publications of the Henry Bradshaw Society: An Annotated Bibliography, with Indexes*. Bibliotheca Ephemerides Liturgicae, Subsidia, 67. Rome, 1992. [Devoted to publishing liturgical materials.]

176. Woolf, Daniel R., ed. *A Global Encyclopedia of Historical Writing*. New York and London, 1998, in 2 volumes.

III. GENERAL, POLITICAL, BIOGRAPHICAL, MILITARY AND DIPLOMATIC HISTORY

177.   Adams, Simon. "Baronial Contexts? Continuity and Change in the Noble Affinity, 1400–1600." In item 97. Pp. 155–97. [Some late medieval interest, though mostly concerned with the Elizabethan earl of Leicester's retinue.]

178.   Allmand, Christopher. *Henry V*. Berkeley and Los Angeles, 1992. [In the English Monarchs series; the definitive biography. Reviewed by G. L. Harriss, *EHR* 108 (1993), 677–79.]

179.   ———. "The English and the Church in Lancastrian Normandy." In item 10. Pp. 287–97. [Policies were mainly political ones; "join us or lose out" worked much of the time.]

180.   Archer, Rowena E. "Parliamentary Restoration: John Mowbray and the Dukedom of Norfolk in 1425." In item 3. Pp. 99–116. [He worked his way back, doing homage in parliament in 1425 as a duke.]

181.   Arthurson, Ian. "Espionage and Intelligence from the Wars of the Roses to the Reformation." *Nottingham* 35 (1991), 134–54. [National identity and open households were magnets for paid spies.]

182.   Arthurson, Ian, and Nicholas Kingwell. "The Proclamation of Henry Tudor as King of England, 3 November

1483." *HR* 63 (1990), 100–06. [Commissioners' returns on rebel estates and light shed on Cornish support for Henry.]

183.   Ashdown-Hill, John. "The Red Rose of Lancaster?" *Ricardian* 10/133 (June 1996), 906–20. [Its use and meaning, how depicted, etc.; limited fifteenth-century evidence on the image.]

184.   ———. "Edward IV's Uncrowned Queen: The Lady Eleanor Talbot, Lady Butler." *Ricardian* 11/139 (December 1997), 166–90. [A widow, a bit of fun, her retirement, and perhaps her skeleton.]

185.   ———. "The Elusive Mistress: Elizabeth Lucy and Her Family." *Ricardian* 11/145 (June 1999), 490–505. [A possible genealogy and Elizabeth Wayte's will of 1487.]

186.   Ayton, Andrew. "Military Service and the Development of the Robin Hood Legend in the Fourteenth Century." *Nottingham* 36 (1992), 126–47. [All those veteran archers were an eager audience for tales of a valiant "enlisted man."]

187.   Ballard, Mark. "An Expedition of English Archers to Liège in 1467, and the Anglo-Burgundian Marriage Alliance." *Nottingham* 34 (1990), 152–74. [A small force but one for which Edward sought a high compensation.]

188.   Barber, Richard. "Malory's *Le Morte Darthur* and Court Culture under Edward IV." *Arthurian Literature* 12 (1993), 133–55. [Royal patronage and Burgundian influences.]

189.   Barron, Caroline M. "The Deposition of Richard II." In item 92. Pp. 132–49. [Crisis of 1399 owed much to chance and ephemeral circumstances that exaggerate the idea of Lancastrian popularity and widespread support for the deposition.]

190.   ————. "Richard II: Image and Reality." In item 1702.
         Pp. 13–19. [Overview of the Wilton Diptych in the
         context of a cultured and image conscious court.]

191.   ————. "Introduction." In item 44. Pp. 9–17. [Looking at
         Richard II's vision of art and kingship.]

192.   Bartlett, Clive, with colored plates by Gerry Embleton.
         English Longbowmen, 1330–1515. Osprey Military
         Warrior series, 11. London, 1995; rev. ed., 1997. [Short
         and heavily illustrated: training, pay, uniforms,
         weapons, battles.]

193.   Peter J. Begent and Hubert Chesshyre. *The Most Noble
         Order of the Garter: 650 Years*. London, 1999. [An elabo-
         rate history with data on personnel: Lisa Jefferson,
         pp. 52–85, covers the statutes, records, and the Order's
         seals.]

194.   Bennett, Matthew. "The Development of Battle Tactics
         in the Hundred Years War." In item 28. Pp. 1–20.
         [Mostly early, but lessons from Edward III and Nicopolis
         were learned and used in the fifteenth century.]

195.   Bennett, Michael J. "The Court of Richard II and the
         Promotion of Literature." In item 48. Pp. 3–20. [The
         English language, bourgeois patronage, and "court
         culture."]

196.   ————. "Edward III's Entail and the Succession to the
         Crown, 1376–1471." *EHR* 113 (1998), 581–609. [A
         Cottonian charter in a fifteenth-century copy; perhaps
         Edward III's attempt to settle the crown in the male
         line.]

197.   ————. "Richard II and the Wider Realm." In item 43.
         Pp. 187–204. [The pull of Ireland and Wales and the
         West; a British rather than just an English realm.]

198.   ———. *Richard II and the Revolution of 1399*. Stroud, 1999. [Leading up to the last years, in detail; informative and thorough.]

199.   Bevan, Bryan. *King Richard III*. London, 1990. [Another general book covering familiar ground.]

200.   ———. *Henry IV*. London and New York, 1994. [A narrative, with many big generalizations in a small book.]

201.   Biggs, Douglas. "'A Wrong Whom Conscience and Kindred Bid Me to Right': A Reassessment of Edmund Langley, Duke of York, and the Usurpation of Henry IV." *Albion* 26 (1994), 253–72. [York's role too easily dismissed: rehabilitation and reevaluation.]

202.   ———. "A Plantagenet Revolution in Government? The Offices of Central Government and the Lancastrian Usurpation of 1399." *Med Pros* 20 (1999), 191–211. [New loyalists were installed; the Ricardian status quo was indeed disturbed.]

203.   Boardman, Andrew W. *The Battle of Towton*. Stroud, 1994. [Political and military history; familiar but thorough.]

204.   Bowers, J. M. "Chaste Marriage: Fashion and Texts at the Court of Richard II." *Pacific Coast Philology* 30 (1995), 15–26. [If we could but know the secrets of the royal bedroom.]

205.   Britnell, Richard. "Richard, Duke of Gloucester and the Death of Thomas Fauconberg." *Ricardian* 10/128 (March 1995), 174–84. [Young Richard, with his royal brother, dealing with an untrustworthy cousin.]

206.   ———. *The Closing of the Middle Ages? England, 1471–1529*. Oxford, 1999. [A general survey, covering politics as well as Britnell's usual focus on economic and urban issues.]

207. Carpenter, Christine. "Who Ruled the Midlands in the
      Later Middle Ages?" *Midland* 19 (1994), 1–20. [Critical
      of the concept of "the county community"; looking rather
      for hierarchies of power and for gentry links with
      monarchy.]

208. ———. *The Wars of the Roses: Politics and The Constitu-*
      tion in England, c. 1437–1509. Cambridge Medieval
      Textbooks, Cambridge, 1997. [Focused on kingship and
      on court and county; not a general or a military survey.]

209. Castor, Helen. "'Walter Blount has gone to serve Tray-
      tours': The Sack of Elveston and the Politics of the North
      Midlands in 1454." *Midland* 19 (1994), 21–39. [Local
      violence and a power vacuum in Derbyshire.]

210. ———. "The Duchy of Lancaster and the Rule of East
      Anglia, 1399–1440: A Prologue to the Paston Letters." In
      item 2. Pp. 53–78. [The Duchy played a powerful role
      between 1399 and Suffolk's rise to power.]

211. ———. "New Evidence of the Grant of Duchy of
      Lancaster Office to Henry Beauchamp, Earl of Warwick,
      in 1444." *HR* 68 (1995), 225–28. [Somerville's study of
      the Duchy missed this, though Warwick had to await
      Buckingham's death to wield power.]

212. Chainey, Graham. "Royal Visits to Cambridge: Henry VI
      to Henry VIII." *Cambridge Antiquarian Society* 80
      (1991), 30–37. [A list of visits, with purpose and duration:
      nine by Henry VI, five by Edward IV, two by Richard III.]

213. Chamberlayne, Joanne L. "A Paper Crown: The Titles
      and Seals of Cecily, Duchess of York." *Ricardian* 10/133
      (June 1996), 329–35. [A Lady of power and possessor of a
      splendid personal seal.]

214. Childs, Wendy R. "Anglo-Portuguese Relations in the
      Fourteenth-Century." In item 37. Pp. 27–49. [A close

look at matters of growing political and diplomatic importance in Richard's day.]

215. Chrimes, Stanley B., Charles D. Ross, and R. A. Griffiths, eds. *Fifteenth Century England, 1399–1509: Studies in Politics and Society.* Stroud, 1995. [A reprint of their classic (or canonical) volume of 1972, with Griffiths' "Foreword to the Second Edition," pp. ix–xiii; for same entry, item 25.]

216. Clark, Linda. "Magnates and Their Affinities in the Parliaments of 1386–1421." In item 19. Pp. 127–53. [A wide look across the years and the entire realm.]

217. Collins, Hugh. "The Order of the Garter, 1348–1461: Chivalry and Politics in Later Medieval England." In item 33. Pp. 155–80. [The Order as an extension of royal policy: military prowess was always at a premium.]

218. Coss, Peter. "Bastard Feudalism Revisited." *Past and Present* 131 (May 1991), 165–203. [Picking up on a 1989 article by Coss, though mainly pre-fifteenth century. A debate with David Crouch (pp. 165–77) and David A. Carpenter (pp. 177–89) and a rejoinder by Coss (pp. 190–203).]

219. Crawford, Anne, introduction. *The Household Books of John Howard, Duke of Norfolk, 1462–1471, 1481–1483.* Stroud, 1992. [Roxburghe Club publications of 1841 and 1844 republished, with some miscellaneous material (1455–1483). Being a great man was expensive.]

220. ———, ed. *Letters of the Queens of England, 1100–1547.* Stroud, 1994. [Basic material, but offering easy access to Margaret of Anjou and the others.]

221. Cron, B. M. "The Duke of Suffolk, the Angevin Marriage, and the Ceding of Maine, 1445." *JMH* 20 (1994), 77–99. [Evidence for who was responsible for the cession; a cloudy narrative, with the finger pointing at Henry VI.]

222.   ———. "Margaret of Anjou and the Lancastrian March on London, 1461." *Ricardian* 11/147 (December 1999), 590–615. [Mainly a narrative, touching her negotiations with the City.]

223.   Crook, David. "Central England and the Revolt of the Earls, January 1400." *HR* 64 (1991), 403–10. [Special interest in the Stathams of Derbyshire, old foes of John of Gaunt.]

224.   Curry, Anne. *The Hundred Years War*. Basingstoke and London, 1993. [A short survey, with attention to the war's wider European context.]

225.   ———. "English Armies in the Fifteenth Century." In item 28. Pp. 38–68. [From Henry V through the 1450s: leaders, organization, garrisons (with dates, size, and maps of their distribution).]

226.   ———. "Lancastrian Normandy: The Jewel in the Crown?" In item 10. Pp. 235–52. [Henry V's decision to invade, and why; the weight of the Norman "legacy" in English history.]

227.   ———. "The Organisation of Field Armies in Lancastrian Normandy." In item 91. Pp. 207–33. [Their size, cost, plans for campaigns, supplies, desertion, and a case study of one John Nelson.]

228.   Daly, Kathleen. "The *Vraie Cronicque D'Escoce* and Franco-Scottish Diplomacy: An Historical Work by John Ireland." *Nottingham* 35 (1991), 106–33. [A French source with much material on Anglo-Scottish-French relations.]

229.   Davies, Clifford S. L. "A Requiem for King Edward in the Sistine Chapel, September, 1483." *Ricardian* 9/114 (September 1991), 162–65. [Was this unexpected memorial for Edward IV or Edward V?]

230.   ———. "Richard III, Brittany, and Henry Tudor, 1483–1485." *Nottingham* 37 (1993), 110–26. [Richard sent archers in 1485 (not 1484); the diplomatic significance of the revised dating.]

231.   ———. "The Wars of the Roses in European Context." In item 76. Pp. 162–85. [England's continental interests, and vice versa.]

232.   ———. "Henry VIII and Henry V: The Wars in France." In item 97. Pp. 235–62. [Some interesting parallels, and a powerful picture of Henry VIII as another warrior king.]

233.   Davies, Rees R. *The Revolt of Owain Glyn Dŵr*. Oxford and New York, 1995. [Likely to remain the last word as far as a full treatment goes. Reviewed by Huw Price, *EHR* 112 (1997), 142–43.]

234.   Daw, Ben. "Elections to the Order of the Garter in the Reign of Edward IV, 1461–83." *Med Pros* 19 (1998), 187–213. [Thirty-six elections, with a stronger political agenda emerging over the years.]

235.   Dawson, Ian. *The Wars of the Roses*. Basingstoke, 1990. [A short volume, designed to introduce the subject to students.]

236.   Dean, James M., ed. *Medieval English Political Writings*. Kalamazoo, Mich., 1996. [In the Middle English Texts series for classroom use: prophetic poems, anti-clerical works, the peasants' rebellion, etc.]

237.   Delaney, Sheila. "Bokenham's Claudian as Yorkist Propaganda." *JMH* 22 (1996), 83–93. [Argues with a 1989 article by John Watts: traces Bokenham's ties with the Yorkists.]

238.   De Vries, Kelly. "The Impact of Gunpowder Weaponry on Siege Warfare in the Hundred Years War." In *The Medieval City under Siege*. Edited by Ivy A. Corfis and

Michael Wolfe. Woodbridge and Rochester, N.Y., 1995. Pp. 227–44. (See item 500.) [Gunpowder, for both offense and defense, was of importance by 1400.]

239.   ———. "The Effectiveness of Fifteenth-Century Shipboard Artillery." *Mariner's Mirror* 84 (1998), 389–99. [Considerable discussion of English material; guns were a-coming.]

240.   Dobson, Richard Barrie. "Politics and the Church in the Fifteenth-Century North." In item 77. Pp. 1–17. [Tale of an attack on the Bishop of Durham's lands to open a discussion of northern "essentialism."]

241.   Dockray, Keith. "Patriotism, Pride, and Paranoia: England and the English in the Fifteenth Century." *Ricardian* 8/110 (September 1990), 430–42. [A survey of contemporary comments on this question.]

242.   ———. "The Battle of Wakefield and the Wars of the Roses." *Ricardian* 9/117 (June 1992), 238–57. [To unravel a clouded story of the battle; see also items 300, 360.]

243.   ———. "Edward IV: Playboy or Politician?" *Ricardian* 10/131 (December 1995), 306–25. [The historiography of the question and a look at contemporary accounts.]

244.   ———. "The Origins of the Wars of the Roses." In item 76. Pp. 65–88. [The historiography of the issue, plus dates and causes in both long- and short-term perspective.]

245.   ———, ed. *Richard III: A Sourcebook*. Stroud, 1997. [Balanced presentation: an introduction and 125 pages of excerpts, mostly from chronicles and narratives, with a few record sources.]

246.   ———, ed. *Edward IV: A Source Book*. Stroud, 1999. [Similar in form to item 245, but now covering a slightly less controversial sibling.]

247. Doig, James A. "Propaganda, Public Opinion, and the Siege of Calais in 1436." In item 2. Pp. 79–106. [The siege had to be sold to the public: devotional poems, appeals for loans, prayers, etc. ("Siege of Calais" is printed from BL Cotton Galba E ix.)]

248. ———. "A New Source for the Siege of Calais in 1436." *EHR* 110 (1995), 404–16. [A tale of English victory, as per BL Add Ms 14848 (and found in the Abbot of Bury's Register).]

249. ———. "Propaganda and Truth: Henry V's Royal Progress in 1421." *Nottingham* 40 (1996), 167–79. [Reminding his subjects of their obligations, with a map of the royal itinerary and list of loans.]

250. ———. "Political Propaganda and Royal Proclamations in Late Medieval England." *HR* 71 (1998), 253–80. [They were a major way of telling news and of softening up audiences; a list of locations where they were read, 1398 and 1404.]

251. Driver, J. T. "A Fifteenth-Century Leicestershire Lawyer and Parliamentary Knight of the Shire: Thomas Palmer of Holt (c. 1400–1475)." *Leicester* 69 (1995), 42–58. [He sat seven times and leaned toward the Yorkists.]

252. ———. "The Career of John Catesby, Esquire: Midland Landholder, Lawyer and Parliamentary Knight of the Shire for Northamptonshire in 1425 and 1429." *Northants* 51 (1998), 7–14. [He was the middle man in a string of five parliamentary Catesbys and in the service of the Earl of Warwick; a deed of 1415 depicted.]

253. ———. "The Career of John Whittokesmode, a Fifteenth-Century Wiltshire Lawyer and Parliamentary 'Carpet Bagger'." *Wiltshire* 92 (1999), 92–99. [Elected MP twelve times: he worked with the bishops of Salisbury and the Hungerfords.]

254. ———. "Sir Thomas Green (c. 1400–1462), Parliamentary Knights for Northamptonshire in the 'Parliament of Bats' (1426)." *Northants* 52 (1999), 7–14. [Biographical: from soldier to active gentry figure and a Yorkist in his later days.]

255. DuBoulay, Francis Robin H. *The England of "Piers Plowman": William Langland and his Vision of the Fourteenth Century.* Woodbridge, 1991. [Using the poem to launch a general survey of society.]

256. Dunlop, David. "The 'Redress and Reparacons of Attemptates': Alexander Legh's Instructions from Edward IV, March–April 1475." *HR* 63 (1990), 340–53. [Diplomatic instructions to his Scottish envoy; a BL Cotton ms. published.]

257. Dunn, Diana. "Margaret of Anjou: Queen Consort of Henry VI: A Reassessment of her Role, 1445–53." In item 2. Pp. 107–43. [Straightening out biographical material; letters read as the letters of a woman of power.]

258. Ellis, Steven G. "The English State and Its Frontiers in the British Isles, 1300–1600." In *Frontiers in Question: Eurasian Borderlands, 700–1700.* Edited by Daniel Power and Naomi Standen. London, 1999. Pp. 153–81. [The "new British history," though mostly on the Tudors.]

259. Falvey, Heather. "William Fleet: More than Just a Castle Builder." *Ricardian* 10/124 (March 1994), 2–15. [An active career in the Southeast, dying in 1444.]

260. Ferster, Judith. *Fictions of Advice: The Literature of Politics of Counsel in Late Medieval England.* Philadelphia, 1996. [*Secretum Secretorum*, Regement of Princes, etc.; how to give advice and stay out of trouble.]

261. Fields, Bertram. *Royal Blood: King Richard III and the Mystery of the Princes.* Stroud, 1998. [The mystery remains unresolved.]

262.   Fisher, John. "A Language Policy for Lancastrian England." *Publications of the Modern Language Association* 107 (1992), 168–80. [English as part of Lancastrian imperialism; emphasis here is on the campaign to promote English, rather than on linguistic issues.]

263.   Fletcher, Alan J. "'The Unity of the State Exists in the Agreement of Its Minds': A Fifteenth-Century Sermon on the Three Estates." *Leeds* n.s. 22 (1991), 103–37. [An estates sermon (of 128 lines), published here from several manuscripts.]

264.   Fletcher, Doris. "The Lancastrian Collar of Esses: Its Origins and Transformations down the Centuries." In item 37. Pp. 191–204. [From 1371 to Henry VIII, with pictures.]

265.   Foss, Peter. *The Field of Redmore: The Battle of Bosworth*. Leicester, 1990; 2nd ed., 1998. [A pamphlet with good local coverage and treating divergent views about location, with a foreword by Ralph A. Griffiths.]

266.   Friel, Ian. "Winds of Change? Ships and the Hundred Years War." In item 28. Pp. 183–93. [Both sides had serious maritime resources: types, some battles, larger ships, better rigging.]

267.   Fryde, Edmund. "Royal Fiscal Systems and State Formation in France from the 13th to the 16th Century, with some English Comparisons." *Journal of Historical Sociology* 4 (1991), 236–87. [To the 1420s, though mostly focused on France.]

268.   Genet, Jean-Philippe. "New Politics or New Language? The Words of Politics in Yorkist and Early Tudor England." In item 97. Pp. 23–64. [Political ideology and partisanship found under every stone, with a computer analysis of word frequency and modes of expression.]

269.   Gill, Louise. *Richard III and Buckingham's Rebellion.*
        Stroud, 1999. [A familiar tale, well illustrated.]

270.   Gillespie, James L. "Richard II: Chivalry and Kingship."
        In item 37. Pp. 115–38. [A chivalric legacy from the Black
        Prince: Richard took it seriously (as he did heraldry).]

271.   ———. "Richard II: King of Battles?" In item 37.
        Pp. 139–64. [Big invasions of Ireland and Scotland, and
        a fairly martial if unsuccessful outlook.]

272.   Gillingham, John. "Contributor" for 1068–1485, in *The
        History Today Companion to British History.* London,
        1995. [Miscellaneous short pieces on a range of subjects.]

273.   Given-Wilson, Christopher. "Wealth and Credit, Public
        and Private: The Earls of Arundel, 1306–1397." *EHR*
        106 (1991), 1–26. [Earl Richard (d. 1376) was of great
        wealth: how he loaned money and used his wealth; a
        receiver's account published.]

274.   ———, ed. and tr. *Chronicles of the Revolution, 1397–
        1400: The Reign of Richard II.* Manchester Medieval
        Sources, Manchester, 1993. [Introduction and many
        extracts in this valuable source book, mostly from chron-
        icles, arranged to "tell the story": *Vita Ricardi Secundi*,
        Walsingham, Short Kirkstall Chronicle, among others.
        Reviewed by George Stow, *Speculum* 70 (1995), 146–48.]

275.   ———. "The Manner of King Richard's Renunciation: A
        'Lancastrian Narrative'?" *EHR* 108 (1993), 365–70. [Text
        was labeled by G. O. Sayles in 1981: "a CCCC manu-
        script, worthy of more respect than usually given."]

276.   ———. "Adam of Usk, the Monk of Evesham and the
        Parliament of 1397–98." *HR* 66 (1993), 329–35. [Adam
        and the monk (*Historia Viotae*): who copied from whom?
        Probably both turned to a common source, a "tract" of
        1398.]

277.   ———. "Richard II, Edward II, and the Lancastrian Inheritance." *EHR* 109 (1994), 553–71. [Mowbray's role in Gloucester's death and other high level plots.]

278.   ———. "The Dating and Structure of the Chronicle of Adam Usk." *Welsh History Review* 17 (1994–95), 529–33. [Written continuously over the years; see item 281 for a final say.]

279.   ———, ed. *An Illustrated History of Late Medieval England.* Manchester and New York, 1996. [General survey, with short contributions by Mark Bailey, Paul Brand, Simone Macdougall, Richard Davies, Ian Johnson, Nigel Ramsay, Ralph A. Griffiths, Michael Hicks, Simon Walker, and Given-Wilson.]

280.   ———. "Late Medieval England, 1215–1485." In item 84. Pp. 102–36. [A quick survey, mostly looking at political events.]

281.   ———, ed. and trans. *The Chronicles of Adam Usk, 1377–1421.* Oxford Medieval Texts, Oxford, 1997. [Comprehensive introduction and an accessible modernized text and translation, superseding E. M. Thompson's work of 1904.]

282.   ———. "Richard II and the Higher Nobility." In item 43. Pp. 107–28. [He had a fair amount of their support but not to his long-term advantage.]

283.   Goodman, Anthony. *John of Gaunt: The Exercise of Princely Power in Fourteenth-Century Europe.* London and New York, 1992. [The major modern treatment. Reviewed: A. J. Tuck, *EHR* 108 (1993), 975–77, and Simon Walker, *Nottingham* 37 (1993), 136–41 (discussing Allmand's *Henry V* as well).]

284.   ———. "Before the Armada: Iberia and England in the Middle Ages." In item 83. Pp. 108–20. [Relations with Spain and Portugal, to 1500.]

285.   ———. "Richard II's Councils." In item 43. Pp. 59–82.
        [Council's role, composition, royal domination thereof.]

286.   ———. "The Defence of Northumberland: A Preliminary
        Survey." In item 91. Pp. 161–72. [Who built castles, and
        when and why; whom did the kings trust for this task?]

287.   Grady, Frank. "The Lancastrian Gower and the Limits
        of Exemplarity." *Speculum* 70 (1995), 552–75. [Writing
        advice poetry for a king was not always a bed of roses.]

288.   Grant, Alexander. "The Otterburn War from the Scottish
        Point of View." In item 42. Pp. 30–64. [The battle was a
        typical border affair, albeit a major one, and it led to the
        truce of 1389.]

289.   ———. "Foreign Affairs under Richard III." In item 38.
        Pp. 113–32. [Dynasty, the royal image, and the impor-
        tance of Brittany in English policy.]

290.   ———. "Richard III and Scotland." In item 77.
        Pp. 115–48. [English ambitions and war aims: Richard
        III had a militant policy toward the northern enemy.]

291.   Griffiths, Ralph A. "The King's Court during the Wars of
        the Roses: Continuities in an Age of Discontinuities." In
        *Princes, Patronage, and the Nobility: The Court at the
        Beginning of the Modern Age, c. 1450–1650.* Edited by
        Ronald G. Asch and Adolf M. Birke. Oxford, 1991.
        Pp. 41–67. [A splendid court that was also business
        oriented; also published in item 46.]

292.   ———. *Sir Rhys ap Thomas and His Family: A Study in
        the Wars of the Roses and Early Tudor Politics.* Cardiff,
        1993. [The family's history and a reprint of the 1796
        version from *The Cambrian Register*, with Griffith's
        learned notes and comments.]

293.   ———. "The Provinces and the Dominions in the Age of the Wars of the Roses." In item 64. Pp. 1–25. [A broad survey that fits the Wars into "the new" British history.]

294.   Griffiths, Rhidian. "Prince Henry and Wales, 1400–1408." In item 54. Pp. 51–61. [Mostly military events and problems.]

295.   Gross, Anthony J. "Langland's Rats: A Moralist's Vision of Parliament." *Parliamentary History* 9 (1990), 286–301. [Worries about the potential for royal tyranny; see item 415 for the issue of the journal.]

296.   ———. "K. B. McFarlane and the Determinists: The Fallibilities of the English Kings, c. 1399–c. 1520." In item 19. Pp. 49–75. [Historiography of kings and kingship, and contemporary views on the king's role.]

297.   ———. *The Dissolution of the Lancastrian Kingship: Sir John Fortescue and the Crisis of Monarchy in Fifteenth-Century England.* Stamford, 1996. [Preface, J. R. Lander, pp. x–xviii. Fortescue as a propagandist and read here as a window upon political change.]

298.   Gunn, Steven J. "Sir Thomas Lovell (c. 1449–1524): A New Man in a New Monarchy?" In item 97. Pp. 117–53. [A career that called for tact and versatility.]

299.   Haigh, Philip A. *The Military Campaigns of the Wars of the Roses.* Stroud, 1995. [Battle by battle, with an appendix on Shrewsbury. Old fashioned, well done.]

300.   ———. *The Battle of Wakefield.* Stroud, 1996. [Figuring out what happened; see items 242 and 360.]

301.   ———. '. . . *Where Both the Host Fought . . .': The Rebellions of 1469–1470 and the Battles of Edgecote and Lose-Cote Field.* Heckmondwike, West Yorkshire, 1997. [Traditional military history: discussion of narrative sources; well illustrated and many maps.]

302.   Hammond, Peter W. *The Battles of Barnet and
        Tewkesbury*. Stroud and New York, 1990. [Informed
        narrative with many illustrations; appendix on legends
        surrounding the death of Edward of Lancaster.]

303.   ———. "The Reputation of Richard III." In item 38.
        Pp. 133–49. [Contemporary and subsequent ups and
        downs.]

304.   Hammond, Peter W., and Livia Visser-Fuchs. "Did
        Edward IV Strike Coins in Burgundy? A Rose Noble in
        Stone in Maastricht." *BNJ* 63 (1993), 129–32. [Carved in
        a doorway (and depicted); not very strong evidence for a
        royal policy.]

305.   Hammond, Peter W., Anne F. Sutton, and Livia Visser-
        Fuchs. "The Reburial of Richard, Duke of York, 21–30
        July, 1467." *Ricardian* 10/127 (December 1994), 122–65.
        [A narrative of the event and a publication (and transla-
        tion) of many scattered and miscellaneous sources.]

306.   Hanham, Alison. "Author? Author? Crowland Revisited."
        Ricardian 11/140 (March 1998), 226–38. [The many
        theories about authorship and the chronicle's origins,
        continuing a controversy from the 1980s.]

307.   Hardy, Robert. "The Longbow." In item 29. Pp. 161–81.
        [Its use and the life of an archer, with attention to what
        has been learned from the raising of "The Mary Rose."]

308.   Harriss, Gerald L. "Political Society and the Growth of
        Government in Late Medieval England." *Past and
        Present* 137 (February 1993), 28–57. [The structure was
        unusually solid, though men and events sapped the
        functioning in the fifteenth century.]

309.   ———. "The King and his Subjects." In item 57.
        Pp. 13–28. [The compact of civil society, working well or
        not so well.]

310.   ———. "The Dimensions of Politics." In item 19. Pp. 1–20. [Land, family, and politics: a valuable general assessment of communities and the nation.]

311.   ———. "Good Duke Humphrey." *Bodleian Library Quarterly* 19 (1994–96), 119–23. [An address at the 555th anniversary of Humphrey's benefaction.]

312.   Harvey, I. M. W. *Jack Cade's Rebellion of 1450.* Oxford, 1991. [First full-length study, with much focus on regional and county activity; little to say on behalf of Henry VI.]

313.   ———. "Was There Popular Politics in Fifteenth-Century England?" In item 19. Pp. 155–74. [How did a common voice make itself heard? Gossip, rumor, government spying.]

314.   Hicks, Michael A. "Did Edward IV Outlive his Reign or Did He Outreign His Life?" *Ricardian* 8/108 (March 1990), 342–45. [Can we accept the Anlaby Cartulary's death date of 22 June?]

315.   ———. *Richard III: The Man Behind the Myth.* London, 1991. [Political biography, with an interest in "the system": chapters on anti-Ricardian propaganda and later myths.]

316.   ———. "Unweaving the Web: The Plot of July, 1483 against Richard III and Its Wider Significance." *Ricardian* 9/114 (September 1991), 106–09. [Probably a real threat, though we have to rely largely on Stow's account.]

317.   ———. "The 1468 Statute of Livery." *HR* 64 (1991), 15–28. [Edward IV's attempt at reform; some prosecutions and the fading use of indentured retainers.]

318.   ———. "Richard, Duke of Gloucester: The Formative Years." In item 38. Pp. 21–37. [The rise and apprenticeship of a youngest son.]

319. ———. *Bastard Feudalism*. London and New York, 1995. [It had a long life, and it contributed to stability within the feudal polity. Valuable summary volume.]

320. ———. "The Forfeiture of Barnard Castle to the Bishop of Durham in 1459." *Northern* 33 (1997), 223–31. [Exemptions to a 1459 act of attainder of 1459; a king's remembrancer exchequer document published.]

321. ———. *Warwick the Kingmaker*. Oxford, 1998. [Thorough political biography with an eye on regional as well as central events: a bit tough on Warwick's moral and personal lapses.]

322. ———. "Cement or Solvent? Kinship and Politics in Late Medieval England: The Case of the Nevilles." *History* 83 (1998), 31–46. [Limits to the power of the Neville network.]

323. ———. "Between Majorities: The 'Beauchamp Interregnum,' 1439–49." *HR* 72 (1999), 27–43. [Duke Henry's daughter Anne held the inheritance together and wielded power.]

324. ———. "From Megaphone to Microscope: The Correspondence of Richard, Duke of York, with Henry VI in 1450 Revisited." *JMH* 25 (1999), 243–53. [York's concern about bad government and his poor communications with Henry as he moved to become "the opposition."]

325. Hodges, Geoffrey. *Owain Glyn Dŵr and the War of Independence in the Welsh Borders*. Almeley, Herefordshire, 1995. [Sympathetic and sensible political history and an assessment of success and failure.]

326. Hooper, Nicholas, and Matthew Bennett. *Cambridge Illustrated Atlas: Warfare, the Middle Ages, 768–1487*. Cambridge, 1996. [The Hundred Years War, 1327–96, pp. 116–23; The Fifteenth-Century (phase of the War),

pp. 128–35; The Wars of The Roses, pp. 140–47. Clear and useful; general chapter at the end, "Theory and Practice of Medieval Warfare."]

327.   Horrox, Rosemary. "The Government of Richard III." In item 38. Pp. 57–74. [How a king worked to get things done.]

328.   ———. "'Caterpillars of the Commonwealth?' Courtiers in Late Medieval England." In item 3. Pp. 1–15. [Held up to scorn, though they were not an aristocratic fifth column; their roles and uses.]

329.   ———. "Personalities and Politics." In item 76. Pp. 89–109. [Contemporary depiction of social stratification: how leaders were judged.]

330.   ———. "Yorkist and Early Tudor England." In *The New Cambridge Medieval History, VII, c. 1415–c. 1500.* Edited by Christopher Allmand. Cambridge, 1998. Pp. 477–95. [Basic survey: England's chapter in the wider tale of late medieval political and economic life.]

331.   Hudson, Graham. *The Battle of Towton.* 2nd ed., Tadcaster, North Yorkshire, 1991. [A booklet covering some very nasty business.]

332.   Hughes, M. E. J. "Counselling the King: Perceptions of Court Politics in the Reign of Richard II." In *France and the British Isles in the Middle Ages and Renaissance: Essays by Members of Girton College, Cambridge, in Memory of Ruth Morgan.* Edited by Gillian Jondorf and David M. Dumville. Woodbridge and Rochester, N.Y., 1991. Pp. 199–206. [The theme of "the king's wicked advisers" as reflected in political and satirical poetry.]

333.   Hughes, Michael. "The Fourteenth-Century French Raids on Hampshire and the Isle of Wight." In item 28. Pp. 121–43. [Mostly town by town: Portsmouth,

Southampton, Winchester, Porchester Castle, and the
Isle of Wight.]

334.   James, Arnold J. "An Amended Itinerary to Bosworth
Field." *Ricardian* 9/113 (June), 1991, 54–69. [The routes
that led to the critical confrontation.]

335.   James, Susan E. "Sir William Parr of Kendal: Part I,
1434–1471." *Cumberland* 93 (1993), 98–114. [Biographi-
cal: times were tough and tricky.]

336.   ———. "Sir William Parr of Kendal: Part II, 1471–83."
Cumberland 94 (1994), 105–20. [He was thick with Glou-
cester and was made a knight of the Garter by Edward
IV in his years of estate-building.]

337.   ———. "Sir John Parr of Kendal, 1437–1475." *Cumberland* 96 (1996), 71–86. [The life of a successful courtier.]

338.   Jamieson, Neil. "The Recruitment of Northerners for
Service in English Armies in France, 1415–50." In item
26. Pp. 102–15. [Large Lancastrian and Cheshire contin-
gents: levies, fees, annuities, contracts with captains.]

339.   Jefferson, Lisa. "Ms. Arundel 48 and the Earliest
Statutes of the Order of the Garter." *EHR* 109 (1994),
356–85. [Probably Henry V was responsible; French
document published.]

340.   ———. "Two Fifteenth-Century Mss. of the Statutes of
the Order of the Garter." *English Manuscript Studies* 5
(1995), 18–35. [*Tempore* Edward IV: one now in Nancy,
one in Modena, both with seals still attached.]

341.   Jewell, Helen. "*Piers Plowman*—A Poem of Crisis: An
Analysis of Political Instability in Langland's England."
In item 92. Pp. 59–80. [We can move through different
versions of the poem and read a story of growing dis-
content.]

342.   Jones, Michael. "The Fortunes of War: The Military
        Career of John, 2nd Lord Bourchier (d. 1400)." *Essex* 26
        (1995), 145–61. [Biographical article, with a look at the
        ransom needed in 1374.]

343.   Jones, Michael, and Simon Walker, eds. *Private
        Indentures for Life Service in Peace and War, 1278–1476.*
        Camden Miscellany 32. Camden Society, 5th series, 3
        (1994), 1–190. [Introduction (pp. 9–33) and 150+ docu-
        ments, mostly after 1377.]

344.   Jones, Michael K. "Richard III as a Soldier." In item 38.
        Pp. 93–112. [A family tradition and Richard's eagerness
        for battle and a martial image.]

345.   ———. "Richard, Duke of Gloucester and the Scropes of
        Masham." *Ricardian* 10/134 (September 1996), 454–60.
        [An indenture of 16 Edward IV: service and loyalty?]

346.   ———. "The Relief of Avranches (1439): An English Feat
        of Arms at the End of the Hundred Years War." In item
        81. Pp. 42–55. [The last field victory, and a triumph for
        chivalry, if nothing else.]

347.   ———. "Edward IV, the Earl of Warwick and the Yorkist
        Claim to the Throne." *HR* 70 (1997), 342–52. [Large
        royal grant to Warwick in 1463, as part of the king's
        gratitude for support in their fugitive days.]

348.   Jones, Michael K., and Malcolm G. Underwood. *The
        King's Mother: Lady Margaret Beaufort, Countess of
        Richmond and Derby.* Cambridge, 1992. [Major
        biography of a powerful woman and a pushy mother.]

349.   Jurkowski, Maureen. "Lancastrian Royal Service,
        Lollardy and Forgery: The Career of Thomas Tykhill." In
        item 2. Pp. 33–52. [A Derbyshire lawyer with family
        tradition of "civil service" but tainted by heresy.]

350.   Keen, Maurice. *English Society in the Later Middle Ages.*
         London, 1990. [A volume in the Penguin Social History
         of Britain series; concise and insightful.]

351.   ———. "Ordinances of War in 1385." In item 3. Pp. 33–48.
         [The large expedition to Scotland and how it was
         arranged and managed.]

352.   ———. "The Wilton Diptych: The Case for a Crusading
         Context." In item 44. Pp. 189–96. [A late date for the
         diptych and the Anglo-French amity of men active in
         crusading orders.]

353.   Keen, Maurice, and Mark Warner, eds. "Morley vs.
         Montagu (1399): A Case in the Court of Chivalry."
         Camden Miscellany 34. Camden Society, 5th series, 10
         (1997), 145–95. [Documents from PRO State Papers
         Misc. on the quarrel, with full introduction on the appeal
         of treason.]

354.   Kekewich, Margaret L. "John Fortescue Junior: An
         Upwardly Mobile Gentleman, c. 1400–1442." *Southern*
         17 (1995), 1–23. [Not a fancy background, but with links
         to the Hungerfords.]

355.   ———. "'Thou shalt be under the power of the man': Sir
         John Fortescue and the Yorkist Succession." *Nottingham*
         42 (1998), 188–230. [Close reading of some later
         Fortescue tracts, with excerpts.]

356.   Kekewich, Margaret L., Colin Richmond, Anne F. Sutton,
         Livia Visser-Fuchs, and John L. Watts. *The Politics of
         Fifteenth-Century England: John Vale's Book.* Stroud,
         1995. [B.L. Add Ms 48031, from 1450–82. A miscellany
         that looks upon political life, with information on the ms.
         Richmond deals with political stability, Visser-Fuchs the
         manuscript, Watts "polemic and politics."]

357.   Kelly, Henry A. "Croyland Observations." *Ricardian* 8/108 (March 1990), 334–41. [See item 306 on this ongoing discussion/controversy.]

358.   ———. "The Case Against Edward IV's Marriage and Off-Spring: Secrecy, Witchcraft; Secrecy; Pre-Contract." *Ricardian* 11/142 (September 1998), 326–35. [The parliament of 1484 worried about Edward and Elizabeth Wydville; see also John Ashdown-Hill, *Ricardian* 11/144 (March 1999), 463–67, on this issue.]

359.   Kenyon, John R. "Coastal Artillery Fortification in England in the Late Fourteenth and Early Fifteenth Centuries." In item 28. Pp. 145–49. [Gunlocks replaced arrow slits.]

360.   Knowles, Richard. "The Battle of Wakefield: The Topography." *Ricardian* 9/117 (June 1992), 258–65. [Very little reliable evidence; see items 242 and 300.]

361.   Leland, John L. "A Further Note on the Dalyngrygge Case." *Med Pros* 11/1 (1990), 85–87. [He was still in the Arundel faction in 1386 in this corrective to an article Leland published in 1988.]

362.   ———. "The Abjuration of 1388." *Med Pros* 15/1 (1994), 115–38. [Fifteen favorites forced to promise to leave the court: a mixed group in age and background.]

363.   ———. "Unpardonable Sinners? Exclusions from the General Pardon of 1388." *Med Pros* 17/2 (1996), 181–95. [Eighteen favorites excluded, some having been in the de Vere circle.]

364.   ———. "The Oxford Trial of 1400: Royal Politics and the County Gentry." In item 37. Pp. 165–89. [The jurors, and how old Ricardians got woven into the fabric of Lancastrian government.]

365.   Loades, David M. *Politics and the Nation: England,*
         1450–1660. 5th ed. Oxford, 1999. [First edition of this
         useful and widely-adopted survey was published in 1974.]

366.   Lomas, Richard A. *Northeastern England in the Middle*
         Ages. Edinburgh, 1992. [Begins with 1066, with chapters
         on government, the Church (both high and popular), and
         the economy.]

367.   ———. "The Impact of Border Warfare: The Scots and
         South Tweedside, c. 1290–c. 1590." *Scottish Historical*
         Review 75 (1996), 143–67. [What the English spent on
         border warfare and defense, set against a society in con-
         siderable distress.]

368.   Luckett, Dominic A. "Crown Patronage and Political
         Morality in Early Tudor England: The Case of Giles,
         Lord Daubeney." *EHR* 110 (1995), 578–95. [His
         checkered record and his fall from favor.]

369.   ———. "Patronage, Violence and Revolt in the Reign of
         Henry VII." In item 2. Pp. 145–60. [Efforts to build a
         king's party, regional difficulties, and the rebellion of
         1497.]

370.   Magee, James. "Sir William Elmham and the
         Recruitment for Henry Despenser's Crusade of 1383.
         Med Pros 20 (1999), 181–90. [The networks whence
         came the men who signed on for the venture.]

371.   Martin, Geoffrey H., ed. and tr. *Henry Knighton:*
         Knighton's Chronicle, 1337–1396. Oxford Medieval
         Texts. Oxford, 1995. [Major project, now making this
         valuable work accessible.]

372.   Matheson, Lister M., ed. *Death and Dissent: Two 15th-*
         Century Chronicles. Woodbridge, 1999. [The first is
         "Dethe of the Kynge of Scotis," trans. John Shirley;
         second is "Warkworth's *Chronicle*: The Chronicle

Attributed to John Warkworth, Master of Peterhouse, Cambridge." Matheson's introduction to the latter work, pp. 61–92, the Chronicle, pp. 93–124.]

373.   McHardy, Alison K. "Haxey's Case, 1397: The Petition and Its Presenter Reconsidered." In item 37. Pp. 93–114. [A Lincolnshire king's clerk who petitioned to curtail royal expenditure; a review of his whole career.]

374.   McNiven, Peter. "Rebellion, Sedition and the Legend of Richard II's Survival in the Reigns of Henry IV and Henry V." *BJRUL* 76 (1994), 93–117. [The many reasons for the myth's persistence; legal sources tapped along with the chronicles.]

375.   Mercer, Malcolm. "Lancastrian Loyalism in the South-West: The Case of the Beauforts." *Southern* 19 (1997), 42–60. [Their network, after 1471, in Somerset and Dorset, plus Stourton family links.]

376.   ———. "Driven to Rebellion? Sir John Lewknor, Dynastic Loyalty and Debt." *Sussex* 137 (1999), 153–59. [With the Lancastrians at Tewkesbury, after his career had crashed under the Yorkists.]

377.   ———. "Lancastrian Loyalism in Kent during the Wars of the Roses." *Arch Cant* 119 (1999), 221–43. [Alliances, networks, and an argument that ties and bonds held up in violent times.]

378.   Milner, John D. "The English Enterprise in France, 1412–13." In item 26. Pp. 80–101. [The Church's contribution to the enterprise and the public's interest.]

379.   Moorhen, Wendy E. A. "William, Lord Hastings and the Crisis of 1483: An Assessment, Part I." *Ricardian* 9/122 (September 1993), 446–66; "Part I." Ibid. 9/123 (December 1993), 482–97. [Loyalty and ambition proved to be fatal bedfellows.]

380. Morgan, D. A. L. "The Political After-Life of Edward III: The Apotheosis of a Warmonger." *EHR* 112 (1997), 856–81. [His fifteenth-century image; war abroad, peace at home.]

381. Morgan, Philip. "Henry IV and the Shadow of Richard II." In item 2. Pp. 1–31. [Political, ideological, and diplomatic aspects of the transition; the world of rumor, conjecture, and conspiracy.]

382. ———. "The Death of Edward V and the Rebellion of 1483." *HR* 68 (1995), 229–32. [A note in the Anlaby Cartulary gives the date (27 June).]

383. ———. "'Those Were the Days': A Yorkist Pedigree Roll." In item 64. Pp. 107–16. [A Rylands pedigree roll as a poster and as propaganda.]

384. Mott, Roger. "Richard II and the Crisis of July, 1397." In item 99. Pp. 167–77. [Gloucester's arrest: short term security and tracking the tale in the chronicles.]

385. Neillands, Robin. *The Hundred Years War*. London and New York, 1990. [Standard narrative, familiar story.]

386. ———. *The Wars of the Roses*. London, 1992. [Standard tale, told once again.]

387. Neville, Cynthia J. "Local Sentiment and the 'National' Enemy in Northern England in the Later Middle Ages." *JBS* 35 (1990), 419–37. [The North was a different world, looking Janus-like in both directions.]

388. ———. *Violence, Custom and Law: The Anglo-Scottish Border Lands in the Later Middle Ages*. Edinburgh, 1998. [Detailed look at a society in constant turmoil: law, violence, local custom, and strategies for coping.]

389. O'Regan, M. *Richard III: A Brief Life*. York, 1999. [A "miscellaneous publication" of the Yorkshire Archaeological Society.]

390.   Ormrod, W. Mark. "The Western European Monarchies in the Later Middle Ages." In *Economic Systems and State Finances*. Edited by Richard Bonney. Oxford, 1995. Pp. 123–60. [Comparing England, France, and Spain.]

391.   ———. *Political Life in Medieval England, 1300–1450*. London and New York, 1995. [In the British History in Perspective series; perceptive but very condensed.]

392.   ———. "The Domestic Response to the Hundred Years War." In item 28. Pp. 84–101. [Selling the war, in the face of high taxes and a crisis in public support and confidence.]

393.   Osberg, Richard H. "The Lambeth Palace Library Manuscript Account of Henry VI's 1432 London Entry." *Mediaeval Studies* 52 (1990), 255–67. [Perhaps an abbreviation of Carpenter's letter, and Lydgate's account offering a pro-London view.]

394.   Parsons, John Carmi. "Ritual and Symbol in the English Medieval Queenship to 1500." In *Women and Sovereignty*. Edited by Louise O. Fradenburg. Edinburgh, 1992. Pp. 60–77. [Their arrival, coronation, intercession with their husbands, and their funerals. Also, item 501.]

395.   ———. "'Never was a body buried in England with such solemnity and honour': The Burials and Posthumous Commemorations of English Queens to 1500." In *Queens and Queenship in Medieval Europe*. Edited by Anne J. Duggan. Woodbridge and Rochester, N.Y., 1995). Pp. 317–37. [The treatment accorded women in the world of high politics and ritual.]

396.   Patterson, Lee. "Making Identities in Fifteenth-Century England." In *New Historical Literary Study: Essays on Reproducing Texts, Representing History*. Edited by Jeffrey N. Cox and Larry J. Reynolds. Princeton, 1993. Pp. 69–107. [The foils used to showcase Henry V and the Lancastrians, plus advice to the prince.]

397.   Payling, Simon. *Political Society in Lancastrian England: The Greater Gentry of Nottinghamshire.* Oxford, 1991. [How county government and society operated (and failed to do so): much general and tabular material on the gentry and their families.]

398.   Payne, Anne, and J. Jefferson. "Edward IV: The Garter and the Golden Fleece." In *L'Ordre de la Toison d'or, de Philippe le Bon à Philippe le Beau (1430–1505): Idéal ou reflet d'une société?* Edited by C. Van den Bergen-Pantens. Brussels, 1996. [The Burgundian court and its luster, affecting English chivalric styles and orders.]

399.   Pearsall, Derek. *The Life of Geoffrey Chaucer: A Critical Biography.* Oxford, 1992. [Life and career: literary work in the context of the career, with a chapter on "The Chaucer Portraits."]

400.   ———. "Hoccleve's *Regement of Princes*: The Poetics of Royal Self-Representation." *Speculum* 69 (1994), 386–410. [Flattering Henry V as the "hammer of Lollards."]

401.   Phillpotts, Christopher J. "John of Gaunt and English Policy toward France, 1389–1395." *JMH* 16 (1990), 363–86. [Gaunt's policies in Guyenne and Richard's intercession in favor of a peace policy in 1396.]

402.   ———. "The Fate of the Truce of Paris, 1396–1415." *JMH* 24 (1998), 61–80. [How the truce could be constructed for conflict, renegotiation, and English ambitions.]

403.   Pollard, Anthony J. *North Eastern England during the Wars of the Roses: Lay Society, War, and Politics, 1450–1500.* Oxford, 1990. [Important regional study merging the North and the nation.]

404.   ———. *Richard III and the Princes in the Tower.* Stroud, 1991. [The Legends, later stories, some documents in the

appendices, and lavishly illustrated. Book discussed by
P. W. Hammond, Livia Visser-Fuchs, and Isolde Wigram,
Ricardian 9/116 (March 1992), 211–21.]

405.   ———. "Dominic Mancini's Narrative of the Events of
1483." *Nottingham* 38 (1994), 152–63. [Not pro-Richard:
how to filter the propaganda; Mancini's sources and
informants.]

406.   ———. "The Crown and the County Palatine of Durham,
1437–94." In item 77. Pp. 67–87. [Episcopal power on the
wane from 1437; a Neville fiefdom and Richard III's
domination.]

407.   ———. "The Lancastrian Constitutional Experiment Revisited: Henry IV, Sir John Tiptoft, and the Parliament
of 1406." *Parliamentary History* 14 (1995), 103–19. [As
speaker, Tiptoft focused on the treasury and the king
accepted that the council and the crown should share the
problem.]

408.   Powell, Edward. "Lancastrian England." In *New Cambridge Medieval History, VII. c 1415–c 1500*. Edited by
Christopher Allmand. Cambridge, 1998. Pp. 457–76.
[Some thematic discussion, but mostly politics
emanating from the throne.]

409.   Prestwich, Michael. "*Miles in Armis Strenuus*: The
Knight at War." *TRHS* 6/5 (1995), 201–20. [Knights in
the military retinues.]

410.   ———. *Armies and Warfare in the Middle Ages: The
English Experience*. New Haven and London, 1996. [A
thorough and valuable survey, mostly on the High
Middle Ages, but some on later times.]

411.   Pugh, Thomas B. "Richard, Duke of York and the Rebellion of Henry Holand, Duke of Exeter, in May 1454."
HR 63 (1990), 248–62. [Richard overcame his son-in-law

and would-be rebel; his letter of rebuke is to Exeter, not to March.]

412.   Radulescu, Aluca. "John Vale's Book and Sir Thomas Malory's *Le Morte Darthur*: A Political Agenda." *Arthuriana* 9 (1999), 69–80. [A political focus, with a look at the ideas of Fortescue and Lydgate.]

413.   Radzikowski, Piotr. "Niclas von Popplau: His Works and Travels." *Ricardian* 11/140 (March 1998), 239–48. [He came from Breslau, met Richard III, and kept a journal of his travels.]

414.   Rawcliffe, Carole. "Parliament and the Settlement of Disputes by Arbitration in the Later Middle Ages." *Parliamentary History* 9 (1990), 316–42. [Case studies; election time quarrels; Commons was often happy to recommend arbitration.]

415.   Rawcliffe, Carole, and Linda Clark. "Introduction." *Parliamentary History* 9 (1990), 233–42. [Introducing an issue devoted to "Parliament and Communities in the Middle Ages," with a survey of topics treated by the subsequent papers; see items 295, 414, 428, and 962.]

416.   Reeves, A. Compton. "The Foppish Eleven of 1483." *Med Pros* 16/2 (1995), 111–34. [Who they were, as singled out by sumptuary legislation.]

417.   Richardson, Geoffrey. *The Hollow Crowns: A History of the Battles of the Wars of the Roses*. Shippey, 1996. [Battle maps and line drawings (by Roy Barton); brief narratives of eleven battles, from St. Albans to Bosworth, with an appendix attacking John Morton for the death of the little princes.]

418.   Richmond, Colin F. *The Paston Family in the Fifteenth Century: The First Phase*. Cambridge, 1990. [The first of three detailed volumes on the family's rise and activity: to know them is not to love them.]

419.   ———. "1483: The Year of Decision (or Taking the
         Throne)." In item 38. Pp. 39–55. [Events, chronology,
         and the sources.]

420.   ———. "The Fifteenth Century: 18 November 1992."
         Journal of Historical Sociology 6 (1993), 471–85. [Rich-
         mond's inaugural lecture at the University of Keele.]

421.   ———. *The Paston Family in the Fifteenth Century:
         Fastolf's Will.* Cambridge, 1996. [Volume 2, following
         item 418, carries the tale into the years of great peril
         and temptation. (Volume 3, *The Paston Family: Endings*
         did not appear until 2000.)]

422.   ———. "The Nobility and the Wars of the Roses,
         1457–1479." *Journal of Historical Sociology* 9 (1996),
         395–409. [Supplements and amends his 1977 paper (on
         who was where, and on which side), published in
         Nottingham in 1977.]

423.   ———. "Richard III, Richard Nixon, and the Brutality of
         Fifteenth-Century Politics: A Discussion." In item 64.
         Pp. 89–97. [And then the conference participants discuss
         the proposition, pp. 97–106.]

424.   ———. "Patronage and Polemic." In item 97. Pp. 65–87.
         [Was political ideology linked to practice or to ethical
         concerns?]

425.   ———. "The Earl of Warwick's Domination of the
         Channel and the Naval Dimension to the Wars of the
         Roses, 1456–1460." *Southern* 20–21 (1998–99), 1–19.
         [The importance of the maritime factor; Warwick filled
         in, as the king proved incapable of taking over.]

426.   Rosenthal, Joel T. "Some Late Medieval and Mid-Tudor
         Norfolk MPs: Compare and Contrast." *Parliamentary
         History* 18/3 (1999), 291–302. [Some changing patterns
         in careers and in the role of men from East Anglia.]

427.   Roskell, John S., with Carole Rawcliffe and Linda Clark.
         The History of Parliament: The House of Commons,
         1386–1421. 4 vols. Stroud, 1993. [Vol. 1 has Roskell's
         introduction and his analyses of the parliaments; vols.
         2–3–4, the biographies. Reviewed by Simon Walker,
         Nottingham 38 (1994), 172–77; A. L. Brown, *EHR* 109
         (1994), 388–90; G. L. Harriss, *Parliamentary History* 13
         (1994), 206–26; J. T. Rosenthal, *Med Pros* 14/2 (1993),
         135–58; Tony Pollard, *Ricardian* 9/123 (December 1993),
         498–504; A. L. Brown (item 515). A vast work and a
         treasure trove of both data and analysis; work on the
         later Lancastrian period now proceeds apace under
         Linda Clark's editorial direction.]

428.   Saul, Nigel. "The Commons and the Abolition of
         Badges." *Parliamentary History* 9 (1990), 302–25. [On
         Henry IV's agenda: Ancient Petition (SC 8/100/4985)
         printed; see item 415.]

429.   ———, ed. *Age of Chivalry: Art and Society in Late*
         Medieval England. London, 1992. [Useful short essays
         on politics, high culture, and patronage, in a well-
         illustrated volume: papers by Saul, Juliet and Malcolm
         Vale, Nigel Ramsay, Peter Draper, Janet Backhouse,
         Brian Stone, Pamela Tudor-Craig, and Veronica
         Sekules.]

430.   ———. "Medieval Britain." In *The National Trust:*
         Historical Atlas of Britain: Prehistoric and Medieval.
         Edited by Nigel Saul. Stroud, 1994. Pp. 115–57. [Clear
         and useful, covering social as well as political
         developments.]

431.   ———. "Henry V and the Dual Monarchy." In item 83.
         Pp. 144–50. [Royal power on the increase, perhaps to a
         dangerous degree.]

432.   ————. "Richard II and the Vocabulary of Kingship."
              EHR 110 (1995), 854–77. [Verbal excess, linked to
              excessive political ideology.]

433.   ————. "Richard II and Westminster Abbey." In item 14.
              Pp. 156–218. [Royal gifts, building, and the abbey as a
              chess piece in political struggles.]

434.   ————. *Richard II.* New Haven and London, 1997. [The
              definitive biography: large, comprehensive, judicious,
              generally convincing in interpretation. Reviewed by
              G. B. Stow, *Speculum* 74 (1999), 493–96.]

435.   ————. "Richard II's Ideas of Kingship." In item 44.
              Pp. 27–32. [Richard's obsession with the imagery of
              exaltation.]

436.   ————. "The Sussex Gentry and the Oath to Uphold the
              Acts of the Merciless Parliament." *Sussex* 135 (1997),
              221–39. [A document with the oath and an analysis of
              the county gentry who had to swear (in July 1388).]

437.   ————. "Richard II, York, and the Evidence of the King's
              Itinerary." In item 37. Pp. 71–92. [Moving royal "head-
              quarters" was never very likely.]

438.   ————. "The Rise of the Dallingridge Family." *Sussex*
              136 (1998), 123–32. [Mostly on the 1380s, with a look at
              family marriages and patronage.]

439.   ————. "The Kingship of Richard II." In item 43.
              Pp. 37–57. [Against a continental backdrop, with a focus
              on the court and royal ideology.]

440.   ————. *Richard II and Chivalric Kingship.* Inaugural
              Lecture of 24 November 1998. Royal Holloway College,
              Egham, 1999. [A peace policy and a love of chivalry were
              awkward bedfellows.]

441.   Seward, Desmond. *The Wars of the Roses Through the
              Lives of Five Men and Women of the Fifteenth Century.*

New York and London, 1995. [Jane Lambert and her daughter Jane Shore, Margaret Beaufort, the earl of Oxford, and John Morton.]

442. Sherborne, James. "The Defence of the Realm and the Impeachment of Michael de la Pole in 1386." In item 92. Pp. 97–116. [War, diplomacy, finance, and the French fleet; others beside de la Pole might have (also) been held accountable.]

443. Silva-Vigier, Anil de. *The Moste Highe Prince . . . John of Gaunt, 1340–1399*. Durham, 1992. [Old style biography, far from the cutting edge.]

444. Smith, Anthony. "'The Greatest Man of that Age': The Acquisition of Sir John Fastolf's East Anglian Estates." In item 3. Pp. 137–53. [He spent £13,000 between 1415–45; men and expenses, with a map of the sites.]

445. Smith, Robert D. "Artillery and the Hundred Years War: Myth and Interpretation." In item 28. Pp. 151–60. [Surveys the evidence on its use, in an area where we have very limited information.]

446. Soper, C. S. "Robert Rydon: Fifteenth-Century Local Boy Makes Good." *D & C N and Q* 36 (1992), 211–13. [Henry VII's clerk of the council.]

447. Spence, Richard T. *The Shepherd Lord of Skipton Castle: Henry Clifford, 10th Lord Clifford, 1454–1523*. Skipton Castle, 1994. [Biographical and appreciative booklet.]

448. Sprakes, Brian. *Historical Notices of the DeMauley Family: Medieval Lords of Doncaster*. Barsley, South Yorkshire, 1997. Pp. 19–38. [Fairly straight political and genealogical history, in the Aspects of Doncaster: Discovering Local History series, edited by Brian Elliott.]

449. Stansfield, Michael. "John Holland, Duke of Exeter and Earl of Huntington (d. 1447) and the Costs of the

Hundred Years War." In item 54. Pp. 103–18. [Political history: ransom, family finances, marriages settlement, and a life shaped by war.]

450.   Stow, George B. "Richard II in John Gower's *Confessio Amantis*: Some Historical Perspectives." *Mediaevalia* 16 (1993), 3–31. [Poetic idealism and a window into historical happenings.]

451.   Strohm, Paul. "Saving the Appearances: Chaucer's *Purse* and the Fabric of the Lancastrian Claim." In item 48. Pp. 21–40. [The new dynasty's propaganda and how the chroniclers dealt with royal spin.]

452.   ———. "The Trouble with Richard: The Reburial of Richard II and Lancastrian Symbolic Strategy." *Speculum* 71 (1996), 87–111. [Lancastrian worries about rumors, legitimation, Lollardy, and Henry V's identity problems.]

453.   ———. *England's Empty Throne: Usurpation and the Language of Legitimation.* New Haven and London, 1998. [New historicism focused on the rhetoric of politics and the fashioning of their interpretation.]

454.   ———. "Hoccleve, Lydgate, and the Lancastrian Court." In item 96. Pp. 640–61. [Poetry, politics, and propaganda.]

455.   Sutton, Anne J. "The Court and Its Culture in the Reign of Richard III." In item 38. Pp. 75–92. [The role of ceremony and display, manners, and literary culture.]

456.   ———. "John Skirwith, King's Pointmaker, (1461–86) and Leatherseller of London." *Ricardian* 11/137 (June 1997), 54–93. [Career, family, his widow and debts; a long inventory of his goods, 1 Henry VII.]

457.   Sutton, Anne J., and Livia Visser-Fuchs. "The Making of a Minor London Chronicle in the Household of Sir

Thomas Frowyk (died 1485)." *Ricardian* 10/126
(September 1994), 86–103. [Some interesting small bits
on the 1480s.]

458.   Sutton, Anne J., Livia Visser-Fuchs, with Peter W.
Hammond. *The Reburial of Richard, Duke of York,
21–30 July 1476*. Richard III Society, London, 1996.
[From Harleian Ms. 4632. French text of Chester
Herald's account, with documents on the hearse and the
feast, plus an English narrative; handsome, well
illustrated booklet.]

459.   Sutton, Anne J., and Livia Visser-Fuchs. "The Royal
Burials of the House of York at Windsor, Part I."
Ricardian 11/143 (December 1998), 366–407. [Much can
be retrieved; routes and processions, with the narratives
in translation. "Part II," *Ricardian* 11/144 (March 1999),
446–62.]

460.   ———. "Laments for the Death of Edward IV: 'It was a
world to see him ride about'." *Ricardian* 11/145 (June
1999), 506–24. [Poems and laments, published in
translation.]

461.   Taylor, Craig. "Sir John Fortescue and the French
Polemical Treatise of the Hundred Years War." *EHR* 114
(1995), 112–29. [Fortescue's use of French material,
especially "Pour ce que plusieurs," by way of Philippa of
Clarence.]

462.   Thompson, Guy Llewelyn. *Paris, Its People Under
English Rule: The Anglo-Burgundian Regime, 1420–
1436*. Oxford, 1991. [Political and urban history of an
occupied city under Henry VI's minority council and by
the people actually on the spot.]

463.   Thornton, Tim. "Scotland and the Isle of Man, c. 1400–
1625: Noble Power and Royal Presumption in the
Northern Irish Sea Province." *Scottish Historical Review*

77 (1998), 1–30. [The Island's long grasp on autonomy
and the complicated politics of the Irish Sea world.]

464.   Tuck, Anthony J. "Richard II and the Hundred Years
War." In item 92. Pp. 116–31. [Foreign policy: money
problems pushed Richard toward a conciliatory position.]

465.   ———. "Henry IV and Europe: A Dynastic Search for
Recognition." In item 19. Pp. 107–25. [The French court's
hostility and how other powers lined up after 1399.]

466.   ———. *Crown and Nobility: England, 1272–1461.*
Oxford, 1999. [The second edition of a valuable study,
first published in 1985. An epilogue: "New Perspectives,
1985–99," pp. 288–300.]

467.   ———. "Richard II and the House of Luxemburg." In
item 43. Pp. 205–29. [Richard was but a small cog in
continental diplomatic wheels.]

468.   Turvey, R. K. "The Marcher Shire of Pembroke and the
Glyndŵr Rebellion." *Welsh History Review* 15 (1990–91),
151–68. [Pembrokeshire spared the worst of the rebellion's destructive path.]

469.   Turville-Petre, Thorlac. "The Persecution of Elizabeth
Swillingtod by Ralph, Lord Cromwell." *Nottingham* 42
(1998), 174–87. [Duress and imprisonment in the 1430s,
over lands; "Compleints" published, 179–83.]

470.   Tyson, Colin. "The Battle of Otterburn: When and Where
Was It Fought?" In item 42. Pp. 65–93. [Squeezing the
sources and A. H. Burne's views on warfare, plus
Froissart's account.]

471.   Vale, Malcolm. "Le tournoi dans la France du Nord,
l'Angleterre et les Pays-Bas." In *Théâtre et Spectacles
hier et aujourd'hui: Moyen Âge et Renaissance.* Actes du
115ᵉ congrès National des Société Savants. Paris, 1991.

472. ———. "The End and Aftermath of the Hundred Years War." In item 83. Pp. 150–62. [The breakdown of the English war machine.]

473. ———. "An Anglo-Burgundian Nobleman and Art Patron: Louis de Bruges, Lord of la Gruthuyse and Earl of Winchester. In item 8. Pp. 115–32. [A central figure in diplomacy and cultural migration (especially architecture).]

474. ———. "The War in Aquitaine." In item 28. Pp. 69–82. [Battles and the course and fortunes of war.]

475. Virgoe, Roger. "The Earlier Knyvets: The Rise of a Norfolk Gentry Family, Part I." *Norfolk* 41/1 (1990), 1–14, and "Part II," 41/3 (1992), 249–79. [The fortunes of an East Anglian family: careers, marriages, and opportunities; also published as number 11, item 94.]

476. ———. "Hugh atte Fenn and Books at Cambridge." *Cambridge Bibliographical Society* 10/1 (1991), 92–98. [Book bequests, paid so slowly as to be of little value.]

477. Visser-Fuchs, Livia. "Edward IV's 'memoir on paper' to Charles, Duke of Burgundy: The So-Called 'Short Version of the arrivall'." *Nottingham* 36 (1992), 167–227. [How the "short version" came to be written; appendix on the ms, printed text, modern use, and the Harpisfeld Newsletter (pp. 210–20).]

478. ———. "'He hardly touched his food, but he talked with me all the time': What Niclas von Popplau Really Wrote about Richard III." *Ricardian* 11/145 (June 1999), 525–30. [Based on the transcription of the Polish account; see item 413.]

479. Walker, Simon E. "Letters of the Duke of Lancaster in 1381 and 1399." *EHR* 106 (1991), 68–79. [Two letters: one being Northumberland's advice to Gaunt, the other a trustworthy newsletter from Lady Joan Pelham.]

480.   ———. "Richard II's Views on Kingship." In item 3.
Pp. 49–63. [Not such radical views, but his ideology
helped tangle the implementation of his policies.]

481.   ———. "Political Saints in Late Medieval England." In
item 19. Pp. 77–106. [Religious support for the opposition; who backed which saints and would-be saints.]

482.   ———. "Between Church and Crown: Master Richard
Andrew, King's Clerk." *Speculum* 74 (1999), 956–91.
[His career: Dean of York, royal secretary, donor of
books to All Souls.]

483.   ———. "Janico Dartasso: Chivalry, Nationality and the
Man-at-Arms." *History* 84 (1999), 31–51. [Janico rode
the crest of chivalry to a good career, though it peaked
well before the end.]

484.   Warner, M. "Chivalry in Action: Thomas Montagu and
the War in France, 1417–1428." *Nottingham* 42 (1998),
146–73. [Mostly his late life and career; warfare before
the heavy reliance on artillery.]

485.   Warner, M. W., and Kay Lacey, "Neville vs. Percy: A
Precedent Dispute circa 1442." *HR* 69 (1996), 211–17. [A
regional quarrel that escalated, with Augmentations
Office documents published.]

486.   Warren, Nancy B. "Kings, Saints, and Nuns: Gender,
Religion, and Authority in the Reign of Henry V." *Viator*
30 (1999), 307–22. [Syon and the Brigittines, and Henry's
aims in his propaganda wars.]

487.   Watts, D. G. "Popular Disorder in Southern England,
1250–1450." In *Conflict and Community in Southern
England.* Edited by Barry Stapleton. London and New
York, 1992. Pp. 1–15. [People with attitude, especially in
but hardly confined to 1381. Also see item 689.]

488.   Watts, John. *"De Consulatu Stiliconis*: Texts and Politics in the Reign of Henry VI." *JMH* 16 (1990), 251–66. [A fifteenth-century translation and an argument on behalf of Richard of York.]

489.   ———. "The Counsels of King Henry VI, ca. 1435–1445." *EHR* 106 (1991), 279–98. [The ordinance of 1444, the nature of the council, and royal weakness rather than governmental norm.]

490.   ———. "When Did Henry VI's Minority End?" In item 26. Pp. 116–39. [Henry's shortcomings, decisions of 1436–37, and the role of the minority council.]

491.   ———. *Henry VI and the Politics of Kingship.* Cambridge, 1996. [Major study of Lancastrian kingship and royal government. Reviewed by R. A. Griffiths, *EHR* 113 (1998), 685–87; M. H. Keen, *Nottingham* 41 (1997), 192–97.]

492.   Webster, Bruce. "Anglo-Scottish Relations, 1296–1389: Some Recent Essays." *Scottish Historical Review* 74 (1995), 99–108. [A review article: border conflict was Edward I's enduring legacy.]

493.   ———. *The Wars of the Roses.* University College London, 1998. [In the Introduction to History series. Short: what happened and a look at why.]

494.   Weir, Alison. *The Princes in the Tower.* New York, 1992. [The myth of the monster still lives.]

495.   Williams, Barrie. "Richard III and the House of Dudley." *Ricardian* 8/108 (March 1990), 346–50. [The elder branch knew how to serve and keep out of the line of fire.]

496.   Williams, Daniel. "Richard III and his Overmighty Subjects: In Defence of the King." In item 81. Pp. 56–71. [Richard's commitment to law and order and his view of kingship.]

497.   Williams, Joann A. M. "The Political Career of Francis,
        Viscount Lovel (1456–?)." *Ricardian* 8/109 (June 1990),
        382–402. [Political biography.]

498.   Wilson, Christopher. "The Tomb of Henry IV and the
        Holy Oil of St Thomas of Canterbury." In item 35.
        Pp. 181–90. [Lancastrian propaganda, the building of
        the tomb, and fading interest in the issue.]

499.   Wiswall, Frank L., III. "Politics, Procedures and the
        'Non-Minority' of Edward III: Some Comparisons." In
        item 37. Pp. 7–25. [Arrangements for a regency, some
        apt comparisons, and Richard exercising power while a
        minor.]

500.   Wolfe, Michael. "Siege Warfare and the *Bonnes Villes* of
        France during the Hundred Years War." See item 238.
        Pp. 49–66. [Fortified cities were more important than
        French kings realized.]

501.   Wood, Charles T. "The First Two Queens Elizabeth."
        See item 394. Pp. 121–31. [Psychology, women, and the
        obstacles to female sovereignty.]

502.   Wright, Edmund. "Henry IV, The Commons and the
        Recovery of Royal Finances in 1407." In item 3.
        Pp. 65–81. [To rebuild confidence in Henry IV and to
        raise money after the confrontation of 1406.]

503.   Wright, Nicholas. "Ransoms of Non-Combatants in the
        Hundred Years War." *JMH* 17 (1991), 323–32. [The best
        advice: try to avoid being captured.]

IV. LEGAL, ADMINISTRATIVE, AND CONSTITUTIONAL HISTORY

504. Allan, David. "A Fourteenth-Century Divorce in Stoke-by-Nayland." *Suffolk* 38/1 (1993), 1–7. [An annulment of 1379; the settlement published.]

505. Ayton, Andrew. "Knights, Esquires and Military Service: The Evidence of the Armorial Cases before the Court of Chivalry." In *The Medieval Military Revolution: State, Society, and Military Change in Medieval and Early Modern Europe*. Edited by Andrew Ayton and J. L. Price. London, 1998. Pp. 81–104. [Mostly looking at the Lovel-Morley dispute.]

506. Baker, John H. *An Introduction to English Legal History*. 3rd ed. London, 1990. [The standard survey. 1st ed. 1971; 2nd ed. 1979.]

507. ———. "The Books of the Common Law." In item 53. Pp. 411–32. [Law libraries, cases and readings, the coming of printing and its impact.]

508. ———, ed. *Reports of Cases by John Caryll, Part I: 1485–1499*. Selden Society, 115 (1999, for 1998). [Caryll died 1523; there will be a second volume.]

509. Barton, J. L. "The Legal Faculties of Late Medieval Oxford." In item 24. Pp. 281–313. [Mostly on the fifteenth century (thanks to the lack of earlier sources): degrees and training.]

510.   Beilby, Mark. "The Profits of Expertise: The Rise of Civil Lawyers and Chancery Equity." In item 54. Pp. 72–90. [Late medieval roots of the Tudor equity courts.]

511.   Bellamy, John G. *The Criminal Trial in Later Medieval England: Felony before the Courts from Edward I to the Sixteenth Century*. Toronto, 1998. [Limited in focus; learned and valuable within its self-determined boundaries.]

512.   Bickersteth, John, and Robert W. Dunning. *Clerks of the Closet in the Royal Household*. Stroud, 1991. [Chapter 3 takes the tale from Henry VI's time to 1603.]

513.   Biggs, Douglas. "Sheriffs and Justices of the Peace: The Patterns of Lancastrian Governance, 1399–1401." *Nottingham* 40 (1996), 149–66. [Assessing the turnover of personnel, with appendix on newly appointed Lancastrian retainers.]

514.   Boatwright, Lesley, ed. *Inquests and Indictments from Late Fourteenth-Century Buckinghamshire*. Buckinghamshire Record Society, 29 (1994). [Coroners' inquests, King's Bench indictments, items calendared, and index of some wills where money may have been extorted for the scribal duty.]

515.   Brown, Alfred L. "The House of Commons, 1386–1421: A Commentary." *Parliament, Estates and Representation* 14/1 (1994), 1–18. [A review article of item 427: mostly complimentary, discussing the limits and problems of the sources and the evidence.]

516.   Brundage, James A. "The Bar of the Ely Consistory Court in the Fourteenth Century: Advocates, Proctors, and Others." *J Eccl H* 43 (1992), 541–60. [Who served? Mostly well trained men; some prosopographical analysis.]

517.   Cannon, Christopher. "*Raptus* in the Chaumpaigne
        Release and a Newly Discovered Document Concerning
        the Life of Geoffrey Chaucer." *Speculum* 68 (1993),
        74–94. [Word-spin and the on-going puzzle about
        Chaucer's behavior and legal problems.]

518.   Carpenter, Christine. "Politics and Constitutional
        History: Before and After McFarlane. In item 19.
        Pp. 175–206. [The old hold of constitutional historians
        and the emergence of fifteenth-century studies.]

519.   Clark, Elaine. "City Orphans and Custody Laws in
        Medieval England." *AJLH* 34 (1990), 168–87. [Towns
        offered protection to orphans; their links with their
        guardian.]

520.   ———. "Charitable Bequests, Deathbed Land Sales, and
        the Manor Court in Later Medieval England." In item
        79. Pp. 143–61. [Manorial courts were called upon to ad-
        minister deathbed charities and bequests; quantitative
        analysis of village life.]

521.   Clark, Linda. "The Benefits and Burdens of Office:
        Henry Bourgchier (1408–83), Viscount Bourgchier and
        Earl of Essex, and the Treasurership of the Exchequer."
        In item 54. Pp. 119–36. [Successful careerism and the
        high profits of high office.]

522.   Clayton, Dorothy J. *The Administration of the County
        Palatine of Chester, 1442–1485.* Chetham Society, 3rd
        series, 35 (1990). [How palatine government functioned,
        personnel, relations with the royal administration, and
        the role of the gentry.]

523.   Clopper, Lawrence M. "Need Men and Women Labor?
        Langland's Wanderer and the Labor Ordinances." In
        item 48. Pp. 110–29. [Charity, begging, and "honest
        labor."]

524.   Condon, Margaret. "From Caitiff and Villain to Pater
        Patriae: Reynold Bray and the Profits of Office." In item
        54. Pp. 137–68. [A career under Henry VII, with com-
        mensurate profits and rewards.]

525.   Cox, A. David M., transcribed; edited by R. H. Darwall-
        Smith. *Account Rolls of University College, Oxford. Vol.
        I: 1381/2–1470/1.* Oxford Historical Society, n.s. 39
        (1999). [Mostly Oxford property in accounts preserved by
        William Smith, a fellow, 1681–1734. A. D. M. Cox died in
        1994, and Smith completed the study.]

526.   Doe, Norman. "The Positivist Thesis in Fifteenth-
        Century Legal Memory and Practice." *JLH* 11 (1990),
        29–39. [Positivist roots of legal thinking traced back to
        Pecock and Fortescue.]

527.   ———. *Fundamental Authority in Late Medieval
        English Law.* Cambridge, 1990. [Law as an expression of
        morality, with an eye on populist contributions and
        thought.]

528.   ———. "Legal Reasoning and Sir Roger Townshend, JCP
        (d. 1493)." *JLH* 11 (1990), 191–99. [The power of analogy
        and extra-legal justifications for the moral foundations
        of law.]

529.   Donahue, Charles, Jr. "Female Plaintiffs in Marriage
        Cases in the Court of York in the Later Middle Ages:
        What Can We Learn from the Numbers." In item 95.
        Pp. 183–213. [A methodological analysis, with numbers
        and cases (by types and categories).]

530.   Driver, J. T. "A Parliamentary Election Indenture for
        Leicestershire, 1433." *Leicester* 70 (1996), 147–49. [Docu-
        ment (published) attests to election results.]

531.   Dyer, Christopher. "Taxation and Communities in Late
        Medieval England." In item 20. Pp. 168–90. [The

sources, local assessments and poll taxes, and the nature of local government.]

532.   Edwards, David G., ed. *Derbyshire Wills Proven in the Prerogative Court of Canterbury*. Derbyshire Record Society 26 (1998). [In modern English; by p. 28 we have reached 1500.]

533.   Fenwick, Carolyn C., ed. *The Poll Taxes of 1377, 1379, and 1381: Part I, Bedfordshire-Leicestershire*. British Academy: Records of Social and Economic History, n.s. 27. London and Oxford, 1998. [Introduction on the tax and then county-by-county statistics: Part II, covering Lincolnshire-Westmorland, appeared in 2001.]

534.   Ferme, Brian. "The Tendency to Roman Law in English Fifteenth-Century Law: Lyndwood's *Provinciale* Re-Examined." In *Proceedings of the Ninth International Congress of Medieval Canon Law, Munich, 13–18 July, 1992*. Edited by Peter Landau and Jörg Müller. Vatican: Monumenta Iuris Canonici, c/10, 1997. Pp. 661–74. [Common law was resistant but not absolutely impermeable.]

535.   Finch, Andrew. "*Repulsa uxore sua*: Marital Difficulties and Separation in the Later Middle Ages." *Continuity and Change* 8 (1993), 11–38. [Compares marital problems, adultery, and separation in Cerisy la Forêt and Bayeux with Hereford.]

536.   Fleming, Peter W. "The Lovelace Dispute: Concepts of Property and Inheritance in Fifteenth-Century Kent." *Southern* 12 (1990), 1–18. [A forty-year struggle over three manors: son vs. father, three brothers, the law, and bad blood.]

537.   Flood, Susan, ed. *St Albans Wills, 1471–1500*. Hertfordshire Record Society Publication, 9 (1993). [In modern

English, from the register of the archdeacon of St
Albans.]

538. Frazer, Constance M., ed., with introduction by Kenneth
Emsley. *Durham Quarter Sessions Rolls, 1471–1625.*
Surtees Society 199 (1991). [Introduction and pp. 39–65
for sessions of 1471–73.]

539. Given-Wilson, Christopher. "Royal Charter Witness
Lists, 1327–1399." *Med Pros* 12 (1991), 35–93. [Tracing
some general patterns of witnessing, with detailed
tabular analysis of lay and clerical witnesses.]

540. Green, Richard Firth. "Ricardian 'Trouthe': A Legal Perspective." In item 67. Pp. 179–202. [The emergence of
the jury trial over compurgation and how literary
materials reflect the transition.]

541. ———. *A Crisis of Truth: Literature and Law in
Ricardian England.* Philadelphia, 1999. [Vast sweep
covering law, literary culture, and religion.]

542. Grummitt, David. "The Financial Administration of
Calais during the Reign of Henry IV, 1399–1414." *EHR*
118 (1993), 277–99. [An expensive business and the
success of special measures to raise the necessary funds,
especially in 1407.]

543. Guth, DeLloyd J. "Climbing the Civil-Service Pole
during Civil War: Sir Reynold Bray c. 1440–1503)." In
item 64. Pp. 47–61. ["Civil" and "service" and Sir
Richard's life and career.]

544. Harvey, Paul D. A., and Andrew McGuiness. *A Guide to
British Medieval Seals.* London, 1996. [A publication of
the British Library and the PRO: a general introduction
and well-illustrated survey, with many late medieval
examples.]

545. [No entry.]

546.   Haskett, Timothy J. "The Judicial Role of the English
         Chancery in Late-Medieval Law and Literacy." In *Écrit
         et pouvoir dans les chancelleries médiévales: Espace
         français, espace anglais.* Edited by Kouky Fianu and
         DeLloyd J. Guth. Louvain, 1997. Pp. 313–32. [A 1995
         conference in Montreal, published as "Textes et Études
         du Moyen Âge, 6." An appeal to chancery in 1438 opens a
         discussion of petitions: statistics, proceedings, etc.]

547.   ———. "The Medieval English Court of Chancery." *LHR*
         14 (1998), 245–313. [Late medieval evolution; the
         changes in scholarship and historiography; plus a report
         on the "Early Court of Chancery in England" project.]

548.   ———. "The Curtys Women in Chancery: The Legacy of
         Henry and Rye Browne." In item 82. Pp. 349–98. ["His"
         and "her" wills compared: patterns, similarities, differ-
         ences.]

549.   Hayes, Rosemary C. E. "'Ancient Indictments' for the
         North of England, 1461–1509." In item 77. Pp. 19–45.
         [Reporting on a project to cover Ancient Indictments of
         King's Bench: numbers, dates, legal-administrative point
         of origin, crimes, and the light they shed on local
         unrest.]

550.   Helmholz, Richard. "Harboring Sexual Offenders: Eccle-
         siastical Courts and Controlling Misbehavior." *JBS* 37
         (1998), 258–68. [A contribution to the MacIntosh sym-
         posium (item 792): society was not soft on those
         shielding the ill-behaved.]

551.   ———. "The Canon Law." In item 53. Pp. 387–98. [A
         survey of the texts that were known and available, both
         foreign and domestic.]

552.   Hettinger, Madonna J. "Defining the Servant: Legal and
         Extra-Legal Terms of Employment in Fifteenth-Century
         England." In *The Work of Work: Servitude, Slavery and*

Labor in Medieval England. Edited by Allen J. Frantzen and Douglas Moffatt. Glasgow, 1994. Pp. 206–28. [Servants and servant-stealing; petitions on a master-servant dispute.]

553.   Hicks, Michael A. "The 1468 Statute of Livery." *HR* 64 (1991), 15–28. [The king's law and order measure against peers who were retaining gentry not of their households.]

554.   Hornsby, Joseph. "Clipped Coins and Heresy: Thomas Hoccleve's Poetics and the Lancastrian Law of Treason." In *Law and Medieval Life and Thought*. Edited by Edward B. King and Susan J. Ridyard. Sewanee Mediaeval Studies, 5 (1990), 217–30. [Loyalty, the royal image, and counterfeiting as a further charge against Oldcastle.]

555.   Ibbetson, David J. "Fault and Absolute Liability in Pre-Modern Contract Law." *JLH* 18 (1997), 1–31. [Liability became stiffer in the fifteenth century.]

556.   Ivall, David E. "The High Sheriffs of Cornwall: A Provisional List." *Cornwall*, n.s. 1, part 2 (1992), 171–93. ["Our" years covered, pp. 177–78.]

557.   Jenks, Stuart. *England, die Hanse und Preusswen: Handel und Diplomatie, 1377–1474*. Cologne and Vienna, 1993. [Vol. 1 covers Handel; vol. 2 Diplomatie; vol. 3 Anhänge. Critical review by T. H. Lloyd, *EcHR* (1993), 675–77.]

558.   Jones, E. D. "Summary Execution at Spalding Priory, 1250–1500." *JLH* 16 (1995), 189–98. [Business was slowing down by the early fourteenth century.]

559.   Jones, Karen, and Michael Zell. "Bad Conversation? Gender and Social Control in a Kentish Borough, c. 1450–c. 1570." *Continuity and Change* 13 (1998),

11–31. [Fordwick, Kent: lots of "social control" presentments; who got punished (by social class).]

560. Kelly, Henry Ansgar. "Statutes of Rape and Alleged Ravishers of Wives: A Context for the Charges against Thomas Malory, Knight." *Viator* 28 (1997), 361–419. [Legal background, including Chaucer (in 1387) and Malory's actions; the tangle is apt to remain tangled.]

561. ———. "Meanings and Use of *Raptus* in Chaucer's Time." *Studies in the Age of Chaucer* 20 (1998), 101–65. [The law: parallels, pardons, the events touching Cecily Champain; with some documents.]

562. Kirby, John L., ed. *Calendar of Inquisitions Post Mortem and Other Analogous Documents, Volume XIX, 7–14 Henry IV (1405–1413).* HMSO, London, 1992. [A volume of great value, as the series is now being continued into the fifteenth century.]

562A. ———, ed. *Calendar of Inquisitions Post Mortem, Volume XX, 1–5 Henry V (1413–1418).* HMSO, London, 1995. [As 562: the Proofs of Age are regularly published in these volumes.]

563. Knapp, Ethan. "Bureaucratic Identity and the Construction of the Self in Hoccleve's *Formulary* and *La male regle.*" *Speculum* 74 (1999), 357–76. [The ground between gossip and autobiography in the setting of a bureaucrat's career.]

564. Lander, Jack Robert. *Justices of the Peace.* Gloucester, 1990. [An office of importance, surprisingly overlooked by modern scholars.]

565. Laughton, Jane. "Women in Court: Some Evidence from Fifteenth-Century Chester." In item 81. Pp. 89–99. [How women made their appearances in court, how often, and in what sorts of cases.]

566.   Lockwood, Shelley, ed. *Sir John Fortescue: On the Laws and Governance of England.* Cambridge, 1997. [In the Cambridge Texts in the History of Political Thought series. Amends Chrimes's 1942 version of *In Praise* (pp. 3–80) and modernizes Plummer's 1885 edition, *The Governance.* Reviewed by Johann P. Sommerville, *Parliamentary History* 17 (1998), 373–75.]

567.   Loengard, Janet Senderowitz. "'Legal History and the Medieval Englishwoman' Revisited: Some New Directions." In *Medieval Women and the Sources of Medieval History.* Edited by Joel T. Rosenthal. Athens, Ga., 1990. Pp. 210–63. [A look at recent work and an examination of the emergence of women's status as a major historiographical issue.]

568.   Marsh, Deborah. "'I see by sizt of evidence': Information Gathering in Late Medieval Cheshire." In item 33. Pp. 71–92. [The gentry and the use (and manipulation) of written evidence.]

569.   McHardy, Alison K. "Clerical Criminals in the Fifteenth Century: Two Cases from the City of York." In item 89. Pp. 105–12. [From William Booth's register: theft and the claim of clerical privilege.]

570.   McIntosh, Marjorie K. "Finding Language for Misconduct: Jurors in Fifteenth-Century Local Courts." In item 50. Pp. 87–122. [Local leaders and disruptive behavior; what was and was not accepted.]

571.   Middleton, Anne. "Acts of Vagrancy: The C Version 'Autobiography' and the Statute of 1388." In *Written Work: Langland, Labor, and Authorship.* Edited by Steven Justice and Kathryn Kerby-Fulton. Philadelphia, 1997. Pp. 208–317. [Statute of Labourers and vagrancy; sweeping legislation and contemporary consciousness of social problems; also, see item 1049.]

572.   Moreton, Charles. "A 'best betrustyd frende': A Late
       Medieval Lawyer and his Clients." *JLH* 11 (1990),
       183–90. [Roger Townshend and the Pastons: a loan to
       John Paston II.]

573.   ———. "The 'Library' of a Late-Fifteenth-Century
       Lawyer." *The Library*, 6th series, 13/4 (1991), 338–46.
       [Roger Townshend's books: forty-four items, about half
       on law and legal matters.]

574.   ———. "The 'Diary' of a Late Fifteenth-Century
       Lawyer." In item 64. Pp. 27–45. [Sir Roger Townshend's
       notebook, from the early 1490s: a lawyer's job on the
       circuit, with a table of Townshend connections and
       marital webs.]

575.   Musson, Anthony, and Mark Ormrod. *The Evolution of
       English Justice: Law, Politics, and Society in the Four-
       teenth Century*. Basingstoke and New York, 1999. [Focus
       is on the center; the judicial system as a structure and
       how it held up in such crises as 1381 and 1399. Appendix
       on sessions and itineraries of King's Bench and parlia-
       ment, 1290–1399.]

576.   Needham, Paul. "The Customs Rolls as Documents for
       the Printed-Book Trade in England." In item 53.
       Pp. 148–63. [A guide to who brought in what, and when
       (or how soon?).]

577.   Neville, Cynthia J. "Local Perspectives and Functions of
       the English Chancery's Legal Instruments in the Later
       Middle Ages: The Anglo-Scottish Border Lands." See
       item 546. Pp. 269–79. [A maritime dispute opens a
       discussion of debt, appeals to chancery, and more such
       fun and games.]

578.   ———. "The Law of Treason in the English Border
       Counties in the Later Middle Ages." *LHR* 3/1 (1990),

1–30. [Acts of 1414 to deal with northern problems; "march treason."]

579.   ———. "Keeping the Peace on the Northern Marches in the Later Middle Ages." *EHR* 109 (1994), 1–25. [Border law was different, and it kept an eye on equitable compensation.]

580.   ———. "War, Women and Crime in Northern English Border Lands in the Later Middle Ages." In *The Final Argument: The Imprint of Violence on Society in Medieval and Early Modern Europe.* Edited by Donald J. Kagay and L. J. Andrew Villalon. Woodbridge and Rochester, N.Y., 1998. Pp. 163–75. [Female thieves often treated leniently by juries of presentment; some statistics on numbers charged.]

581.   Newman, Christine. "Local Court Administration in the Liberty of Allertonshire, 1470–1540." *Archives* 22 (April 1995), 13–24. [When and why cases wound up in the borough court and when and why in the baronial.]

582.   Ormrod, Mark. "England in the Middle Ages. In *The Rise of the Fiscal State in Europe, c. 1200–1815.* Edited by Richard Bonney. Oxford, 1999. Pp. 19–52. [Survey of state mechanisms for tax collecting and a general look at revenues.]

583.   Owen, Arthur E. B. "The Custom of Romney Marsh and the Statute of Sewers of 1427." *Arch Cant* 116 (1997), 93–99. [Customs and practices: the customs of the Marsh were influenced by Midland practices.]

584.   Payling, Simon J. "Arbitration, Perpetual Entails, and Collateral Warranties in Late Medieval England: A Case Study." *JLH* 13 (1992), 32–62. [Cromwell and Fitzhugh fought over the Marmyon inheritance; the importance of arbitration.]

585.   ———. "A Disputed Mortgage: Ralph, Lord Cromwell,
Sir John Gra and the Manor of Multon Hall." In item 3.
Pp. 117–36. [Cromwell held the cards, but his will
opened the door for Gra, whereas chancery had not been
much help.]

586.   ———. "Murder, Motive and Punishment in Fifteenth-
Century England: Two Gentry Case Studies." *EHR* 113
(1998), 1–17. [A Rutland dispute, a murder, the
wife/widow and her lover, and the role played by royal
mercy.]

587.   Penn, Simon A. C., and Christopher Dyer. "Wages and
Earnings in Late Medieval England: Evidence from the
Enforcement of the Labour Laws." *EcHR* 43 (1990),
356–76. [The flexibility of wage earners' lives, their
mobility, and the high incidence of short-term employ-
ment.]

588.   Poos, Lawrence R. "Sex, Lies and the Church Courts of
Pre-Reformation England." *JIH* 25 (1995), 585–607.
[Networks of revenues and gossip (and defamation) that
reported people to the authorities, with a table of categories of defamation.]

589.   ———. "The Heavy-Handed Marriage Counsellors:
Regulation of Marriage in Some Late-Medieval English
Local Ecclesiastical-Court Jurisdictions." *AJLH* 39
(1995), 293–309. [Ways in which ecclesiastical courts
intervened under the eyes of the community and secular
judicial scrutiny.]

590.   Poos, Lawrence R., and Lloyd Bonfield, eds. *Selected
Cases in Manorial Courts, 1250–1550.* Selden Society,
114 (1997). [Following Maitland's lead on manorial court
materials, though mostly prior to 1377. Long introduction covers manorial court proceedings in detail.]

591.   Powell, Edward. "The Strange Death of Sir John
         Mortimer: Politics and the Law of Treason in
         Lancastrian England." In item 3. Pp. 83–97. [An
         execution of 1424; the jury acquitted but his escape was
         seen as treason (by words).]

592.   ———. "Law and Justice." In item 57. Pp. 29–41. [Local
         communities and/or a centralized legal system.]

593.   ———. "After 'After McFarlane': The Poverty of Patron-
         age and the Case for Constitutional History." In item 26.
         Pp. 1–16. [Constitutional history and a balanced view of
         the reciprocities of patronage.]

594.   Ramsay, Nigel L. "What Was the Legal Profession?" In
         item 54. Pp. 62–71. [The inns, serjeants, and lesser legal
         ranks of chancery and common law.]

595.   ———. "Scriveners and Notaries as Legal Inter-
         mediaries in Later Medieval England." In item 59.
         Pp. 118–31. [Their skills, roles, and fees; some
         individuals and cases.]

596.   Rawcliffe, Carole. "'That Kindliness Should Be
         Cherished More, and Discord Driven Out': The Settle-
         ment of Commercial Disputes by Arbitration in Later
         Medieval England." In item 59. Pp. 99–117. [The
         importance of arbitration and how it was encouraged by
         municipal authorities, with anecdotes and cases.]

597.   Richardson, Malcolm. "Early Equity Judges: Keepers of
         the Rolls of Chancery, 1415–1447." *AJLH* 36 (1992),
         440–65. [The office and the string of competent men who
         held it (plus their duties and perquisites); some career
         biographies.]

598.   ———. *The Medieval Chancery under Henry V.* List and
         Index Society, Special series 30 (1999). [Analysis of
         officials and level of bureaucracy; prosopographical
         analysis and biographies.]

599.   Saul, Nigel. "The Brockworth Poll Tax Return, 1377."
       HR 72 (1997), 112–25. [The tax return (in a Westminster
       Abbey muniment): roll published, showing considerable
       mobility and migration.]

600.   Sinclair, Shelley A. "The 'Ravishing of Isabel Boteler:'
       Abduction and the Pursuit of Wealth in Lancastrian
       England." *Ricardian* 11/146 (September 1999), 546–57.
       [Some cases: the law was much better than practice
       often turned out to be.]

601.   Smith, Carrie. "Medieval Coroners' Rolls: Legal Fiction
       or Historical Fact?" In item 33. Pp. 93–115. [Statistics
       and many problems: maybe a lot of legal fiction, but also
       some substance.]

602.   Summerson, Henry. "The Criminal Underworld of Medi-
       eval England." *JLH* 17 (1996), 197–224. [Amusing
       survey of an un-funny topic, with many late medieval
       examples.]

603.   Thorne, Samuel E., in collaboration with Michael E.
       Hager and Margaret MacVeagh Thorne, with a com-
       mentary of cases by Charles Donahue, Jr. *The Year
       Books of Richard II: 6 Richard II, 1382–83.* Ames
       Foundation, 1986. [Project begun by Thorne in the
       1950s, with much commentary by the others; cases in
       French with translations.]

604.   Thornton, Tim. "Local Equity Jurisdiction in the Terri-
       tories of the English Crown: The Palatinate of Chester,
       1450–1540." In item 33. Pp. 27–52. [Waning days of
       palatinate jurisdiction, with a close look at the appoint-
       ment of commissioners.]

605.   Tilsley, David. "Arbitration in Gentry Disputes: The
       Case of Bucklow Hundred in Cheshire, 1400–1465." In
       item 33. Pp. 53–70. [Survey of many cases and the
       frequent resort to arbitration.]

606.   Tucker, Penny. "Relationships between London's Courts and the Westminster Courts in the Reign of Edward IV." In item 33. Pp. 117–37. [How the sheriffs' courts worked, and how the City held out against Westminster encroachment.]

607.   ———. "London's Courts of Law in the 15th Century: The Litigants' Perspective." In *Communities and Courts in Britain, 1150–1900.* Edited by Christopher Brooks and Michael Lobhan. London and Rio Grande, Ohio, 1997. Pp. 25–41. [Why private litigants chose the City of Westminster, and how business fell between the Hustings Courts, the Mayor's, and the Sheriff's.]

608.   Virgoe, Roger. "The Will of Hugh atte Fenn, 1476." *A Norwich Miscellany, Norfolk Record Society* 56 (1993), 31–57. [Tracking the East Anglian gentry in death as in life.]

609.   ———. "Inheritance and Litigation in the Fifteenth Century: The Buckenham Dispute." *JLH* 15 (1994), 23–40. [Also printed in item 94, as paper number 11.]

610.   ———. "The Ravishment of Joan Boys." In *East Anglian Studies: Essays Presented to J. C. Barriger on His Retirement.* Edited by Adam Longcroft and Richard Joby. Norwich, 1995. Pp. 276–81. [Also published in item 94 as paper no. 10.]

611.   Visser-Fuchs, Livia. "Nicholas Harrisfeld: Clerk of the Signet, Author, and Murderer." *Ricardian* 10/125 (June 1994), 42–59. [A civil servant who killed John Blakeney in 1471.]

612.   Walker, Simon. "Yorkshire Justices of the Peace, 1389–1413." *EHR* 108 (1993), 281–313. [How independent and powerful were the justices, many of whom had parliamentary links and Yorkist loyalties; includes tables on their attendance.]

613.   ———. "Between Church and Crown: Master Richard
        Andrew, King's Clerk." *Speculum* 74 (1999), 956–91.
        [Detailed career study of an active figure (and a man
        with an extensive library).]

614.   Ward, Kevin J., ed., with introduction by John S.
        Thompson and Kevin Ward. *Eggington Court Rolls
        (1297–1572)*. Bedfordshire Historical Record Society, 69,
        a volume devoted to *Hundreds, Manors, Parishes and
        the Church: A Selection of Early Documents for Bedford-
        shire*, 1990. [Ward wrote the commentary on the text:
        ten courts covered, 1377–1509.]

615.   Watts, John L. "Ideas, Principles and Politics." In item
        76. Pp. 110–33. [Contemporary views of a (or "the")
        constitution and of political expression and theory.]

616.   Wijffels, Alain. "The Civil Law." In item 53. Pp. 399–410.
        [Growth of such literature and the English market; the
        contents of a basic collection, and then beyond.]

617.   Woolgar, Christopher M., ed. *Household Accounts from
        Medieval England: Part 1. Introduction, Glossary, Diet
        Accounts, Part II. Diet Accounts: Cash, Corn and Stock
        Accounts: Wardrobe Accounts*. Records of Social and
        Economic History, n.s. 18 (1991 and 1993). [Twenty-
        eight documents (some of considerable length); a
        valuable presentation of familiar but relatively
        inaccessible materials.]

V. SOCIAL AND ECONOMIC, REGIONAL AND FAMILY HISTORY, NUMISMATICS, AND DEMOGRAPHY

618. Acheson, Eric. *A Gentry Community: Leicestershire in the Fifteenth Century, c. 1422–c.1485.* Cambridge, 1992. [Little aristocratic domination and a four-tier gentry structure.]

619. Adams, Terence. "Aliens, Agriculturalists and Entre- preneurs: Identifying the Market-Makers in a Norfolk Port from the Water-Bailiffs' Accounts, 1400–60." In item 26. Pp. 140–57. [Whence agricultural goods and commodities came (largely by water), and the route of imported goods.]

620. Ainsworth, Peter. "Froissardian Perspectives on Late- Fourteenth-Century Society." In *Orders and Hierarchies in Late Medieval and Renaissance Europe.* Edited by Jeffrey Denton. Basingstoke, 1999. Pp. 56–73, 179–82. [Chivalry, aristocratic readers, and the wider social scene.]

621. Allen, Martin. "Documentary Evidence for the Henry VI Annulet Coinage of York." *BNJ* 65 (1995), 120–34. [Accounts of gold received and denominations struck; documents on authority to mint published; see item 729.]

622. Appleby, John C. "Devon Privateering from Early Times to 1688." In item 32. Pp. 90–97. [But mostly covering Tudor times.]

623.   Arnold, Hilary. "The Kitchens of Medieval York: The
        Evidence of the Inventories." *York Historian* 16 (1999),
        2–9. [Kitchen implements, cooking strategies, food and
        condiments, with a list of inventories consulted.]

624.   Aston, Margaret. "Death." In item 57. Pp. 202–28.
        [Terrors of hell, choice of burial sites, popularity of
        saints.]

625.   Bailey, Mark. "Coastal Fishing off Southeast Suffolk in
        the Century after the Black Death." *Suffolk* 37/2 (1990),
        102–14. [Some unusual documents published, plus
        tables of masters and boats and all in pursuit of a thin
        evidentiary trail.]

626.   ———. "Demographic Decline in Late Medieval
        England: Some Thoughts on Recent Research." *EcHR* 49
        (1996), 1–19. [Mortality still a paramount factor, though
        it would soon yield to fertility.]

627.   ———. "Historiographical Essay: The Commercialization
        of the English Economy, 1086–1500." *JMH* 24 (1998),
        297–311. [Early growth and commercialization; a review
        essay covering thirteen contributions.]

628.   [No entry.]

629.   Barrell, Andrew D. M., and M. H. Brown. "A Settler
        Community of Post-Conquest Rural Wales: The English
        in Dyffryn Clwyd, 1294–1399." *Welsh History Review* 17
        (1994–95), 322–35. [Separate communities but reason-
        ably amicable relations.]

630.   Bennett, Judith M. "Conviviality and Charity in
        Medieval and Early Modern England." *Past and Present*
        134 (February 1992), 19–41. [Church ales and village
        life; with a discussion. See also ibid. 154 (February
        1997), for a "Comment" by Maria Moisa, pp. 223–34, and
        a reply by Bennett, pp. 235–42, over the distinction
        between charity and consumerism.]

631.   ———. "Women and Men of the Brewers Gild of London, ca. 1420." In item 30. Pp. 181–232. [Male brewers sought to take control, with women's major role becoming at risk.]

632.   ———. *Ale, Beer, and Brewsters in England: Women's Work in a Changing World, 1300–1600.* New York and Oxford, 1996. [Women's initiative in a major industry, but in a world not inclined to cut them much slack.]

633.   Blake, Norman. "Introduction" and "The Literary Language." In *Cambridge History of the English Language, Volume II: 1066–1476.* Cambridge, 1992. Pp. 1–22 and 500–541. [General background on the language spoken by most of the folk, both the learned and the not-so-learned; see also item 654.]

634.   Blanchard, Ian S. W. *International Lead Production and Trade in the 'Age of the Saigerprozess', 1460–1560.* Stuttgart, 1995. [New technology, silver crisis; appendices 2 (pp. 231–88) and 3 (pp. 289–313) look at English and Welsh production and exports in a book mostly dealing with Germany.]

635.   Bradley, Helen. "The Datini Factors in London, 1380–1410." In item 26. Pp. 55–79. [Correspondence survives, showing their agents and the cost of shipping goods home.]

636.   Britnell, Richard H. *The Commercialisation of English Society, 1000–1500.* Manchester, 1993; 2nd ed. 1996. [The money economy and the role of commerce, in an important treatment. Reviewed by J. L. Bolton, *EHR* 1993, 971–73.]

637.   ———. "Commerce and Capitalism in Late Medieval England: Problems of Description and Theory." *Journal of Historical Sociology* 6 (1993), 359–76. [The years between 1300 and 1500 as years of arrested development, rather than of "progress."]

638.   ———. "The Economic Context." In item 76. Pp. 42–65.
            [Hard times, instability, and what people did for a living;
            important not to over-emphasize the economic impact of
            domestic warfare.]

639.   [No entry.]

640.   ———. "The English Economy and the Government,
            1450–1550." In item 97. Pp. 89–116. [Old problems, new
            lines of development and growth, and the role of the
            state in such areas.]

641.   Caple, C. "The Detection and Definition of an Industry:
            The English Medieval and Post-Medieval Pin Industry."
            Arch J 148 (1991), 241–55. [The threat of cheap imports,
            developing the technology, and the role of zinc in the
            process.]

642.   Carlin, Martha. "Fast Food and Urban Living Standards
            in Medieval England." In item 23. Pp. 27–51. [A style of
            life that long antedated the coming of McDonalds.]

643.   Carpenter, Christine. *Locality and Polity: A Study of
            Warwickshire Landed Society, 1401–1499.* Cambridge,
            1992. [With appendices on the county gentry and their
            affinity; a large and important study of the "county
            community." Reviewed by R. A. Archer, *Ricardian*
            10/125 (June 1994), 60–65; Simon Payling, *Parliamentary
            History* 13 (1994), 322–32; Colin Richmond, *EHR* 107
            (1994), 127–29; and Steven J. Gunn, *Historical Journal*
            35 (1992), 999–1003.]

644.   ———. "Gentry and Community in Medieval England."
            JBS 33 (1994), 340–80. [Examines the idea of the county
            community with historiographical background and a dim
            view of it as an "organic community."]

645.   ———. "The Stonor Circle in the 15th Century." In item
            3. Pp. 175–200. [A dense network, but still in need of
            friends and money.]

646. ———, ed., with introduction. *Kingsford's Stonor Letters and Papers, 1290–1483.* Cambridge, 1996. [Reprint of Camden Society volumes of 1919 (3rd series, vols. 3, 29, 30) and 1924 (3rd series, vol. 34). Introduction (pp. 1–31), plus some materials not included by Kingsford. Major source, now readily accessible. See Alison Hanham, "Varieties of Errors and *Kingsford's Stonor Letters and Papers*," *Ricardian* 11/142 (September 1993), 345–52.]

647. ———, ed., with introduction. *The Armburgh Papers: The Brokholes Inheritance in Warwickshire, Hereford-shire and Essex, c. 1417–c. 1453.* Woodbridge, 1998. [A Chetham manuscript: a major collection of family papers, if not quite on a par with its famous rivals for general reflections or striking personalities.]

648. Challis, Christopher E. "Lord Hastings to the Great Silver Recoinage, 1464–1699." In *A New History of the Royal Mint.* Edited by C. E. Challis. Cambridge, 1992. Pp. 179–228. [Carrying the story down to 1544; see also item 739.]

649. Childs, Wendy R. "'To oure losse and hindraunce': English Credit to Alien Merchants in the Mid-Fifteenth Century." In item 59. Pp. 68–98. [Practices and problems: appendix analyzes 110 cases and names of prosecuted creditors.]

650. ———. "Anglo-Portuguese Trade in the Fifteenth Century." *TRHS*, 6th series, 2 (1992), 195–219. [Good political relations; modest volume of trade but increasing toward the end of the period.]

651. ———. "Devon's Overseas Trade in the Late Middle Ages." In item 32. Pp. 79–89. [Goods, men, economic trends.]

652. ———. "The 'George' of Beverley and Olav Olavesson: Trading Conditions in the North Sea in 1464." *Northern*

31 (1995), 108–22. [The ship was attacked in Bergen; settlement finally reached.]

653.　　———. "The Commercial Shipping of South-Western England in the Later Fifteenth Century." *Mariner's Mirror* 83 (1997), 272–92. [Ships, their points of origin, cargoes, the pilgrim trade, etc.]

654.　　Clark, Cecily. "Onomastics." In item 633. Pp. 542–606. [Naming patterns in post-Conquest England: origins, roots, and families of names; changes over the centuries.]

655.　　Clark, Elaine. "The Quest for Security in Medieval England." In *Aging and the Aged in Medieval Europe.* Edited by Michael M. Sheehan. Pontifical Institute of Mediaeval Studies, Toronto, Papers in Medieval Studies, 11 (1991). Pp. 189–200. [From a conference held in 1983: accords and arrangements between parents and children, with some published here; see also item 782.]

656.　　Cook, Barrie J., with Ray Carey and Kevin Leahy. "Medieval and Early Modern Coin Finds from South Ferriby, Humberside." *BNJ* 68 (1998), 95–118. [Pp. 103–04 and 112–13 for late medieval materials in a general survey of numbers, denominations, and sites.]

657.　　Coss, Peter. *The Knight in Medieval England, 1000–1400.* Stroud, 1993. [Mostly earlier: politics and power, culture and chivalry; well illustrated and wide-ranging.]

658.　　———. "Knights, Esquires and the Origins of Social Gradation in England." *TRHS*, 6th series, 5 (1995), 155–78. [Searching for a basis of distinction: "the emergence of esquires."]

659.　　Cox, John D. "Drama, The Devil, and Social Conflict in Late Medieval England." *American Benedictine Review* 45 (1994), 341–62. [Ideological sources and roots of social conflict.]

660.   Crowfoot, Elisabeth, Frances Pritchard, and Kay
         Staniland. *Textiles and Clothing, c. 1150–c. 1450:
         Museum of London: Medieval Finds from Excavations in
         London: 4*. HMSO, London, 1992. [Much late medieval
         material: digs, technology, kinds of cloth, etc.
         Photography by Edwin Baker; illustrations by Christina
         Unwin; excavations, Alan Vince; appendix on dyes by
         Penelope Walton.]

661.   Davies, Clifford S. L. "The Crofts: Creation and Defence
         of a Family Enterprise under the Yorkists and Henry
         VII." *HR* 68 (1995), 241–65. [The family's background
         and rise; life in Herefordshire and the border.]

662.   Dinn, Robert. "'Monuments Answerable to Men's Worth':
         Burial Patterns, Social Status and Gender in Late
         Medieval Bury St. Edmunds." *J Eccl H* 46 (1995),
         237–55. [Wills: how people chose sites (mostly in
         churchyards), and with whom; burial patterns followed
         secular and social ones.]

663.   Dockray, Keith, ed. *The Plumpton Correspondence,
         edited by Thomas Stapleton*. Gloucester, 1990. [A new
         introduction to this reprint of the original edition of
         1839.]

664.   Dyer, Alan. *Decline and Growth in English Towns*.
         Basingstoke, 1991; Cambridge, 1995. [A booklet written
         for the Economic History Society, covering recent work
         and main lines of explanation.]

665.   Dyer, Christopher. "Were There Any Capitalists in Fif-
         teenth-Century England?" In item 59. Pp. 1–24. [Schools
         of interpretation, with Richard Heritage of Warwick-
         shire as a case study.]

666.   ———. "The Hidden Trade of the Middle Ages: Evidence
         from the West Midlands of England." *Journal of Histor-
         ical Geography* 18 (1992), 141–57. [Much economic life

outside "official" channels, involving a healthy high
percentage of the populace.]

667.   ———. "The Economy and Society." In item 84.
        Pp. 137–73. [A survey and summary.]

668.   ———. "Peasants and Coins: The Uses of Money in the
        Middle Ages." *BNJ* 67 (1997), 30–47. [The Howard
        Linecar Lecture, 1997: peasant coin hoards, mostly of
        pennies, and a look at some inventories.]

669.   Dymond, David. "Five Building Contracts from
        Fifteenth-Century Suffolk." *Antiq J* 78 (1998), 269–87.
        [Structural details of four houses and a barn near Bury;
        the houses were in high fashion.]

670.   Edwards, James F., and Brian P. Hindle. "The Trans-
        portation System of Medieval England and Wales."
        Journal of Historical Geography 17 (1991), 123–34. [An
        overview: road, navigable rivers, ports, and the strategic
        siting of borough; see item 726 for a different interpre-
        tation.]

671.   Epstein, Stephan R. "Regional Fairs, Institutional Inno-
        vation, and Economic Growth in Late Medieval Europe."
        EcHR 47 (1994), 459–82. [A general sweep; after 1350
        England lagged behind with little new growth, few new
        fairs.]

672.   Fleet, Peter. "Markets in Medieval Lincolnshire." *East
        Midland Historian* 3 (1993), 7–14. [Mostly begun earlier,
        but a few new ones.]

673.   Friedrichs, Rhoda L. "The Two Last Wills of Ralph Lord
        Cromwell." *Nottingham* 34 (1990), 93–112. [A rich man
        with no children, many enemies, and a perennial need
        for powerful friends.]

674.   Friel, Ian. "Devon Shipping from the Middle Ages to
        ca. 1600." In item 32. Pp. 73–78. [Ship types.]

675.	Fudge, John D. *Cargoes, Embargoes, and Emissaries: The Commercial and Political Interaction of England and the German Hanse, 1450–1510.* Toronto, 1995. [Foreword by Ian Blanchard. An economic narrative, with appendices on trade statistics, cloth exports, documents on litigation, and a glossary.]

676.	Galloway, James A. "Driven by Drink? Ale Consumption and the Agrarian Economy of the London Region, c. 1300–1400." In item 23. Pp. 87–100. [Per capita consumption, moving the grain, and the increasing role of barley.]

677.	Galloway, James A., and I. Murray, "Scottish Migration to England, 1400–1560." *Scottish Geography Magazine* 112 (1996), 29–38. [How many took the high road to England.]

678.	Gardiner, Mark. "The Exploitation of Sea-Mammals in Medieval England: Bones and their Social Context." *Arch J* 154 (1997), 173–95. [Little serious whaling, though "big" fish were high prestige food; mostly stranded porpoises, with an appendix of big bone finds.]

679.	Gerchow, Jan. "Gilds and Fourteenth-Century Bureaucracy: The Case of 1388–9." *Nottingham* 40 (1996), 109–48. [A royal inquiry into local practice: documents published (though the plates are almost undecipherable).]

680.	Gies, Frances, and Joseph Gies. *A Medieval Family: The Pastons of Fifteenth-Century England.* New York, 1998. [Presented via a chronological narrative; an easy story to follow.]

681.	Goldberg, P. J. P. "Marriage, Migration, and Servanthood: The York Cause Paper Evidence." In item 41. Pp. 1–15. [By sex, age, and age at marriage, plus migration (into and out of York).]

682.   Hammond, Peter W. *Food and Feast in Medieval
        England.* Stroud, 1993. [A general treatment, well
        illustrated, looking at class differences, town and
        country, nutrition, and table manners.]

683.   Hanawalt, Barbara A. *Growing Up in Medieval London:
        The Experience of Childhood in History.* Oxford and New
        York, 1993. [Some touches of an imaginative approach
        mixed with archival work; a sympathetic treatment.]

684.   ———. "Ballads and Bandits: Fourteenth-Century Out-
        laws and the Robin Hood Poems." In item 48. Pp. 154–75.
        [Myths of social banditry.]

685.   ———. "'Good Governance' in the Medieval and Early
        Modern Context." *JBS* 37 (1998), 246–57. [A contribu-
        tion to the symposium on Marjorie McIntosh; see item
        792: types of misbehavior, with an eye on gender
        distinctions.]

686.   Hanawalt, Barbara, and Ben R. McRee. "The Guilds of
        Homo Prudens in Late Medieval England." *Continuity
        and Change* 7 (1992), 163–79. [Functioning institutions
        in the setting of urban life and of popular religion.]

687.   Harding, Vanessa. "Cross-Channel Trade and Cultural
        Contacts: London and the Low Countries in the Later
        Fourteenth Century." In item 8. Pp. 153–68. [Numbers,
        ships, ports, volume of trade; many questions are beyond
        the extant data.]

688.   Hare, J. N. "The Growth of the Roof-Tile Industry in
        Later Medieval Wessex." *Med Arch* 35 (1991), 86–103. [A
        growing enterprise: sites, maps, centers of production
        and distribution.]

689.   ———. "The Lords and Their Tenants: Conflict and
        Stability in Fifteenth-Century Wiltshire." See item 487.
        Pp. 16–34. [Serfdom declining and some thriving
        industrial areas, though landlords remained in control.]

690.   ————. "Growth and Recession in the Fifteenth-Century
          Economy: The Wiltshire Textile Industry and the
          Countryside." *EcHR* 52 (1999), 1–26. [Growth up to the
          slump of c. 1450: wool production squeezed the arable,
          with data on rent values.]

691.   Harren, Michael J. "The Will of Master John de Belvoir,
          Official of Lincoln (1391)." *Mediaeval Studies* 58 (1996),
          119–47. [A diocesan administrator with the usual be-
          quests; will published (pp. 138–47).]

692.   Harris, Eric. "Die Pairing on the Transitional Coins of
          Henry IV and Henry V." *BNJ* 67 (1997), 20–29. [New
          dies were needed for the newly debased coins and for
          small coins.]

693.   ————. "Halfgroats in the Henry IV–Henry V Period."
          BNJ 68 (1998), 147–48. [Amplification of points in his
          1997 article; see item 692.]

694.   ————. "Dies for the Heavy and Light Pence, 1399–1422."
          BNJ 69 (1999), 215–19. [Plates and a table of distin-
          guishing features.]

695.   Harris, Eric, and Michael Sharp. "The Roshleigh Henry
          IV Half-Groat." *BNJ* 67 (1997), 105. [The die is depicted.]

696.   Harvey, Barbara. *Living and Dying in England: The
          Monastic Experience.* Oxford, 1993. [Major study setting
          the monks of Westminster into the context of diet,
          demography, communal life, and rituals of death.
          Reviewed by R. B. Dobson, *EHR* 19 (1994), 960–62.]

697.   Haskett, Timothy S. "'I have ordeyned and make my
          testament and last wylle in this Forme': English as a
          Testamentary Language, 1387–1450." *Mediaeval Studies*
          58 (1996), 149–206. [The search for English, with a list
          (pp. 193–206) of English-language testators.]

698.   Hatcher, John. "England in the Aftermath of the Black
        Death." *Past and Present* 144 (August 1994), 3–35. [A
        survey of interpretations and an emphasis on slow but
        long-term change.]

699.   ———. "The Great Slump of the Mid-Fifteenth Century."
        In item 20. Pp. 237–72. [Export numbers show a collapse
        in 1440s and 1450s; agriculture less affected, though
        land values fell.]

700.   ———. "Plague, Population and the English Economy,
        1348–1530." In *British Population History from the
        Black Death to the Present Day*. Edited by Michael
        Anderson. Cambridge, 1996. Pp. 9–93. [A reworking of
        his 1977 booklet written for the Economic History
        Society.]

701.   Heal, Felicity. "Reciprocity and Exchange in the Late
        Medieval Household." In item 50. Pp. 178–98. [A center
        of honor and of consumption.]

702.   Hieatt, Constance C. "The Middle English Culinary
        Recipes in MS Harley 5401: An Edition and Commen-
        tary." *Medium Aevum* 65 (1996), 54–71. [Ninety-six
        short recipes printed, mostly early fifteenth century.]

703.   Holmes, George A. "Anglo-Florentine Traders in 1451."
        EHR 108 (1993), 371–86. [Documents of the Salivati
        family, preserved in Pisa, telling how large shipments
        from England were handled.]

704.   ———. "Lorenzo de' Medici's London Branch." In item
        20. Pp. 273–85. [Hard times in the 1460s and 1470s: bad
        loans, the dangers of dealing with kings, and in-house
        personality conflicts.]

705.   Horrox, Rosemary. "Service." In item 57. Pp. 61–78. [A
        key to social hierarchy and structure.]

706.   James, Susan E. "Parr Memorials in Kendal Parish
         Church." *Cumberland* 92 (1992), 99–163. [There are but
         few family remains.]

707.   Jefferson, Lisa. "Tournaments, Heraldry, and the
         Knights of the Round Table: A Fifteenth-Century
         Armorial with Two Accompanying Texts." *Arthurian
         Literature* 14 (1996), 69–157. [A private manuscript
         published; the heraldry of the mythical.]

708.   ———. "Neville Babthorpe, and the Serjeants: Three
         Fifteenth-Century Feast Menus." *Oxon* 63 (1998),
         241–49. [What they served at some fancy dinners in
         1427; documents published.]

709.   Johnston, Alexandra F. "Traders and Playmakers:
         English Guildsmen and the Low Countries." In item 8.
         Pp. 99–114. [They also transported an interest in plays
         and pageants back to England.]

710.   ———. "William Revetour, Chaplain and Clerk of York,
         Testator." *Leeds* n.s. 29 (1998), 153–71. [A will of 1446
         from a man with an interest in the drama; the will
         published here.]

711.   Jones, E. D. "A Few Bubbles More: The Myntling
         Register Revisited." *JMH* 17 (1991), 263–69. [More
         controversy about its demographic reliability, as first
         argued in 1989.]

712.   Keen, Maurice. "Heraldry and Hierarchy: Esquires and
         Gentlemen." In item 29. Pp. 94–108, 184–87. [Upward
         mobility, to some extent.]

713.   Keiser, George R. "Practical Books for the Gentleman."
         In item 53. Pp. 470–94. [The how-to-do-it literature, on a
         wide range of topics for the needs of both high and low.]

714.   Kermode, Jennifer I. "Money and Credit in the Fifteenth
         Century: Some Lessons from Yorkshire." *Business*

History Review 65 (1991), 475–501. [European economic crisis hit local credit arrangements.]

715.   ———. "Medieval Indebtedness: The Regions versus London." In item 81. Pp. 72–88. [Mainly York: a thorough exploration of a neglected but basic topic: tables and quantitative data.]

716.   Kirby, Joan. "A Northern Knightly Family in the Waning Middle Ages." *Northern* 31 (1995), 86–107. [The Plumptons, based on their coucher book and letters.]

717.   ———, ed. *The Plumpton Letters and Papers*. Camden Society, 5th series, 8 (1996). [Valuable edition to replace that of 1839. Reviewed by R. B. Dobson, *Northern* 34 (1998), 239–41.]

718.   Kirby, John L., ed. *The Hungerford Cartulary: A Calendar of the Earl of Radnor's Cartulary of the Hungerford Family*. Wiltshire Record Society, 99 (1993). [One of the few late medieval secular, family cartularies.]

719.   Knight, Stephen, ed. *Robin Hood: An Anthology of Scholarship and Criticism*. Woodbridge, 1999. [Included are Hanawalt's essay from item 48, pp. 263–84, and Colin Richmond's (from *Nottingham Mediaeval Studies*, item 777), pp. 363–76.]

720.   Kowaleski, Maryanne. *Local Markets and Regional Trade in Medieval Exeter*. Cambridge, 1995. [Important study, with emphasis on the wider region as well as the city as the center of economic life.]

721.   ———. "The Grain Trade in Fourteenth-Century Exeter." In item 30. Pp. 1–52. [How much came in, and the role of Exeter men in the import business.]

722.   Kümin, Beat A. *The Shaping of a Community: The Rise and Reformation of the English Parish, c. 1400–1560*. Aldershot and Brookfield, Vt., 1996. [Valuable general look at the center of local life.]

723. Lambdin, Laura C., and Robert J. Lambdin, eds. *Chaucer's Pilgrims: An Historical Guide to the Pilgrims in "The Canterbury Tales."* Westport, Conn., and London, 1996. [Thirty-two short papers setting the historical and social context of each pilgrim, in a useful introduction to trades, ranks, and social roles.]

724. Landman, James H. "The Laws of Community, Margery Kempe, and the 'Canon's Yeoman's Tale'." *JM & EMS* 28/2 (1998), 389–425. [Crafts, community, and the regulation of behavior; some chancery petitions published.]

725. Langdon, John. "Water-Mills and Windmills in the West Midlands, 1086–1500." *EcHR* 44 (1991), 424–44. [After the plague it was mostly water mills, mainly for grain; a detailed look at several manorial estates.]

726. ————. "Inland Water Transport in Medieval England." *Journal of Historical Geography* 19 (1993), 1–11. [A response to item 670, saying it overestimates the role of inland water transport.]

727. Lepine, David. "The Courtenays and Exeter Cathedral in the Later Middle Ages." *Devon* 124 (1992), 41–58. [Close regional links: patronage, burials, and noblesse oblige.]

728. Lerer, Seth. "William Caxton." In item 96. Pp. 720–83. [His work, role, and influence.]

729. Lessen, Marvin. "York Annulet Silver Coins of Henry VI." *BNJ* 63 (1993), 59–64. [The York mint was reopened on a temporary basis; see item 621.]

730. Lessen, Marvin, Mary F. Streigel, and Peter P. Gaspar. "Counterfeit 'Scowling Bust' Groats of Henry V." *Numismatic Chronicle* 153 (1993), 218–25. [Table compares them with genuine coins of Henry V and Edward IV.]

731.   Lester, Geoffrey A. "The Earliest English Sailing Instructions." In item 60. Pp. 330–67. [From a French manual and covering English, French, Spanish, and Portuguese waters.]

732.   Lloyd, Terence H. *England and the German Hanse, 1157–1611: A Study in Their Trade and Commercial Diplomacy.* Cambridge, 1991. [The political currents and much economic data.]

733.   Lock, Roy. "The Black Death in Walsham-le-Willows." *Suffolk* 37/4 (1992), 316–37. [40–50 percent mortality, and then following the tale to 1400, when things bounced back a bit.]

734.   Loschky, David, and Ben D. Childers. "Early English Mortality." *JIH* 23 (1993), 85–97. [Perhaps declining by the mid-fifteenth century (down to 50 per thousand?).]

735.   Maddern, Philippa C. *Violence and Social Order: East Anglia, 1422–1442.* Oxford, 1992. [Setting local and private violence into the context of lawful government and of local disorder; an important statement, if not quite drastic revisionism.]

736.   ———. "'Best Trusted Friends': Concepts and Practices of Friendship among Fifteenth-Century Norfolk Gentry." In item 81. Pp. 100–17. [A close look at Simeon Fyncham's world of contacts and a salutary reminder of amicable relationships.]

737.   ———. "Friends of the Dead: Executors, Wills, and Family: Strategy in Fifteenth-Century Norfolk." In item 3. Pp. 155–74. [The will as part of a long-term plan, with tables of beneficiaries, executors, etc.]

738.   Masschaele, James. "The Multiplicity of Medieval Markets Reconsidered." *Journal of Historical Geography* 20 (1994), 255–71. [Patterns of development prior to

1350 still prevailed, even if there were few new developments.]

739.   Mayhew, Nicholas J. "From Regional to Central Minting, 1158–1464." See item 648. Pp. 83–178, especially 149–78. [Money, minters, government policies, and metallurgy.]

740.   McIntosh, Marjorie K. *Controlling Misbehavior in England, 1370–1600.* Cambridge, 1998. [Ambitious study of community values and social control; discussed in an issue of *JBS* 37 (1998); see item 792.]

741.   ———. "Response." *JBS* 37 (1998), 291–305. [Her comments about a session devoted to item 740; see item 792 for a listing of the participants. The challenge of macrohistory and micro-history and the links between values and behavior.]

742.   ———. "The Diversity of Social Capital in English Communities, 1300–1640 (with a glance at modern Nigeria)." *JIH* 29 (1999), 459–90. [Local organization, credit, sexuality, and symbolic capital.]

743.   McSheffrey, Shannon. "Jurors, Respectable Masculinity, and Christian Morality: A Comment on Marjorie McIntosh's *Controlling Misbehavior.*" *JBS* 37 (1998), 269–78. [Jurors and masculinity and the inter-twining of religion, culture, and ideology; part of the discussion of McIntosh's work, as per item 792.]

744.   ———. "Men and Masculinities in Late Medieval London: Civil Culture: Governance, Patriarchy and Reputation." In *Conflicted Identities and Multiple Masculinities: Men in the Medieval West.* Edited by Jacqueline Murray. Garland Medieval Casebooks, 25. London and New York, 1999. Pp. 243–78. [Marriage strategies and negotiations, in the setting of local community, sex, behavior, and reputation.]

745.   Mertes, Kate. "Aristocracy." In item 57. Pp. 42–60.
        [Nobility, lordship, and courtesy.]

746.   Middleton-Stewart, Judith. "'Down to the Sea in Ships':
        Decline and Fall on the Suffolk Coast." In *Counties and
        Communities: Essays in East Anglian History Presented
        to Hassell Smith*. Edited by Carole Rawcliffe, Roger
        Virgoe, and Richard Smith. Norwich, 1996. Pp. 69–83.
        [With considerable focus on the fifteenth century.]

747.   Moon, J. H., and Thomas Rolff. "An Examination of the
        Structure of Society within the Kentish High Weald
        Based on a Study of a Fifteenth-Century Parish Clerk."
        Arch Cant 112 (1993), 193–212. [Bequests, land trans-
        fers and gifts, local families; list of Lamberhurst wills.]

748.   Moreton, Charles E. "A Social Gulf? The Upper and
        Lesser Gentry of Later Medieval England." *JMH* 17
        (1991), 255–62. [Community? Links across the divides,
        drawing on Townshend family material.]

749.   ———. *The Townshends and Their World: Gentry, Law,
        and Land in Norfolk, c. 1450–1551*. Oxford, 1992. [De-
        tailed examination of a family, legal careers, estates,
        and the county community.]

750.   Morgan, Philip. "Gentry Households in Fifteenth-
        Century Cheshire." *BJRUL* 79/2 (1997), 21–26. [An
        indenture of 21 Henry VI concerning the Mainwaring
        family.]

751.   Munby, Lionel M., introduction. *All My Worldly Goods:
        An Insight into Family Life from Wills and Inventories,
        1447–1742*. St Albans, 1991. [Only a few wills before
        1510.]

752.   Munro, John H. "Urban Wage Structures in Late-Medi-
        eval England and the Low Countries: Work-Time and
        Seasonal Wages." In *Labour and Leisure in Historical*

Perspective, Thirteenth to Twentieth Centuries. Edited by Ian Blanchard. Stuttgart, 1994. Pp. 65–78. [Seasonal variations and leisure time; a paper from the 11th International Economic History Congress, Milan, September 1994).]

753. Newman, Christine M. "Order and Community in the North: The Liberty of Allertonshire in the later Fifteenth Century." In item 77. Pp. 47–66. [A look at a relatively stable society.]

754. Nightingale, Pamela. "Monetary Contraction and Mercantile Credit in Later Medieval England." *EcHR* 43 (1990), 560–75. [Credit got tougher when monetary supplies shrank; few hands were in control by the fifteenth century.]

755. Norris, Malcolm. "Later Medieval Monumental Brasses: An Urban Funerary Industry and Its Representation of Death." In item 9. Pp. 184–209 (and appendix, 248–51). [Major workshops and how "mortality" was depicted.]

756. North, Jeffrey J. *North English Hammered Coinage, Volume 2.* London, 1991. Pp. 60–98. [Covering Richard II–Richard III: principal styles and denominations.]

757. Orme, Nicholas. "Medieval Hunting: Fact and Fancy." In item 48. Pp. 133–53. [Social theories and information on how to do it.]

758. ———. "The Culture of Children in Medieval England." *Past and Present* 148 (August 1995), 48–88. [A wide survey: toys, games, the children's year, school books, etc.]

759. [No entry.]

760. ———. "Children and Literature in Medieval England." *Medium Aevum* 68 (1999), 218–46. [Children as a reading public; a wide survey of books and audiences.]

761.   Ormrod, William Mark. "Finance and Trade under
         Richard II." In item 43. Pp. 155–86. [Taxes, customs,
         wool and cloth exports; many graphs, charts, and
         statistics.]

762.   Payling, Simon J. "Social Mobility, Demographic Change,
         and Landed Society in Late Medieval England." *EcHR*
         45 (1992), 51–73. [Heiresses became more important
         after the plague; the long-term drift toward the con-
         solidation of land and wealth was checked a bit.]

763.   Pearsall, Derek. "Chaucer's Tomb: The Politics of Re-
         burial." *Medium Aevum* 64 (1995), 51–73. [Chaucer's
         desire for an abbey burial site and a possible reconstruc-
         tion of the original tomb.]

764.   Peberdy, R. B. "Navigation on the River Thames
         between London and Oxford in the Late Middle Ages."
         Oxon 61 (1996), 311–40. [Quite a lively scene; river
         perhaps more navigable than generally thought.]

765.   Pedersen, Frederick. "Demography in the Archives:
         Social and Geographical Factors in Fourteenth-Century
         York Cause Paper Marriage Litigation." *Continuity and
         Change* 10 (1995), 405–36. [Who got involved, how many,
         their ages and gender.]

766.   Phythian-Adams, Charles V. "Rituals of Personal Con-
         frontation in Late Medieval England." *BJRUL* 73/1
         (1991), 65–90. [Reading some anecdotes of violence and
         behavior, though much (alas) is from Tudor times.]

767.   Platt, Colin. *King Death: The Black Death and Its After-
         math in Late-Medieval England.* London, 1996. [Social
         and cultural ramifications, alongside demographic and
         economic ones.]

768.   Poos, Lawrence. *A Rural Society after the Black Death:
         Essex, 1350–1525.* Cambridge, 1991. [Major regional
         study, with emphasis on demography and mobility.]

769.   Postles, David. "Personal Naming Patterns of Peasants
        and Burgesses in Late Medieval England." *Med Pros*
        12/1 (1991), 29–56. [A case study in the use of naming
        patterns as a window into social structure and
        morphology.]

770.   ———. "Brewing and the Peasant Economy: Some
        Manors in Late Medieval Devon." *Rural History* 3 (1992),
        133–44. [Looking at presentments: the transition from
        household production to an industry in which both men
        and women were active.]

771.   Pritchard, Gillian. "Religion and the Paston Family." In
        item 18. Pp. 65–82. [They were pious and conventional;
        not a topic the letters are likely to explicate at much
        length.]

772.   Razi, Zvi. "The Myth of the Immutable English Family."
        Past and Present 140 (August 1993), 3–44. [Manorial
        records argue for change; people come and go; nuclear
        and extended families are both to be found.]

773.   Reeves, A. Compton. "Histories of English Families
        Published in the 1980s." *Med Pros* 13/2 (1992), 83–120.
        [A survey of recent work.]

774.   ———. *Pleasures and Pastimes in Medieval England.*
        Stroud, 1995. [There was play as well as work; a survey
        of leisure and recreation and a look at popular culture.]

775.   Renfrew, Cindy. *Take a Thousand Eggs or More: A
        translation of medieval recipes from Harleian MS. 279,
        Harleian MS. 4016 and extracts of Ashmole MS. 1439,
        Laud MS. 553, and Douce MS. 55.* 2 vols. Sussex, N.J.,
        1998. [As in an EETS volume of 1888: repr. 1964, with
        material modernized.]

776.   Richmond, Colin. "The English Gentry and Religion,
        c. 1500." In item 52. Pp. 121–50. [A tale of limited

commitment and devotion, somewhat to the author's disappointment.]

777.   ———. "An Outlaw and Some Peasants: The Possible
            Significance of Robin Hood." *Nottingham* 37 (1993),
            90–101. [Included in item 719: social consciousness and
            an identification with "fictitious" characters.]

778.   Riddy, Felicity. "'Mother Knows Best': Reading Social
            Change in a Courtesy Text." *Speculum* 71 (1996), 66–86.
            ["What the goodwife taught her daughter" is the launching text for inter-generational communication and
            gender roles.]

779.   Rigby, Steven H. *English Society in the Later Middle
            Ages: Class, Status, and Gender*. Basingstoke and New
            York, 1995. [Structural analysis, informed by sociology
            and the "closure theory" of interaction.]

780.   Robertson, Mary L. "'Sires remembre we are
            neyghbours': English Gentry Communities in the 15th
            Century." *JBS* 34 (1995), 112–18. [A review article
            covering items 618, 643, and 749.]

781.   Rosenthal, Joel T. *Patriarchy and Families of Privilege
            in Fifteenth-Century England*. Philadelphia, 1991. [Case
            studies of different types of family structure and of
            upper class widows.]

782.   ———. "Retirement and the Life Cycle in Fifteenth-
            Century England." See item 655. Pp. 173–88. [The
            concept of retirement and the need to provide for it was
            sometimes recognized and even implemented.]

783.   ———. *Old Age in Late Medieval England*. Philadelphia,
            1996. [A sampling of some folks, and some groups, who
            made it to their three score and ten.]

784.   ———. "When Did You Last See Your Grandfather?" In
            item 2. Pp. 223–44. [Material on three-generation
            families.]

785.   [No entry.]

786.   Rosser, Gervase. "Going to the Fraternity Feast: Com-
         mensality and Social Relations in Late Medieval
         England." *JBS* 33 (1994), 430–46. [Nothing like eating
         and drinking together.]

787.   Rothwell, William F. "The Trilingual England of
         Geoffrey Chaucer." *Studies in the Age of Chaucer* 16
         (1994), 45–67. [Language as a guide to social and
         cultural changes.]

788.   Rubin, Miri. "Small Groups: Identity and Solidarity in
         the Late Middle Ages." In item 59. Pp. 132–50. [Reflec-
         tions on "community" and its value in historical analysis:
         hierarchy, ceremony, tension.]

789.   ———. "The Poor." In item 57. Pp. 169–82. [Institutions
         and the social ideology that provided (some) help.]

790.   Ryder, M. L. "Fleece Grading and Wool Sorting." *Textile
         History* 26/1 (Spring, 1995), 3–22. [Types of grades and
         the importance of wool's original position on the sheep's
         body.]

791.   Saul, Nigel. "Chaucer and Gentility." In item 48.
         Pp. 41–55. [Gentility, class, behavior, and links with
         status and income.]

792.   Seaver, Paul. "Introduction to Symposium: Controlling
         (Mis)Behavior." *JBS* 37 (1998), 231–45. [Introduces
         papers on McIntosh's *Controlling Misbehavior* (item
         740); see also items 550, 684, 741, and 743; local courts,
         local values, social stability.]

793.   Singerman, Jeffrey L., and Will McLean. *Daily Life in
         Chaucer's England*. Westport, Conn., 1995. [Life and
         time: clothes, food and drink, entertainment.]

794.   Spring, Eileen. *Law, Land, and Family: Aristocratic
         Inheritance in England, 1300 to 1800*. Chapel Hill, N.C.,

1993. [Takes issue with Lawrence Stone's views of family
and aristocracy. Reviewed by Linda Mitchell, *Speculum*
70 (1995), 429–31.]

795.   Staniland, Kay. "Extravagance or Regal Necessity? The
         Clothing of Richard II." In item 44. Pp. 84–93. [A royal
         yen for fancy clothes, but little innovation or shocking
         extravagance.]

796.   Stell, P. M. "Forenames in Thirteenth- and Fourteenth-
         Century Yorkshire: A Study Based on a Biographical
         Database Generated by Computer." *Med Pros* 20 (1999),
         95–128. [Name frequencies and root stocks through the
         end of the fourteenth century.]

797.   Stewartby, Lord. "Calais Quarter-Nobles of Henry VI."
         BNJ 69 (1999), 220–21. [Distinctions between coins
         struck at London, York, and Calais.]

798.   Stopford, J. "Modes of Production among Medieval
         Tilers." *Med Arch* 37 (1993), 93–108. [Some were
         itinerant, some worked but intermittently.]

799.   Stow, George B. "Richard II and the Invention of the
         Pocket Handkerchief." *Albion* 27 (1995), 221–35. [Give
         Richard II some credit, whatever his larger short-
         comings.]

800.   Sutton, Anne F. "Order and Fashion in Clothes: The
         King, His Household, and the City of London at the End
         of the Fifteenth Century." *Textile History* 22/9 (1991),
         253–76. [Comparing the court of Edward IV and Henry
         VII, and the minimal impact of sumptuary legislation.]

801.   ———. "Caxton Was A Mercer: His Social Milieu and
         Friends." In item 81. Pp. 118–48. [The recreation of a
         social circle and the routines of life and trade.]

802.   ———. "Dress and Fashions, c. 1470." In item 18.
         Pp. 5–26. [Useful survey.]

803. ————. "Some Aspects of the Linen trade, c. 1130s to
1500, and the Part Played by the Mercers of London."
Textile History 30/2 (Autumn 1999), 155–75. [Important
activity, off the mainline of the wool trade.]

804. Swanson, Robert N. "A Medieval Staffordshire Fraternity: The Guild of St John Baptist, Walsall." In item 68.
Pp. 47–65. [Accounts of 1468–95 and 1495–1505:
numbers, fees, etc.]

805. Thornton, Tim. "A Defence of the Liberties of Cheshire,
1451–2." *HR* 68 (1995), 338–54. [County fought to keep
its privileges; documents on resumption of honor.]

806. Threlfall-Holmes, Miranda. "Late Medieval Iron Production and Trade in the North-East." *Arch Ael*, 5th series,
27 (1999), 109–22. [Based on the purchases of Durham
Cathedral Priory, 1464–1510; growing use of local
material and list of local suppliers.]

807. Tuck, Anthony. "The Percies and the Community of
Northumberland in the Later Fourteenth Century." In
item 42. Pp. 178–95. [Ties to local gentry, local traditions,
and networks.]

808. ————. "A Medieval Tax Haven: Berwick upon Tweed
and the English Crown, 1336–1461." In item 20.
Pp. 148–67. [Wool exports and the usual pleas of urban
decline and poverty.]

809. Virgoe, Roger. "Aspects of the County Community in the
Fifteenth Century." In item 54. Pp. 1–13. [Putting flesh
on the phrase by looking at elections and shire courts:
also in item 94.]

810. Virgoe, Roger, with A. Hassell Smith. "Norfolk." In
*English County Histories: A Guide: A Tribute to C. R.
Elrington.* Edited by R. J. Currie and C. P. Lewis.
Stroud, 1994. Pp. 280–90. [A tribute to a long tradition
of serious local history and historiography.]

811.   Walker, Simon. "Sir Richard Abberbury (c. 1330–1399) and His Kinsmen: The Rise and Fall of a Gentry Family." *Nottingham* 34 (1990), 113–40. [Long and successful career, though the family declined after 1399.]

812.   Watkins, Andrew. "The Woodland Economy of the Forest of Arden in the Later Middle Ages." *Midland* 18 (1993), 19–36. [Much parked land, with wood a valuable cash crop (as thieving peasants well knew).]

813.   Wayment, Hilary. "Sir John Savile, Steward of Wakefield, 1482, d. 1505." *YAJ* 68 (1996), 181–89. [He lies in Thornhill Church, with a tomb of 1528 and a depiction in a window.]

814.   White, Eileen. "The Great Feast." *Leeds* n.s. 29 (1998), 401–10. [George Neville's installation as archbishop, 6 Edward IV; they ate far too much.]

815.   Whittle, Jane. "Individualism and The Family-Land Bond: A Reassessment of Land Transfer Patterns among the English Peasantry." *Past and Present* 160 (August 1998), 25–63. [The market vs. an in-the-family dynamic, with an active market in evidence.]

816.   Williams, Alan, and Elizabeth Williams. "Excavation of a Late Medieval Lime Kiln on Breadwell Point, Northumberland." *Arch Ael*, 5th series, 24 (1996), 109–17. [A small affair of the fifteenth century, explicated by a sixteenth-century description.]

817.   Woodhead, Peter. *The Herbert Schneider Collection: English Gold Coins, 1257–1603.* London, 1996. [Volume I, pp. 16–43, covers Richard II–Richard III: mints and issues, well illustrated.]

818.   Woodward, Donald. *Men at Work: Labourers and Building Craftsmen in the Towns of Northern England, 1450–1750.* Cambridge, 1995. [Mostly later: wages,

working life cycle, living standards: the wage series only
begin in the sixteenth century.]

819.   Woolgar, Christopher. "Diet and Consumption in Gentry
and Noble Households: A Case Study from around the
Wash." In item 3. Pp. 17–31. [Four big households ex-
amined: supplies, seasonable change, prices, regional
peculiarities.]

820.   Wright, Laura. "Trade between England and the Low
Countries: Evidence from Historical Linguistics." In item
8. Pp. 169–79. [Mixed- and multi-language documents as
signs of cultural exchange.]

821.   Zeepvat, R. J., and H. Cooper-Reade. "Excavations
within the Outer Bailey of Hertford Castle."
Hertfordshire Archaeology 12 (1994–96), 15–40. [Of
interest because of "notable assemblage" of late medieval
food debris, pp. 33–37: with contributions by Deborah
Jacques and Keith Dobney.]

VI. WOMEN, DOMESTICITY, MARRIAGE, SEX AND SEXUALITY (AND MARGERY KEMPE)[3]

822.   Archer, Rowena E. "'How ladies . . . who live on their manors ought to manage their households and estates': Women as Landholders and Administrators in the Later Middle Ages." In item 41. Pp. 149–81. [Mostly aristocratic ladies and drawing heavily on East Anglian families.]

823.   Armstead, Wendy. "Interpreting Images of Women with Books in Misericords." In *Women and the Book: Assessing the Visual Evidence*. Edited by Lesley Smith and Jane H. M. Taylor. Toronto, 1997. Pp. 57–74. [A 1993 St Hilda's Conference; depictions of women reading, praying, writing—with humor and hints of sex.]

824.   Armstrong, Elizabeth P. "'Understanding by Feeling' in Margery Kempe's Book." In item 61. Pp. 17–35. [She was not an hysteric; her serious spirituality compared with that of St Teresa.]

825.   Ashley, Kathleen. "Historicizing Margery: *The Book of Margery Kempe* as Social Text." *JM & EMS* 28/2 (1998), 371–88. [Auto-hagiography in a society where spiritual self-justification was an accepted theme.]

---

[3] Material relating to Margery Kempe—even if focused largely on her spirituality and religious expression—is included in this chapter.

826.   Bardsley, Sandy. "Women's Work Reconsidered: Gender and Wage Differentiation in Late Medieval England." *Past and Present* 165 (November 1999), 3–29. [Even in times of rising wages, women rarely caught up to men.]

827.   Barratt, Alexandra. "Margery Kempe and the King's Daughter of Hungary." In item 61. Pp. 189–201. [Comparison with Elisabeth, matching their revelations.]

828.   Barron, Caroline M. "Johanna Hall (d. 1441) and Johanna Sturdy (d. c. 1460), Bell-Founders." In item 7. Pp. 99–111. [Unusual women, with material on the bells these widows oversaw.]

829.   Beckwith, Sarah. "Problems of Authority in Late Medieval English Mysticism: Language, Agency, and Authority in *The Book of Margery Kempe.*" *Exemplaria* 4 (1992), 171–200.

830.   ———. "A Very Material Mysticism: The Medieval Mysticism of Margery Kempe." In *Gender and Text in the Later Middle Ages.* Edited by Jane Chance. Gainesville, Fla., 1996. Pp. 195–215.

831.   Bennett, Judith M. "Medieval Women, Modern Women: Across the Great Divide." In *Culture and History, 1350–1600: Essays on English Communities, Identities, and Writing.* Edited by David Aers. Detroit and London, 1992. Pp. 147–75. [The paradigms for studying women and "their history"; there was no golden age, and things were usually tough or tougher.]

832.   ———. "Women's History: A Study in Continuity and Change." *Women's History Review* 2/2 (1993), 173–84. [See item 869 for a debate on interpreting long-term contours of women's social and historical roles.]

833.   Bhattacharji, Santha. *God Is An Earthquake: The Spirituality of Margery Kempe.* London, 1997. [Foreword

by Benedicta Ward, pp. xi–xiii; heresy, conversations
with Christ, and Margery as a teacher.]

834.   Boyd, David L., and Ruth Mazo Karras. "The Interro-
gation of a Male Transvestite Prostitute in Fourteenth-
Century London." *GLQ: A Journal of Lesbian and Gay
Studies* 1 (1995), 459–65. [There have always been
boundary crossings.]

835.   Bradbury, Kristine G. "The World of Etheldreda
Gardner: Viewing a Woman in the Late Fifteenth
Century Through the Lives of her Husbands." *Ricardian*
9/115 (December 1991), 146–53. [Three marriages, the
last to an MP and lord mayor of London.]

836.   Bradley, Helen. "Lucia Visconti, Countess of Kent (d.
1424)." In item 7. Pp. 77–84. [Her life as an aristocratic
outsider, after a short-lived English marriage.]

837.   Bremner, Eluned. "Margery Kempe and the Critics: Dis-
empowerment and Deconstruction." In item 61.
Pp. 117–35. [Crossing lots of boundaries, but not to be
written off as a deviant or a crank.]

838.   Cleve, Gunnel. "Margery Kempe: A Scandinavian Influence in Medieval England?" In item 39. Pp. 163–78.
[Birgitta's example and teachings, and how Margery
might have learned of and from them.]

839.   Copeland, Rita. "Why Women Can't Read: Medieval Her-
meneutics, Statutory Law, and the Lollard Heresy
Trials." In *Representing Women: Law, Literature, and
Feminism*. Edited by Susan Heinzelman and Zipporah
B. Wiseman. Durham, N.C., and London, 1994.
Pp. 253–86. ["Official" views against women as readers,
and instances of subversive reading.]

840.   Coss, Peter. *The Lady in Medieval England, 1000–1500*.
Stroud, 1998. [A general treatment: perceptive and well
illustrated.]

841.   Cullum, P. H. "'And Hir Name was Charite': Charitable
        Giving by and for Women in Late Medieval Yorkshire."
        In item 41. Pp. 182–211. [As found in wills: types and
        categories of giving, to women and to men.]

842.   Davies, Matthew. "Dame Thomasine Percyvale, 'The
        Maid of Week' (d. 1514)." In item 7. Pp. 184–207. [She
        married three London tailors; her neighborhood
        networks.]

843.   Dickman, Susan. "A Showing of God's Grace: *The Book
        of Margery Kempe.*" In item 78. Pp. 159–76. [A compari-
        son to continental mysticism.]

844.   Dillon, Janette. "The Making of Desire in *The Book of
        Margery Kempe.*" *Leeds* n.s. 26 (1995), 113–44.
        [Sexuality, the Lollards, and the inter-personal
        dynamics of dictation and the confessional.]

845.   ———. "Margery Kempe's Sharpe confessor/s." *Leeds*,
        n.s. 27 (1996), 131–38. [She was met with skepticism
        and also by some support.]

846.   ———. "Holy Women and Their Confessors or Confes-
        sors and Their Holy Women? Margery Kempe and
        Continental Tradition." In *Prophets Abroad: The
        Reception of Continental Holy Women in Late-Medieval
        England.* Edited by Rosalynn Voaden. Cambridge, 1996.
        Pp. 115–40. [Margery's tears and her confessor's
        preaching formed an alliance.]

847.   [No entry.]

848.   Ellis, Deborah S. "Margery Kempe and King's Lynn." In
        item 61. Pp. 139–63. [The town, urban life, and a
        woman's world in this setting, with a map of the town
        and a list of the neighbors.]

849.   Ellis, Roger. "Margery Kempe's Scribe and the Miracu-
        lous Books." In item 75. Pp. 161–75. [The scribe could be

caught in the middle; references to other mystical
writings.]

850.   Erler, Mary C. "Margery Kempe's White Clothes."
        Medium Aevum 62 (1993), 78–83. [How she came to
        adopt them, and what she was thereby proclaiming.]

851.   ———. "Three Fifteenth-Century Vowesses." In item 7.
        Pp. 165–83. [Case studies and then tables listing some of
        London's vowed women, 1367–1537.]

852.   French, Katherine L. "'To Free Them from Binding':
        Women in the Late Medieval English Parish." *JIH* 27
        (1997), 387–412. [Hocktide: graphs show the money
        collected in this traditional women's area.]

853.   Friedrichs, Rhoda L. "Marriage Strategies and Younger
        Sons in Fifteenth-Century England." *Med Pros* 14/1
        (1993), 53–69. [A survey, with many cases of sons going
        their own way.]

854.   Gallyon, Margaret. *Margery Kempe of Lynn and
        Medieval England*. Norwich, 1995. [General treatment,
        with a look at urban life; Margery approached via
        themes (secular clergy, friars, etc.).]

855.   Gibson, Gail McMurray. "Blessing from Sun and Moon:
        Churching as Women's Theater." In item 50. Pp. 139–54.
        [Explicated as drama: the triumph of Mary over Eve.]

856.   ———. "St Margery: *The Book of Margery Kempe*." In
        Equally in God's Image: Women in the Middle Ages.
        Edited by Julia Bolton Holloway, Constance S. Wright,
        and Joan Bechtold. New York, 1990. Pp. 144–63.
        [Margery was very literal minded and her experience in
        childbirth and as a fecund mother affected her religious
        views.]

857. ———. "Scene and Obscene: Seeing and Performing Late Medieval Childbirth." *JM & EMS* 29/1 (Winter, 1999), 7–24. [Descriptions and depictions.]

858. Glück, Robert. *Margery Kempe.* New York, 1994. [A retelling of her tale, specially aimed at children and general readers.]

859. Goldberg, P. J. P. "Women's Work, Women's Role, in the Late-Medieval North." In item 54. Pp. 34–50. [Opportunities in towns, occupations, crafts, and kinds of work.]

860. ———. "Marriage, Migration, and Servanthood: The York Cause Paper Evidence." In item 41. Pp. 1–15. [As the title indicates, a survey of the lives of the young, especially of girls.]

861. ———. "'For Better, For Worse': Marriage and Economic Opportunity for Women in Town and Country." In item 41. Pp. 108–25. [Towns were the place, and women's opportunities therein included more control over and within marriage.]

862. ———. *Women, Work, and Life Cycle in A Medieval Economy: Women in York and Yorkshire, c. 1300–1500.* Oxford, 1992. [Important study of (regional) economic and demographic alternatives.]

863. ———. "Women in Later Medieval English Archives." *JSA* 15/1 (1994), 59–71. [What is well documented, and what is not.]

864. ———. "Women." In item 57. Pp. 112–31. [Social roles, decorum, life possibilities.]

865. ———, ed. and trans. *Women in England, c. 1275–1525.* Manchester, 1995. [Long introduction and then a book of sources in English: by stages through the life cycle, economic activity, law and custom, etc.]

866.   Goodman, Anthony. *Katherine Swynford.* Lincoln, 1994.
        [A cathedral booklet; biographical, as appropriate from
        her paramour's biographer (item 283).]

867.   Goodman, Jennifer R. "'That Wommen Holde In Ful
        Greet Reverence': Mothers and Daughters Reading
        Chivalric Romances." In item 90. Pp. 25–30. [Some
        fifteenth-century women as readers, and some examples
        of women reading as found in the literature itself.]

868.   Graham, Helena. "'A Woman's Work . . .': Labour and
        Gender in the Late Medieval Countryside." In item 41.
        Pp. 126–48. [Court rolls from Abrewas (Staffordshire):
        many active women, brewsters, their fines, etc.]

869.   Hall, Bridget. "Women's History: A Study in Change,
        Continuity, or Standing Still?" *Women's History Review*
        2/1 (1993), 5–22. [An exchange with Bennett; see item
        832.]

870.   Hanawalt, Barbara A. "The Widow's Mite: Provision for
        Medieval London Widows." In *Upon My Husband's
        Death: Widows in the Literature and Histories of
        Medieval Europe.* Edited by Louise Mirrer. Ann Arbor,
        Mich., 1992. Pp. 21–45. [Dower and remarriage: rights,
        options, and harassment. Also see 918.]

871.   ———. "Remarriage as an Option for Urban and Rural
        Widows in Late Medieval England." In item 95.
        Pp. 141–64. [Some statistics: normative literature and
        personal options.]

872.   ———. "Female Networks for Fostering: Lady Lisle's
        Daughters." In 74. Pp. 239–58. [Mostly a story of warm
        relationships.]

873.   ———. "'The Childe of Bristowe' and the Making of
        Middle-Class Adolescence." In item 50. Pp. 155–78.
        [Uneasiness about the young, as shown in this poem in a
        Harleian manuscript.]

874.   Harding, Wendy. "Body and Text: *The Book of Margery Kempe*. In *Feminist Approaches to the Body in Medieval Literature*. Edited by Linda Lomperis and Sarah Stanbury. Philadelphia, 1993. Pp. 168–87. [A gulf between Margery's illiterate orality and the written text, and how we close this gap.]

875.   Haskett, Timothy S. "The Curteys Women in Chancery: The Legacy of Henry and Rye Brown." In item 82. Pp. 349–98. [Comparing their bequests, with transcripts of the wills.]

876.   Helmholz, Richard H. "Married Women's Wills in Later Medieval London." In item 95. Pp. 165–82. [Procedures, case studies, and the disappearance of such wills.]

877.   Holbrook, Sue Ellen. "'About Her': Margery Kempe's Book of Feeling and Working." In *The Idea of Medieval Literature: New Essays on Chaucer and Medieval Culture in Honor of Donald R. Howard*. Edited by James M. Dean and Christian K. Zacher. London and Toronto, 1992. Pp. 265–84. [Margery's struggles to find a mode of discourse so she could talk to God and tell her tale to God and to us.]

878.   Holloway, Julia Bolton. "Bridget, Margery, Julian, and Alice: Bridget of Sweden's Textual Community in Medieval England." In item 61. Pp. 203–22. [A group of late medieval religious women.]

879.   Hopkins, Andrea. *Most Wise and Valiant Ladies*. London, 1997. [An enthusiastic approach with nice illustrations: for Margery Kempe, pp. 61–83; for Margaret Paston, pp. 133–55.]

880.   [No entry.]

881.   Jewell, Helen. *Women in Medieval England*. Manchester and New York, 1996. [A general survey with an eye on

rural-urban and class distinctions between and among women.]

882.   Joensen, Leyvoy. "'The Flesh Made Word': Allegory in *The Book of Margery Kempe.*" *A/B: Autobiographic Studies*, 6 (1991), 169–82.

883.   Johnson, Lynn S. "The Trope of the Scribe and the Question of Literary Authority in the Works of Julian of Norwich and Margery Kempe." *Speculum* 66 (1991), 820–38. [Strategies that were used when mediating the female voice.]

884.   ———. "Margery Kempe: Social Critic." *JM & RS* 22/2 (Spring, 1992), 159–84. [Separates Margery the author from Margery the subject: how she used her own creation to step outside and discuss herself.]

885.   Jones, Ernest D. "The Medieval Leyrwite: A Historical Note on Female Fornication." *EHR* 107 (1992), 945–53. [The Mytling Register, again: did leyrwite fines "run in families" or do they pinpoint brothels?]

886.   ———. "The Spalding Priory Merchet Evidence from the 1250s to the 1470s." *JMH* 24 (1998), 155–75. [Husbands paid most fines, and fewer widows seem to have remarried after 1380.]

887.   ———. "Merchet Practice on the Spalding Manor of Sutton from 1253 to 1477." *Lincolnshire* 33 (1998), 79–84. [Statistics on the incidence of merchet and who paid the fine; the best extant data, taken from four manors.]

888.   Karras, Ruth Mazo. "The Latin Vocabulary of Illicit Sex in English Ecclesiastical Court Records." *Journal of Medieval Latin* 1 (1991), 1–17. [Connotations, distinctions, and popular and received usage.]

889.   ———. "Two Models, Two Standards: Moral Teaching
and Sexual Mores." In item 50. Pp. 123–38. [Behavior
and literature: *Dives and the Pauper*.]

890.   ———. *Common Women: Prostitution and Sexuality in
Medieval England*. New York and Oxford, 1996.
[Covering behavior, social history, and gender analysis.]

891.   Kelliher, Hilton. "The Rediscovery of Margery Kempe: A
Footnote." *British Library Journal* 23 (1987), 259–63.
[Tracking the manuscript, between Mountgrace and
1934.]

892.   Kelly, Henry Ansgar. "Shades of Incest and Cuckoldry:
Pardoners and John of Gaunt." *Studies in the Age of
Chaucer* 13 (1991), 121–40. [How much did John of
Gaunt sleep around? With Phillipa Chaucer?]

893.   Kettle, Ann J. "Ruined Maids: Prostitutes and Servant
Girls in Later Medieval England." In *Matrons and Mar-
ginal Women in Medieval Society*. Edited by Robert R.
Edwards and Vickie Ziegler. Woodbridge, 1995. Pp. 19–31.
[Focus on Lichfield: sad tales, moral supervision, sex as
business.]

894.   Kirby, Joan W. "Women in the Plumpton Correspondence: Fiction and Reality." In 94. Pp. 219–32. [See item
717 for her edition of the Letters.]

895.   Lacey, Kay. "Margaret Croke (d. 1491)." In item 7.
Pp. 143–64. [A figure in the Stonor Letters; her daughter
Elizabeth married Sir William Stonor in a string of
"good" marriages.]

896.   Lawes, Richard. "The Madness of Margery Kempe." In
item 40. Pp. 147–67. [Cross-cultural psychiatry and its
limitations.]

897.   Lawton, David. "Voice, Authority, and Blasphemy in *The
Book of Margery Kempe*." In item 61. Pp. 93–115. [Her

learning and theological sophistication, and her desire to be read "univocally."]

898.   Leyser, Henrietta. *Medieval Women: A Social History of Women in England*. London, 1995. [A survey, with much on the later Middle Ages, and discussion of the sources; especially valuable for teaching purposes.]

899.   Lochrie, Karma. *Margery Kempe and Translations of the Flesh*. Philadelphia, 1991. [Mostly looking at literary and linguistic issues in her story; important treatment of everybody's pet topic.]

900.   Mahoney, Dhira B. "Margery Kempe's Tears and the Power over Language." In item 61. Pp. 37–50. [Tears as a sign of power.]

901.   Mate, Mavis L. *Daughters, Wives and Widows after the Black Death: Women in Sussex, 1350–1435*. Woodbridge, 1998. [Change and continuity, with no single path as the dominant one; a study informed by case studies and much background in the local communities of the shire.]

902.   ———. *Women in Medieval English Society*. Cambridge, 1999. [A short book, tracking historiography and current views, in the Economic History Society's New Studies in Economic and Social History series. Chapter 3 (pp. 27–95) covers 1250–1530.]

903.   McEntire, Sandra J. "The Journey into Selfhood: Margery Kempe and Feminine Spirituality." In item 61. Pp. 51–69. [An assertion of the (re)integration of memory, loss, sorrow, and pain.]

904.   McRae-Spencer, Alison. "Putting Women in Their Place: Social and Legal Attitudes towards Violence in Marriage in Late Medieval England." *Ricardian* 10/128 (March 1995), 185–93. [Some case studies that argue for controlling the violence.]

905.   McSheffrey, Shannon, selected, introduced, and trans-
        lated. *Love and Marriage in Late Medieval London.*
        TEAMS Documents of Practice series. Kalamazoo,
        Mich., 1995. [A source book of documents designed for
        teaching purposes; see item 1600.]

906.   ———. "'I will never have none ayenst my Faders Will':
        Consent and the Making of Marriage in the Late
        Medieval Diocese of London." In item 82. Pp. 153–74.
        [Young people, often on their own, made more conserva-
        tive and conformist choices than we might imagine.]

907.   Moorhen, Wendy E. A. "Lady Katherine Gordon: A
        Genealogical Puzzle." *Ricardian* 11/139 (December
        1997), 191–213. [Perkin Warbeck's wife and almost as
        mysterious as her spouse.]

908.   Murray, Jacqueline. "Individualism and Consensual
        Marriage: Some Evidence from Medieval England." In
        item 82. Pp. 121–51. [Theories and case studies of
        marital tension and accommodation.]

909.   Myers, Michael B. "A Fictional-True Self: Margery
        Kempe and the Social Reality of the Merchant Elite of
        King's Lynn." *Albion* 31 (1999), 377–94. [Some social
        realities behind her construction of her life.]

910.   O'Connor, Stephen. "Joan Pyel (d. 1412)." In item 7.
        Pp. 71–75. [She took over the project of building Irthling-
        borough College.]

911.   Partner, Nancy F. "Reading the *Book of Margery Kempe.*"
        Exemplaria 3 (1991), 29–66.

912.   Payling, Simon. "The Politics of Family: Late Medieval
        Marriage Contracts." In item 19. Pp. 21–47. [Uses and
        settlements, plus the usual range of marriage arrange-
        ments and negotiations.]

913.   Payne, Paddy, and Caroline M. Barron. "The Letters and
        Life of Elizabeth Despenser, Lady Zouche (d. 1408)."
        Nottingham 41 (1997), 126–56. [Her will and five letters;
        among the earliest such materials for an English woman.]

914.   Pedersen, Frederik. "Did the Medieval Laity Know the
        Canon Law Rules on Marriage? Some Evidence from
        Fourteenth-Century York Cause Papers." *Mediaeval
        Studies* 56 (1994), 111–52. [Sometimes they were well
        informed on these matters.]

915.   Provost, William. "Margery Kempe and Her Calling." In
        item 61. Pp. 3–16. [Wife and/or heretic; Margery com-
        pared to the Wife of Bath and Julian of Norwich.]

916.   Rawcliffe, Carole. "Margaret Stodeye, Lady Philipot
        (d. 1436)." In item 7. Pp. 85–98. [Her marriages trace a
        path through London politics and bourgeois life.]

917.   Riddy, Felicity. "'Women talking about things of God': A
        Late Medieval Sub-culture." In item 63. Pp. 104–27.
        [Women as readers: who did read Julian of Norwich and
        how was she interpreted.]

918.   Rosenthal, Joel T. "Other Victims: Peeresses as War
        Widows, 1450–1500." See item 870. Pp. 131–52. [Re-
        printed from *History* 1987.]

919.   ———. "Fifteenth-Century Widows and Widowhood:
        Bereavement, Reintegration, and Life Choices." In item
        95. Pp. 33–58. [Options open to widows and the ones
        that some of them chose.]

920.   ———. "Looking for Grandmother: The Pastons and
        their Counterparts in Late Medieval England." In item
        74. Pp. 259–77. [Grandmothers are a much-neglected
        topic.]

921.   ———. "Three-Generation Families: Searching for
        Grandpa and Grandma in Late Medieval England." In

Medieval Family Roles: A Book of Essays. Edited by Cathy Jorgensen Itnyre. New York and London, 1996. Pp. 225–37. [Also see item 925.]

922.   Smith, Richard M. "Geographical Diversity in the Resort to Marriage in Late Medieval Europe: Work, Reputation, and Unmarried Females in the Household Formation Systems of Northern and Southern Europe." In item 41. Pp. 16–59. [Firm data on Florence and sketchier English material: labor, sex ratios, servants, and marriage patterns. A paper based on very wide reading.]

923.   Staley, Lynn. *Margery Kempe's Dissenting Fictions.* University Park, Penn., 1994. [Good analysis of feminism and spirituality.]

924.   ———, ed. *The Book of Margery Kempe.* TEAMS Middle English Texts series. Kalamazoo, Mich., 1996. [An edition designed for the classroom; useful introduction and an uncluttered edition.]

925.   Stoertz, Fione Harris. "Suffering and Survival in Medieval English Childbirth." See item 921. Pp. 101–20. [Mostly on the earlier period, but some interesting late medieval material.]

926.   Stork, Nancy P. "Did Margery Kempe Suffer from Tourette's Syndrome?" *Mediaeval Studies* 59 (1997), 261–300. [History of the diagnosis of the syndrome and an analysis of Kempe's "acting out" episodes.]

927.   Stratford, Jenny. "Joan Buckland (d. 1462)." In item 7. Pp. 113–28. [Long-time widow; years of litigation and estate management.]

928.   Sutton, Anne F. "Alice Claver, Silkwoman (d. 1489)." In item 7. Pp. 129–42. [She continued the business, with a good-sized workshop and sales to the court.]

929.   Sutton, Anne F., and Livia Visser-Fuchs. "A 'most Benevolent Queen': Queen Elizabeth Woodville's Reputation, her Piety and her Books." *Ricardian* 10/129 (June 1995), 214–45. [Many books can be linked to the queen; see also Isolda Wigram, ibid. 10/131 (December 1995), 327–30.]

930.   Swabey, Ffiona. "The Letter Book of Alice de Bryene and Alice de Sutton's List of Debts." *Nottingham* 42 (1998), 121–45. [Following on the trail of Edith Rickert's pioneering scholarship: eight letters and a list of debts.]

931.   ———. "The Household of Alice de Bryene, 1412–13." In item 23. Pp. 133–44. [Hospitality and meals: to whom, how many, and of what.]

932.   ———. *Medieval Gentlewoman: Life in a Widow's Household in the Later Middle Ages.* Stroud, 1999. [A full exposition of the material on Alice de Bryene's household; a case study set in a wide and thoughtful context.]

933.   Szell, Timea K. "From Woe to Weel and Weal to Woe: Notes on the Structure of *The Book of Margery Kempe.*" In item 61. Pp. 73–91. [To be read as auto-hagiography.]

934.   Taylor, Helen Clare. "'Mulier, Quid Ploras?' Holy Tears in the *Book of Margery Kempe.*" *Mediaevalia* 19 (1996 for 1993), 363–84. [Argues for a familiarity with patristic writers and the Psalms.]

935.   Thiébaux, Marcelle, introduction and trans. *The Writings of Medieval Women.* New York, 1998. [Julian of Norwich (pp. 441–65), Margery Kempe (pp. 471–78, 488–503), and some letters of Margaret of Anjou (pp. 480–83).]

936.   Triggs, Tony D., trans. with introduction. *The Book of Margery Kempe: The Autobiography of the Wild Woman of God.* Tunbridge Wells, 1995. [She was illiterate, but readable prose resulted; maps follow her wanderings at home and abroad.]

937.   Veale, Elspeth. "Matilda Penne, Skinner (d. 1932–3)." In
        item 7. Pp. 47–52. [Another widow who maintained the
        business after her husband's death.]

938.   Visconsi, Elliott. "'She Represents the Person of Our
        Lord': The Performance of Mysticism in the *Vita* of
        Elisabeth of Spalbeek and *The Book of Margery Kempe*."
        Comitatus 28 (1997), 76–89. [Writing was a spiritual
        labor pain, suffered to enhance an identification with
        Jesus.]

939.   Voaden, Rosalynn. "Beholding Men's Members: The
        Sexualizing of Transgression in *The Book of Margery
        Kempe*." In *Medieval Theology and the Natural Body*.
        Edited by Peter Biller and A. J. Minnis. Woodbridge and
        Rochester, N.Y., 1997. Pp. 175–90.

940.   ———. *God's Word, Women's Voices: The Discernment of
        Spirits in the Writings of Late-Medieval Women Vision-
        aries*. York, 1999. [Chapter iv, "Margery Kempe: The
        Woman Who Would Not Go Away," pp. 109–54.]

941.   Ward, Jennifer C. *English Noblewomen in the Later
        Middle Ages*. London, 1992. [General survey, based on
        some well-recorded case studies.]

942.   ———, ed. and trans. *Women of the English Nobility and
        Gentry, 1066–1500*. Manchester, 1995. [A source book,
        with some late medieval material: marriage, family,
        land, households, spiritual life.]

943.   ———. "English Noblewomen and the Local Community
        in the Later Middle Ages." In *Medieval Women and
        Their Communities*. Edited by Diane Watt. Toronto and
        Buffalo, 1997. Pp. 186–203. [Households, economic
        responsibilities, and local ties.]

944.   ———. "Townswomen and their Households." In item
        18. Pp. 27–42. [Husbands and wives, widows and
        remarriage, business and family life.]

945.   Watt, Diane. "'No Writing for Writing's Sake': The Language of Service and Household Rhetoric in the Letters of the Paston Women." In *Dear Sister: Medieval Women and the Epistolary Genre*. Edited by Karen Cherewatuk and Ulrike Wiethaus. Philadelphia, 1993. Pp. 122–38. [Taking a leaf from Virginia Wolfe, a close reading of constricted roles and a woman's freedom to set an epistolary agenda.]

946.   ———. *Secretaries of God: Women Prophets in Late Medieval and Early Modern England*. Cambridge, 1997. [Chapter 2 deals with Margery Kempe: "A Prophet in Her Own Country: Margery Kempe and the Medieval Tradition," pp. 15–50; in the context of medieval feminist prophecy.]

947.   Whittle, Jane. "Inheritance, Marriage, Widowhood and Remarriage: A Comparative Perspective on Women and Landholding in North-East Norfolk, 1440–1580." *Continuity and Change* 13 (1998), 33–72. [Women were active in the land market, but not as much as "their" menfolk.]

948.   Wilson, Janet. "Communities of Dissent: The Secular and Ecclesiastical Communities of Margery Kempe's *Book*." See item 943. Pp. 155–85. [Setting Margery into a social context.]

949.   ———. "Margery and Alison: Women on Top." In item 61. Pp. 223–37. [Speaking out, and without Chaucer's cop-out reversal.]

950.   Winstead, Karen A. "Capgrave's *St Katherine* and the Perils of Gynecocracy." *Viator* 25 (1994), 361–76. [Written 1445–46, and warning Henry VI against being ruled by a woman.]

951.   Wood, Robert A. "Poor Widows, c. 1393–1415." In item 7. Pp. 55–69. [Bequests and donations by women of different economic strata.]

952.   Yates, Julian. "Mystic Self: Margery Kempe and the Mirrors of Narrative." *Comitatus* 26 (1995), 75–93.

953.   Yoshikawa, Naoë-Kukita. "The Role of the Virgin Mary and the Structure of Meditation in *The Book of Margery Kempe*." In item 40. Pp. 169–92. [Her identification with the Virgin's life and woes.]

VII. URBAN AND MUNICIPAL HISTORY

954.   Alexander, Jennifer S., ed. *Southwell and Nottingham-shire: Medieval Art, Architecture, and Industry.* British Archaeological Association, Conference Proceedings, 17 (1996). [This volume—and the others in this series—contains relevant articles that are too short for individual listings; see items 1009, 1019, 1732, 1733, and 1820.]

955.   Alsford, Stephen. "The Town Clerks of Medieval Colchester." *Essex* 24 (1993), 125–35. [Evolution of the office; men and careers, as the office's status went up in the world.]

956.   Archer, Ian W. *The History of the Haberdasher's Company.* Chichester, 1991. [Pp. 1–31 take us to the Reformation; well illustrated.]

957.   Attreed, Lorraine, ed. *The York House Books, 1461–1490.* Stroud, 1991, 2 vols., for the Richard III and Yorkist History Trust. [Urban records, Latin and English, reflecting a rich data base for town government: vol. 1 covers 1476–49 and 1480–86; vol. 2 covers 1483–89 and 1488–90.]

958.   ———. "Arbitration and the Growth of Urban Liberties in Late Medieval England." *JBS* 31 (1992), 205–35. [With the town of Exeter vs. the bishop in the 1440s as the main case study.]

959.   ———. "The Politics of Welcome: Ceremonies and Constitutional Development in Later Medieval English Towns."

In item 49. Pp. 208–31. [Much on York in the fifteenth century, in the setting of a more general treatment.]

960.   ——. "Poverty, Payments, and Fiscal Policies in English Provincial Towns." In *Portraits of Medieval and Renaissance Living: Essays in Memory of David Herlihy.* Edited by Samuel K. Cohen and Steven R. Epstein. Ann Arbor, Mich., 1996). Pp. 325–48. [How towns tried to cope with their financial problems and obligations.]

961.   Bailey, Mark. "A Tale of Two Towns: Buntingford and Standon in the Later Middle Ages." *JMH* 19 (1993), 351–71. [Small towns in Hertfordshire, after the plague: signs of growth in Buntingford, longer tale of decline in Standon.]

962.   Barron, Caroline M. "London and Parliament in the Lancastrian Period." *Parliamentary History* (1990), 343–67. [Level of interest in elections shows guild involvement and financial commitment; appendix of election indentures and other relevant sources; see item 415.]

963.   ——. "William Langland: A London Poet." In item 48. Pp. 91–109. [Tracing the City's imprint and records of the poem's London reception.]

964.   ——. "Centers of Conspicuous Consumption: The Aristocratic Town House in London, 1200–1550." *London Journal* 20/1 (1995), 1–16. [There were seventy-five such houses in 1520, thirty being of the wealthy laity.]

965.   ——. "The Expansion of Education in Fifteenth-Century London." In item 14. Pp. 219–245. [Covering both young men and young women: many opportunities.]

966.   ——. "Richard II and London." In item 43. Pp. 129–54. [The king's failed relations with the City as a microcosm of his larger failure.]

967. Barron, Caroline M., and Laura Wright. "The London Middle English Guild Certificates of 1388–9." *Nottingham* 39 (1995), 108–45. [Historical introduction (pp. 108–18) by Barron, text of certificates (pp. 119–45) edited by Wright.]

968. Bateman, Nicholas. "The dedication of Guildhall Chapel." *London & Middlesex* 50 (1999), 23–28. [Dedicatory stones to Thomas Knolles and Henricus Frowyk in the 1440s; signs of rebuilding.]

969. Bolton, J. L., ed. *The Alien Communities of London in the 15th Century: The Subsidy Rolls of 1440 and 1483–4.* Richard III and Yorkist History Trust, Stamford, 1998. [North Sea migrants made up about 6–7 percent of London's population; a tale of considerable tension.]

970. Bonney, Margaret. *Lordship and the Urban Community: Durham and Its Overlords, 1250–1540.* Cambridge and New York, 1990. [Topography, archaeology, economic life, and relations with the ecclesiastical powers.]

971. Britnell, Richard H. "Bailiffs and Burgesses in Colchester, 1400–1525." *Essex* 21 (1990), 103–09. [How elections and office worked in the context of an urban oligarchy.]

972. ———. "York under the Yorkists." In item 18. Pp. 175–94. [Construction, falling rents, taxes, public health, competing jurisdictions, population, and urban life and culture.]

973. Bryant, Lawrence M. "Configurations of the Community in Late Medieval Spectacles: Paris and London during the Dual Monarchy." In item 49. Pp. 3–33. [How to study spectacle, and what the performances encompassed.]

974. Burgess, Clive. "Strategies for Eternity: Perpetual Chantry Foundation in Late Medieval Bristol." In item 52. Pp. 1–32. [General reflections and then examples of varieties of behavior, with a list of Bristol chantries.]

975.   ———. *The Parish Church and the Laity in Late Medieval Bristol.* Bristol Branch, The Historical Association and the University of Bristol, 1992. [A pamphlet covering ecclesiastical structure, urban piety, and lay wills.]

976.   ———. "London Parishes: Development in Context." In item 18. Pp. 151–74. [Penitence, chantries, and parish finances.]

977.   ———. "The Churchwardens' Accounts of St Andrew Hubbard, Eastcheap, and Their Implication." *London & Middlesex* 50 (1999), 61–66. [A minor church, not rebuilt after the Fire; accounts begin c. 1456.]

978.   Carlin, Martha. *London and Southwark Inventories, 1316–1650.* Centre for Metropolitan History and Institute of Historical Research, University of London, 1995. [An invaluable reference aid for material culture and related issues: handlist for extents for debts, by items and dates.]

979.   ———. *Medieval Southwark.* London and Rio Grande, Ohio, 1996. [Thorough urban/suburban study, mostly late medieval: trade, demography, government, pressure from The Big City just across the river.]

980.   Carr, David R. "The Problem of Urban Patriciates: Office Holders in Fifteenth-Century Salisbury." *Wiltshire* 83 (1990), 118–35. [Municipal ledger of 1397–1452: many constituencies sent men into the front ranks, with tables on trade, 1437 and on taxation and rents.]

981.   ———. "From Pollution to Prostitution: Supervising the Citizens of Fifteenth-Century Salisbury." *Southern* 19 (1997), 24–41. [The bishop's heavy hand on town government and the murder of bishop Aiscough.]

982.   Childs, Wendy. "The Trade and Shipping of Hull, 1300–1500." *East Yorkshire Local History Society* 1990.

[A pamphlet: imports, exports, cargoes, men and ships, local details and larger trends.]

983.   Christianson, C. Paul. "The Rise of London's Book-Trade." In item 49. Pp. 128–47. [Sellers, prices, the market, and case studies of some successful aliens.]

984.   Cobb, Harry S., ed. *The Overseas Trade of London: Exchequer of Customs Accounts, 1480–1.* London Record Society, 27 (1990). [Petty customs accounts of imports and exports, introduction, a glossary, and a few miscellaneous documents. Material in calendar form.]

985.   Combes, Helen. "Piety and Belief in Fifteenth-Century London: An Analysis of the Fifteenth-Century Churchwardens' Inventory of St Nicholas Shambles." *London & Middlesex* 48 (1997), 137–52. [Reconstruction of "popular piety" from inventories, chantry records, vestments, and furnishings.]

986.   Conheeny, Jan. "Reconstructing the Demography of Medieval London from Studies of Human Skeletal Material: Problems and Potential." *London & Middlesex* 50 (1999), 78–86. [Digs of the 1970s, revealing age and size of those interred; caution urged in interpretation.]

987.   Coulson, Charles. "Battlements and the Bourgeoisie: Municipal Status and the Apparatus of Urban Defence in Later-Medieval England." In *Medieval Knighthood, V (Papers from the Sixth Strawberry Hill Conference, 1994.* Edited by Stephen Church and Ruth Harvey. Woodbridge, 1995. Pp. 119–95. [A general survey with much fifteenth-century material covered in the discussion.]

988.   Cowie, Robert, and Alan Pipe, with contributions by John Clark and Jacqueline Pearse. "A Late Medieval and Tudor Horse Burial Ground: Excavations at Elverton Street, Westminster." *Arch J* 155 (1998), 226–51. [Horses skinned but not butchered: seventy-six animals, with the pathology of their skeletons.]

989.   Crout, Patricia. "Settlement, Tenure, and Land Use in
        Medieval Stepney: Evidence of a Field Survey, c. 1400."
        London Journal 22/1 (1997), 1–15. [A survey of all strips
        in the bishop of London's manor, plus its internal organi-
        zation and its ties with London (with two maps).]

990.   Davies, Clifford S. L. "The Alleged 'Sack of Bristol':
        International Ramifications of Breton Privateering,
        1484–85." *HR* 67 (1994), 230–39. [Bristol ships probably
        lost a sea battle, but later tales of a sacking of the city
        are not to be trusted.]

991.   Davies, Matthew. "The Tailors of London: Corporate
        Charity in the Late Medieval Town." In item 2.
        Pp. 161–90. [The role of craft guilds: role, size and
        number, money for alms, the tailors' almshouse, the men
        and their wives.]

992.   ———. "Artisans, Guilds, and Government in London."
        In item 18. Pp. 125–50. [Organization of the guilds,
        inter-guild relations, and municipal government.]

993.   Davis, Virginia. "Medieval English Ordination Lists: A
        London Case Study." *Local Population Studies* 50
        (Spring 1993), 51–60. [A progress report on a larger
        project, with list of canons of Elsyng Spital, 1362–1448.]

994.   Dinn, Robert. "Baptism, Spiritual Kinship, and Popular
        Religion in Late Medieval Bury St Edmunds." *BJRUL*
        72 (1990), 93–106. [Baptism, testamentary references;
        ways of assessing the push and pull of social and kinship
        ties.]

995.   ———. "Death and Rebirth in Late Medieval Bury St
        Edmunds." In item 9. Pp. 151–69. [What wills tell about
        prayers, funerals, attendance, and related expenditures.]

996.   Dobson, Richard Barrie. "Citizens and Chantries in Late
        Medieval York." In *Church and City, 1000–1500: Essays*

in Honour of Christopher Brooke. Edited by David
Abulafia, Michael Franklin, and Miri Rubin. Cambridge,
1992. Pp. 311–32. [A survey of York's chantries: health
and wealth, founders, and a brief for sustained or even
rising popularity.]

997.   Doree, Stephen G., ed. *The Early Churchwardens'
Accounts of Bishops Stortford, 1431–1558.* Hertfordshire
Record Society, 10 (1994). [English documents, or in
translation, with glossary and helpful introduction.]

998.   Draper, Jo, with M. E. King. "The Topography of Dorchester in the 15th Century." *Dorset* 117 (1995), 21–50.
[The Dorchester Domesday (1395–1500) permits a
street-by-street analysis: property owners, rents, and
analysis, with diagrams and maps.]

999.   Dyer, Christopher. "Small-town Conflicts in the Later
Middle Ages: Events at Shipston-on-Stour." *Urban
History* 19 (1992), 183–210. [Classic problem: conservative ecclesiastical landlord (the priory) and pushy
townsmen, with a blow-up, 1395–1406.]

1000.   ———. "Trade, Towns and the Church: Ecclesiastical
Consumers and the Urban Economy of the West
Midlands, 1290–1540." In item 88. Pp. 55–75. [Con-
sumption patterns, spending power, and the Church not
being so different from lay society in these areas.]

1001.   Farnhill, Ken. "The Religious Gilds of Wymondham,
c. 1470–1550." *Norfolk* 42/3 (1996), 321–31. [Wills and
guild books furnish information on wealth and property.]

1002.   Galloway, James A. "Metropolitan Market Networks:
London's Economic Hinterland in the Later Middle
Ages." *London & Middlesex* 50 (1990), 91–97. [A report
from the "Feeding the City" and "Market Networks"
projects; the city's catchment and distribution basin.]

1003.   ———. "Driven by Drink? Ale Consumption and the
             Agrarian Economy of the London Region, c. 1300–1400."
             In item 23. Pp. 87–100. [Getting enough food and drink
             into the City was a major socio-economic problem.]

1004.   Galloway, James A., Derek Keene, and Margaret
             Murphy. "Fuelling the City: Production and Distribution
             of Firewood and Fuel in London's Region, 1290–1400."
             EcHR 49 (1996), 447–72. [Where wood came from,
             transport costs, and growing scarcity by 1400 (with coal
             on the way).]

1005.   Gittings, Clare. "Urban Funerals in Late Medieval and
             Reformation England." In item 9. Pp. 170–83. [Public
             display, costs, and an opportunity for socialization.]

1006.   Glover, Elizabeth. *A History of the Ironmongers' Com-
             pany*. London, 1994. [Pp. 1–24 take the story to 1509.]

1007.   Goldberg, P. J. P. "Lay Book Ownership in Late
             Medieval York: The Evidence of Wills." *The Library*, 6th
             series, 16/3 (1994), 181–89. [Only 5 percent of the wills
             mention books (mostly service books).]

1008.   ———. "Performing the Word of God: Corpus Christi
             Drama in the Northern Province." In item 98.
             Pp. 145–70. [Urban craft guilds and civic pageantry,
             with Wakefield and its drama as the main case study.]

1009.   Gransden, Antonia, ed. *Bury St Edmunds: Medieval Art,
             Architecture, Archaeology and Economy*. BAA
             Conference Transaction 20 (1998). [Many aspects of
             building, art, and the town's support for such activities;
             see item 954.]

1010.   Hanawalt, Barbara A. "The Host, the Law, and the
             Ambiguous Space of Medieval London Taverns." In item
             51. Pp. 204–23. [Published also as Chapter 7 of her
             Gender and Social Control in Medieval England; see
             item 1858.]

1011.   Harding, Vanessa. "Burial Choice and Burial Location in
        Later Medieval London." In item 9. Pp. 119–35. [By
        parishes and precincts: wills, bequests, and the range of
        choices.]

1012.   Harding, Vanessa, and Laura Wright, eds. *London
        Bridge: Selected Accounts and Rentals, 1381–1538.*
        London Record Society, 31 (for 1994), 1995. [Various
        accounts for the Bridge House and Bridgemaster, with a
        full introduction; documents calendared.]

1013.   Hebert, N. M. *Medieval Gloucester.* Gloucester, for the
        Gloucestershire Record Office, 1993. [By the editor of the
        county's *Victoria County History.*]

1014.   Hilton, Rodney. *English and French Towns in Feudal
        Society: A Comparative Study* (Cambridge, 1992). [Com-
        parisons across the Channel, and the links between
        urban and rural.]

1015.   ———. "Status and Class in the Medieval Town." In
        item 88. Pp. 9–19. [An overview of class relations and
        structure.]

1016.   Howes, Audrey M. "The Career of Robert Michelson,
        Merchant, Ship Master and Burgess of Kingston upon
        Hull, 1464–90." *Ricardian* 8/110 (September 1990),
        443–48.

1017.   Jones, Tom Beaumont. "The Black Death and Hamp-
        shire." *Hampshire Papers* 18 (1999). [Its effects traced
        into the fifteenth century.]

1018.   Justice, Steven. "Inquisition, Speech and Writing: The
        Case from Late Medieval Norwich." In item 1316.
        Pp. 289–322. [John Burrell was mouthing off in 1429,
        which was not a wise thing to do.]

1019.   Keen, Laurence. *"Almost the Richest City": Bristol in the Middle Ages*. BAA Conference Transaction, 19 (1997). [See item 954 for volumes in this series.]

1020.   Kermode, Jenny. *Medieval Merchants: York, Beverley and Hull in the Later Middle Ages*. Cambridge, 1998. [Detailed comparisons and a wide range of urban, economic, and social and family topics explored at length; much prosopography and quantitative data.]

1021.   Kettle, Ann J. "'Behaving Badly': Lichfield Women in the Later Middle Ages." In item 68. Pp. 67–81. [A survey of what was said about them, as misbehavior was defined and perceived by the many "prying eyes."]

1022.   Kowaleski, Maryanne. "The Port Town of 14th-Century Devon." In item 32. Pp. 62–72. [With comparative statistics.]

1023.   Langdon, John. "City and Countryside in Medieval England." *AgHR* 43 (1995), 67–72. [A review article of James Campbell, et al., *A Medieval Capital and Its Grain Supply* (London, 1993).]

1024.   Laughton, Jane. "The Alewives of Later Medieval Chester." In item 2. Pp. 191–208. [Urban brewing as a business: production, the trade, the role of women; see also item 632.]

1025.   Laughton, Jane, and Christopher Dyer. "Small Towns in the East and West Midlands in the Later Middle Ages: A Comparison." *Midland* 24 (1999), 24–52. [Towns in the East Midlands were faring better than in the West.]

1026.   Leech, Roger H. *The Topography of Medieval and Early Modern Bristol: Part I: Property Holdings in the Early Walled Town and Marsh Suburb North of the Avon*. Bristol Record Society 48 (1997). [By tenements, by streets, by owners; twenty-one streets covered, with detailed maps.]

1027. Lewis, Elisabeth A., ed. *The Southampton Port and Brokerage Books, 1448–9.* Southampton Record Series 36 (1993). [A very busy town, now a county; text in Latin, without extensions.]

1028. Lindenbaum, Sheila. "The Smithfield Tournament of 1390." *JM & RS* 20/1 (Spring, 1990), 1–20. [Urban rituals and the underlying cracks in the political structure.]

1029. ———. "London Texts and Literate Practice." In item 96. Pp. 284–309. [Chronicles and other material, often critical of the social and political scene.]

1030. Macleod, Roderick. "The Topography of St Paul's Precinct, 1200–1500." *London Topographical Society* 26 (1990), 1–14. [Buildings and changes, with maps.]

1031. Massey, Robert. "Lancastrian Rouen: Military Service and Property Holding, 1419–49." In item 10. Pp. 269–86. [Some English settled there; who held office, did military service, gained property.]

1032. McRee, Ben R. "Religious Gilds and Civic Order: The Case of Norwich in the Later Middle Ages." *Speculum* 67 (1992), 69–97. [Important article on an important case study.]

1033. ———. "Charity and Gild Solidarity in Late Medieval England." *JBS* 32 (1993), 195–225. [A wide survey and then a focus on Norwich. Not a very sanguine picture.]

1034. ———. "Peacemaking and Its Limits in Late Medieval Norwich." *EHR* 109 (1994), 831–66. [Many crises; old procedures and practices were breaking down by the 1430s.]

1035. ———. "Unity or Division? The Social Meaning of Gild Ceremonies in Urban Communities." In item 49. Pp. 189–207. [General treatment, many different examples.]

1036.   Megson, Barbara E. "The Bowyers of London,
          1300–1550." *London Journal* 18/1 (1993), 1–13.
          [Development of the company from 1363 on, though in
          decline by the 1470s.]

1037.   ———. *Such Goodly Company: A Glimpse of the Life of
          the Bowyers of London*. The Worshipful Company of
          Bowyers, London, 1993. [With a foreword by Robert
          Hardy.]

1038.   ———. "Life Expectation of Widows and Orphans of
          Freemen in London, 1375–1399." *Local Population
          Studies* 57 (Autumn, 1996), 18–29. [Better survival and
          longevity than we might have anticipated, with wills and
          the Letter Books as the sources.]

1039.   Muggleton, J. "Some Aspects of the Two Late Medieval
          Chamberlains' Account Books of York. " *YAJ* 67 (1995),
          133–46. [How the accounts worked, with a table of pay-
          ments, 1448–51, from the eighty-five freemen admitted,
          and how they paid their fines.]

1040.   Munby, Julian, with John Ashdown, Brian Durham,
          D. Haddon-Reece, Martin Henig, and Christian
          Jeuckens. "Zackarias's: A Fourteenth-Century Oxford
          New Inn and the Origins of the Medieval Urban Inn."
          Oxon 57 (1992), 245–309. ["Zac's for Macs" store was on
          the site of New Inn: details, plus a general treatment of
          Oxford inns and a list of them in c. 1400.]

1041.   Nightingale, Pamela. *A Medieval Mercantile Commun-
          ity: The Grocers' Company and the Politics and Trade of
          London, 1000–1485*. New Haven and London, 1995. [The
          grocers and the economy, and their decline after 1380 in
          this detailed monograph. Reviewed by J. L. Bolton, *The
          Ricardian* 11/136 (March 1997), 25–30, and critical of
          the partisan view of London politics.]

1042.   O'Connor, S. J., ed. *A Calendar of the Cartularies of John Pyel and Adam Fraunceys*. Camden Society, 5th series, 2 (1993). [Rich source for two rich London merchants: Fraunceys d. 1375, and Pyel d. 1382.]

1043.   ———. "Perceptions of Status among Merchants in Fourteenth-Century London." In item 26. Pp. 17–35. [Careers: status and mobility, office holding, and some pursuit of economic careers and fortunes.]

1044.   Oliver, Kingsley M. *Hold Fast, Sir: The History of the Worshipful Company of Saddlers of the City of London, 1160–1960*. Chichester, 1995. [Pp. 1–52 run the tale to Henry VIII's time, with reference to company charters and a fifteenth-century rent roll.]

1045.   Ormrod, W. M. "Urban Communities and Royal Finance in England during the Later Middle Ages." In *Actes: Colloqui Corona, municipis i fiscalitat a la baixa edat mitjana*. Edited by Manuel Sanchez et Antoni Furio. Lleida, Institut d'Estudis Ilerdenes, n.d. Pp. 45–60.

1046.   Palliser, David M. "Urban Society." In item 57. Pp. 132–49. [Size, rankings, guilds, and merchants; community and civic pageantry.]

1047.   ———. "The York Freeman's Register, 1273–1540: Amendments and Additions." *York Historian* 12 (1995), 21–27. [Corrects and amplifies Collins's 1896 publication of the register.]

1048.   Pearsall, Derek. "Strangers in Late-Fourteenth-Century London." In *The Stranger in Medieval Society*. Edited by F. R. P. Akehurst and Stephanie Cain Van D'Elden. Minneapolis and London, 1997. Pp. 46–62. [Kinds and types of outsiders; how Chaucer's usage helps open this window.]

1049.   ———. "Langland's London." See item 471. Pp. 185–207. [Taverns, commerce, and lots of sin.]

1050.   Postles, David. "An English Small Town in the Later
         Middle Ages: Loughborough." *Urban History* 20 (1993),
         7–29. [Little evidence of serious decline in a quiet
         setting.]

1051.   Rigby, Steven H. *Medieval Grimsby: Growth and
         Decline.* University of Hull: Monographs in Regional and
         Local History, 3 (1993). [From pp. 48 on: "Grimsby in the
         Later Middle Ages": a fishing town hit hard times, under
         its urban oligarchy.]

1052.   Roberts, Edward, and Karen Parker, eds. *Southampton
         Probate Inventories, 1447–1575.* Southampton Record
         Series 34 (1991) and 35 (1992). [But by the third
         inventory we have reached the sixteenth century.]

1053.   Rose, Susan. *Southampton and the Navy in the Age of
         Henry V.* Hampshire Papers, 14 (1998). [Where and how
         ships were built; town declined as a naval center by 1440.]

1054.   Rosser, Gervase. "Crafts, Guilds and the Negotiation of
         Work in the Medieval Town." *Past and Present* 154 (Feb.
         1997), 3–31. [Across much of Europe, as "work" became a
         negotiated relationship.]

1055.   ———. "Conflict and Political Community in the
         Medieval Town: Disputes between Clergy and Laity in
         Hereford." In item 88. Pp. 20–42. ["Conflict was in-
         herent"; lay government versus ecclesiastical franchise.]

1056.   Sacks, David H. *The Widening Gate: Bristol and the
         Atlantic Economy, 1450–1700.* Berkeley, Los Angeles,
         and London, 1991. [Most chapters of this urban
         economic study begin with late medieval material.]

1057.   Schofield, John. "The Capital Re-Discovered: Archaeology
         in the City of London." *Urban History* 20 (1993), 211–24.
         [Pp. 218–22 cover the years 1100–1500.]

1058.   Seaborne, Gwen. "Controlling Commercial Morality in
         Late Medieval London: The Usury Trials of 1421." *JLH*
         19 (1998), 116–42. [Twenty-four cases from London's
         plea rolls; sophisticated business, claimed and handled
         by the civic authorities.]

1059.   Shaw, David Gary. *The Creation of a Community: The
         City of Wells in the Middle Ages.* Oxford, 1993. [Urban
         history shaped under the cathedral's shadow; a case
         study that conforms to the usual models of urban life
         and municipal contours.]

1060.   Shaw, Diane. "The Construction of the Private in
         Medieval London." *JM & EMS* 26/3 (Fall 1996), 447–66.
         [Neighbors' complaints about gazes and behavior, as
         property triumphed over people; an innovative assess-
         ment of the evidence.]

1061.   Simpson, James. "'After Craftes Conseil clotheth yow
         and fede': Langland and London City Politics." In item
         80. Pp. 109–27. [The civic procession after Pentecost and
         Piers Plowman on the role of guilds and fraternities.]

1062.   Stell, P. M. "The Constables of York." *York Historian* 15
         (1998), 16–25. [1380–1500: the watches and the social
         level of those serving in this office.]

1063.   Strohm, Paul, "Politics and Poetics: Usk and Chaucer in
         the 1380s. In *Literary Practice and Social Change in
         Britain, 1380–1530.* Edited by Lee Patterson. Berkeley
         and Los Angeles, 1990. Pp. 83–112. [Literary and
         secular careers against the background of the court and
         London politics.]

1064.   ———. "Hochon's Arrow: Social Drama and Fictional
         Truth." *JM & RS* 21/2 (Fall 1991), 225–49. [The London
         elections of 1384 and a text about treason and (dis)order.]

1065.   ———. "Trade, Treason, and the Murder of Janus Im-
            perial." *JBS* 35 (1996), 1–23. [A dead Genoese in London,
            1379; putting a confusing tale into a political and
            cultural setting.]

1066.   Summerson, Henry. *Medieval Carlisle: The City and the
            Border from the Late 11th to the Mid-16th Century.* 2
            vols. Cumberland and Westmorland Antiquarian and
            Archaeological Society, e.s., 25 (1993). [Chapters 5–7
            cover 1349–1561.]

1067.   ———. "Responses to War: Carlisle and the West March
            in the Late Fourteenth Century." In item 42. Pp. 155–77.
            [Truces and non-truces, and the toll of war in an area
            remote from the royal reach.]

1068.   ———. "Carlisle and the English West March in the
            Later Middle Ages." In item 77. Pp. 89–113. [York and
            Lancaster both saw its importance, though local loyalty
            tilted toward the Yorkists.]

1069.   Sutton, Anne F. *A Merchant Family of London, Coventry,
            and Calais: The Tates, c. 1450 to 1515.* London, for the
            Mercers' Company, 1998. [The family produced three
            lord mayors.]

1070.   Swanson, Robert N. "Urban Rectories and Urban For-
            tunes in Late Medieval England: The Evidence from
            Bishop's Lynn." In item 88. Pp. 100–30. [Most parishes
            saw revenues decline in the fifteenth century, as did the
            priory.]

1071.   Tanner, Norman. "The Cathedral and the City." In item
            6. Pp. 255–80. [Especially pp. 262–69 for these years: the
            rising of 1443.]

1072.   Tringham, Nigel J., ed. *Charters of the Vicars Choral of
            York Minster: City of York and Its Suburbs to 1546.*
            Yorkshire Record Series 148 (1993). [Only a little on the

fifteenth century; tables of grants and loans, church by church.]

1073.   Twycross, Meg. "Some Aliens in York and their Overseas Connections." *Leeds* n.s. 29 (1998), 359–80. [People and families and their legal and economic position; a report of the York Domesday Project.]

1074.   Verduyn, Anthony. "The Revocation of Urban Peace Commissions in 1381: The Lincoln Petition." *HR* 65 (1992), 108–11. [The Lincoln petition that triggered the council's blanket suspension of the commissions.]

1075.   Wade, J. E. "The Overseas Trade of Newcastle upon Tyne in the Late Middle Ages." *Northern* 30 (1994), 31–48. [Basically, the introduction to the material published in item 1076.]

1076.   ———, ed. *The Customs Accounts of New Castle upon Tyne, 1454–1500*. Surtees Society, 202 (1995). [Accounts transcribed; see item 1075 for a full explanation.]

1077.   Wallace, David. "Chaucer and the Absent City." In item 48. Pp. 59–90. [Chaucer (and Boccaccio) as windows into urban government and social structure.]

1078.   Watkins, Andrew. *Small Towns in the Forest of Arden in the Fifteenth Century*. Dugdale Society Occasional Papers, 38 (1998). [Economic life, guilds, markets; small towns resisted the domination of larger ones.]

1079.   Wayment, Hilary. "Sir John Savile, Steward of Wakefield 1482, d. 1505." *YAJ* 68 (1996), 181–89. [A civic figure; tomb in Thornhill church, c. 1528; and Sir John also looks down from a window.]

1080.   Wood, Charles T. "Froissart, Personal Testimony, and the Peasant Revolt of 1381." In item 1708. Pp. 40–49. [No one expected a chronicler of chivalry to be overly generous.]

1081. Woodward, Donald. "The Accounts of the Building of Trinity House, Hull, 1467–1476." *YAJ* 62 (1990), 153–70. [Seafarers' guild; accounts published, showing construction costs.]

1082. Wright, Laura. "Early Modern London Business English." In *Studies in Early Modern English*. Edited by Dieter Kastovsky. Berlin and New York, 1994. Pp. 449–65. [Monolingualism gradually prevailed.]

VIII. Rural, Manorial, and Agricultural History, and Uppity Peasants

1083.   Aers, David. "*Vox Populi* and the Literature of 1381." In item 96. Pp. 432–53. [A survey of contemporary voices and views: monks, Chaucer and Langland, Gower, and others of the gang.]

1084.   Arvanigian, Thomas E. "Free Rents in the Palatinate of Durham and the Crisis of the Late 1430s." *Arch Ael*, 5th series, 24 (1996), 99–108. [Economic contraction, with excused rents for the sake of political stability and to appease powerful tenants.]

1085.   Bailey, Mark. "The Prior and Convent of Ely and their Management of the Manor of Lakenheath in the Fourteenth Century." In item 36. Pp. 1–19. [Uneasy relations with the peasants; some labor services, still, after the plague.]

1086.   ———. "Rural Society." In item 57. Pp. 150–68. [Landlords and estates, lord-peasant relations, village communities and leisure.]

1087.   Bainbridge, Virginia. *Gilds in the Medieval Countryside: Social and Religious Change in Cambridgeshire, c. 1350–1558*. Woodbridge and Rochester, N.Y., 1996. [350 rural guilds (as against 60 in the returns of 1388–89), mostly treated in the setting of lay religion; a large study of a neglected topic.]

1088.   Barrell, A. D. M., R. R. Davies, O. J. Padel, and Ll. B.
          Smith. "The Dyffryn Clwyd Court Roll Project, 1340–1352
          and 1389–1399: A Methodology and Some Preliminary
          Findings." In item 79. Pp. 260–97. [A Welsh marcher
          lordship: kin, officials, land transfers.]

1089.   Beadle, Richard. "Prolegomena to a Literary Geography
          of Later Medieval Norfolk." In *Regionalism in Late
          Medieval Manuscripts and Texts.* Edited by Felicity
          Riddy. Cambridge, 1991. Pp. 89–108. [A York manu-
          script conference in 1989: regional identity, linguistic
          peculiarities, and literary activity; see also item 1153.]

1090.   Bean, John Malcolm W. "Landlords." In item 65.
          Pp. 526–86. [Incomes from categories of lands, tenure
          and inheritance, the land market, revenues. Stability or
          a looming crisis?]

1091.   Beckerman, John S. "Procedural Innovation and Institu-
          tional Changes in Medieval English Manorial Courts."
          LHR 10 (1992), 197–252. [Growing importance of
          written records in disputes.]

1092.   Birrell, Jean. "Deer and Deer Farming in Medieval
          England." *AgHR* 40 (1992), 112–26. [An efficient and
          economical activity, as well as a status symbol.]

1093.   Bonfield, Lloyd, and Lawrence R. Poos. "The Develop-
          ment of the Deathbed Transfer in Medieval English
          Manorial Courts." In item 79. Pp. 117–42. [Its growing
          importance, as one of the available strategies for land
          transfer and transmission; most examples cited are late.]

1094.   Britnell, Richard H. "Eastern England." In item 65.
          Pp. 53–67, 194–210, and 611–24. [See item 65 for an
          explanation of the standard or uniform approach of each
          contributor in covering his or her segment of rural
          England.]

1095.   Bush, Michael. "The Risings of the Commons in England, 1381–1549." In item 29. Pp. 109–25, 187–87. [Class feelings and the continuity of the common themes.]

1096.   Butler, Lawrence A. S. "Rural Buildings in England and Wales." In item 65. Pp. 891–919. [Covering types, sizes, and designs.]

1097.   Campbell, Bruce M. S. "A Fair Field Once Full of Folk: Agrarian Change in an Era of Population Decline, 1348–1500." *AgHR* 41 (1993), 60–70. [Review article of item 65: complimentary but critical, assessing the commercialization of society in those critical years in the transition from feudalism to capitalism.]

1098.   Campbell, Bruce M. S., Kenneth C. Barley, and John P. Powers. "The Demesne-Farming Systems of Post Black Death England: A Classification." *AgHR* 44 (1996), 131–79. [Seven types identified, with explanation of typologies on regional/national lines (using Norfolk, London, and the entire realm as bases of comparisons).]

1099.   [No entry.]

1100.   Campbell, Bruce M. S., and Mark Overton. "A New Perspective on Medieval and Early Modern Agriculture: Six Centuries of Norfolk Farming, c. 1250–c. 1850." *Past and Present* 141 (November 1993), 38–105. [In defense of medieval agriculture, linking it to later developments and emphasizing continuities in yields and prices.]

1101.   Carnwath, Julia. "The Churchwarden's Accounts of Thame, Oxfordshire, c. 1443–1524." In item 26. Pp. 177–97. [Who the wardens were and their duties.]

1102.   Clark, Elaine. "Social Welfare and Mutual Aid in the Medieval Countryside." *JBS* 33 (1994), 381–406. [Who took care of whom; generally a sanguine and generous assessment.]

1103.   Crane, Susan. "The Writing Lesson of 1381." In item 48.
Pp. 201–21. [What to make of the peasants, and what is
peasant consciousness?]

1104.   Cripps, Judith, Richard Holton, and Janet Williamson.
"Appendix: A Survey of Medieval Manorial Court Rolls
in England." In item 79. Pp. 596–637. [Listed by counties
and then by manors, with dates of extant rolls (into the
early sixteenth century).]

1105.   DeWindt, Anne Reiber. "Local Government in a Small
Town: A Medieval Leet Jury and Its Constituents."
Albion 23 (1991), 627–54. [Who the jurors were and their
turnover; some statistics and an appraisal of village self
government.]

1106.   ———. "The Town of Ramsey: The Question of Economic
Development, 1290–1523." In item 30. Pp. 53–116. [Tax
assessments and other sources allow for the reconsti-
tution of family and community patterns and an
occupational survey.]

1107.   Dyer, Christopher. "The Past, The Present, and The
Future in Medieval Rural History." *Rural History* 1
(1990), 37–49. [The Postan legacy, new views, new
directions for research.]

1108.   ———. "The English Medieval Village Community and
Its Decline." *JBS* 33 (1994), 407–29. [Had it ever been
more cohesive? And if so, how do we make such a
judgment?]

1109.   ———. "The West Midlands." In item 65. Pp. 77–92,
222–38, and 636–47.

1110.   Eiden, Herbert. "Joint Action against 'Bad' Lordship:
The Peasants' Revolt in Essex and Norfolk." *History* 83
(1998), 5–30. [A high level of organization, focusing on
deep causes: map shows centers of resistance.]

1111.   ———. "Norfolk, 1382: A Sequel to the Peasants' Revolt."
          EHR 114 (1999), 370–77. [Walsingham tells of a rising in
          September 1382: middling men involved, with ten execu-
          tions and an escheator's inquisition of their lands.]

1112.   Farmer, David. "Marketing the Produce of the Country-
          side, 1200–1500." In item 65. Pp. 324–430. [Markets,
          fairs, transport, and the world of bargaining and its
          rules.]

1113.   ———. "Prices and Wages, 1350–1500." In item 65.
          Pp. 431–525. [Statistics on prices, yields, piece rate,
          wages, and the statute of laborers.]

1114.   ———. "The *famuli* in the Later Middle Ages." In item
          20. Pp. 207–236. [Carries Postan's 1954 study into the
          fourteenth century and beyond, showing a slow improve-
          ment of their lot.]

1115.   Fox, Harold S. A. "Devon and Cornwall." In item 65.
          Pp. 152–74, 303–23, and 722–43.

1116.   Fryde, Edmund B. *Peasants and Landlords in Later
          Medieval England, c. 1380–c. 1525*. Stroud, 1996. [A col-
          lection of essays on manorial history, both before and
          after 1381, and looking at the crisis of the fifteenth
          century; critically reviewed, item 126.]

1117.   Fryde, Edmund B., and Natalie Fryde. "Peasant Rebel-
          lion and Peasant Discontent." In item 65. Pp. 744–819.
          [Economic background, a narrative, and themes that ran
          through the fifteenth century.]

1118.   Gardiner, Mark. "The Geography and Peasant Rural
          Economy of the Eastern Sussex High Weald, 1300–1420."
          Sussex 134 (1996), 125–39. [A region of mixed agri-
          culture and pastoral farming; too far from London for
          easy economic development.]

1119.   Goldberg, P. J. P. "Urban Identity and the Poll Taxes of 1377, 1378, and 1381." *EcHR* 43 (1990), 194–216. [The first tax is rich for demographic content, the others for occupational structure and rural-urban differences.]

1120.   Greatrex, Joan. "The Reconciliation of Spiritual and Temporal Responsibilities: Some Aspects of the Monks of St Swithins as Landowners and Estate Managers." *Hampshire* 51 (1995), 77–87. [Serving many masters.]

1121.   Green, Richard Firth. "John Ball's Letters: Literary History and Historical Literature." In item 48. Pp. 176–200. [The culture of protest and its various forms of expression.]

1122.   Hargreaves, Paul V. "Seignorial Reaction and Peasant Responses: Worcester Priory and Its Peasants After the Black Death." *Midland* 24 (1999), 53–78.

1123.   Harvey, Paul D. A. "The Home Counties." In item 65. Pp. 106–19, 254–68, and 662–79.

1124.   Harvey, R. B., and B. K. Harvey. "Bradford-on-Avon in the Fourteenth Century." *Wiltshire* 86 (1993), 118–29. [Some Shaftesbury Abbey accounts, 1367 and later; manorial produce on the demesne, and the town's post-plague decline.]

1125.   Haydon, Edwin S., and John H. Harrop, eds. *Widworthy Manorial Court Rolls, 1453–1617.* Honiton, Devon, 1997. [Photostats of documents, transcriptions, and translations, though only one is prior to Henry VII.]

1126.   Justice, Steven. *Writing and Rebellion: England in 1381.* Berkeley and Los Angeles, 1994. [New historicism meets the sophisticated rhetoric of the rebels.]

1127.   King, Edmund. "The East Midlands." In item 65. Pp. 67–77, 210–21, and 624–35.

1128.   Komlos, John, and Richard Landes. "Anachronistic
        Economics: Grain Storage in Medieval England." *EcHR*
        44 (1991), 36–45. [The cost of storing grain; an exchange
        with D. McCloskey and J. Nash (1984).]

1129.   Le Patourel, Hilda Elizabeth J. "Rural Building in
        England and Wales." In item 65. Pp. 820–90. [Types,
        sizes, designs.]

1130.   Marvin, William P. "Slaughter and Romance: Hunting
        Reserves in Late Medieval England." In item 51.
        Pp. 224–52. [Class, gender, and control of space; some
        late fourteenth-century cases.]

1131.   Mate, Mavis. "Kent and Sussex." In item 65. Pp. 119–36,
        268–85, and 680–703.

1132.   ———. "The Economic and Social Roots of Medieval
        Popular Rebellion: Sussex in 1450–1451." *EcHR* 45
        (1992), 661–76. [More social and economic than in Kent,
        fueled by the mid-century recession.]

1133.   ———. "The East Sussex Land Market and Agrarian
        Class Structure in the Late Middle Ages." *Past and
        Present* 139 (May 1993), 46–65. [An active land market,
        with complex land holding, much turn-over and
        mobility.]

1134.   Miller, Edward. "Yorkshire and Lancashire." In item 65.
        Pp. 42–52, 182–94, and 596–611.

1135.   ———. "The Southern Counties." In item 65. Pp. 136–51,
        285–303, and 703–22.

1136.   Munby, Julian, and John M. Steane, with contributions
        by R. A. Chambers, A. J. Fleming, B. Holden, H. Philip
        Powell, Mark K. Taylour. "Swalcliffe: A New College
        Barn in the Fifteenth Century." *Oxon* 60 (1995), 333–78.
        [Barn built c. 1401–08; now a museum.]

1137.   Olson, Sherri. "Jurors of the Village Court: Local
        Leadership before and after the Plague in Ellington,
        Huntingdonshire." *JBS* 30 (1991), 237–52. [Men (and
        women), families, village responsibility, and civic life.]

1138.   ———. "Family Linkages and the Structure of the Local
        Elite in the Medieval and Early Modern Village." *Med
        Pros* 13/2 (1992), 53–82. [Who, and for how long: two
        families followed in detail in rural Huntingdonshire.]

1139.   ———. "'Families Have Their Fate and Periods':
        Varieties of Family Experience in the Pre-Industrial
        Village." In item 30. Pp. 409–48. [Tracing some families
        for three to four generations; some rose, some fell, some
        disappeared.]

1140.   ———. *A Chronicle of All that Happens: Voices from the
        Village Court in Medieval England.* Studies and Texts,
        124, Pontifical Institute of Mediaeval Studies. Toronto,
        1996. [Life in Upwood and Ellington, Huntington:
        families, village dynamics, and a comparison between a
        lowland and an upland community.]

1141.   Ormrod, W. M. "The Peasants' Revolt and the Govern-
        ment of England." *JBS* 29 (1990), 1–30. [How the rebel-
        lion affected the royal administration and its personnel,
        as popular wrath extended beyond manorial records.]

1142.   Owen, A. E. B. "Share and Share Alike: Some Partitions
        of Medieval Manors." *Lincoln* 31 (1996), 20–21. [A
        common practice, with a partition deed of 1418 (and one
        of 1317).]

1143.   ———. *The Medieval Lindsey Marsh: Select Documents.*
        Lincoln Record Society, 85 (1996). [Many calendared
        from 1377–1485: wills, land transfers, a scrappy
        chronicle, accounts, etc., arranged by communities.]

1144.   Owen, D. Huw. "Wales and the Marches." In item 65.
         Pp. 92–106, 238–54, and 648–61.

1145.   Papworth, Martin. "The Medieval Manorial Buildings of
         Kingston Lacy: Survey and Excavation Results with an
         Analysis of Medieval Account Rolls, 1295–1462." *Dorset*
         120 (1998), 45–62. [A ruin by 1573, forgotten by 1774,
         but the Lancastrian building can be discerned. Tiles
         described by Laurence Keen, petrology by D. F. Williams,
         metal work by Nancy Grace, painted plaster by Lisa
         Oestreicher, the foundation remains by A. M. Lockes.]

1146.   Postles, David. "Review" of *Agrarian History of England
         and Wales, III*. EHR 107 (1992), 388–90. [Appreciative.]

1147.   ———. "Demographic Change in Kibworth Harcourt,
         Leicestershire, in the Later Middle Ages." *Local Popula-
         tion Studies* 48 (Spring 1992), 41–48. [Wide fluctuations,
         wider than the extant data allow us to track.]

1148.   ———. "Personal Pledgings in Manorial Courts in the
         Later Middle Ages." *BJRUL* 75/1 (1993), 67–78. [How
         the system functioned late in its day: by whom, to/for
         whom.]

1149.   Raftis, J. Ambrose. "Peasants and the Collapse of the
         Manorial Economy on Some Ramsey Abbey Estates." In
         item 20. Pp. 191–206. [Eight peasant strategies and the
         end of traditional serfdom (as marked by the end of labor
         services).]

1150.   Rampton, Martha. "The Peasants' Revolt of 1381 and the
         Written Word." *Comitatus* 24 (1993), 45–60. [A look at
         how contemporaries commented on events of the day.]

1151.   Razi, Zvi. "Interfamilial Ties and Relationships in the
         Medieval Village: A Quantitative Approach Employing
         Manor-Court Rolls." In item 79. Pp. 369–91. [Data up to
         1400: intra-familial interaction, land transfers, and
         pledging patterns.]

1152.   Richmond, Colin F. "Landlord and Tenant: The Paston
         Evidence." In item 59. Pp. 25–42. [Being a landlord was
         not a bed of roses.]

1153.   ———. "What a Difference a Manuscript Makes: John
         Wyndham of Felbrigg, Norfolk (d. 1475)." In item 1089.
         Pp. 129–41. [A case study in the inter-weaving of East
         Anglian gentry society.]

1154.   Schofield, Phillip R. "Tenurial Developments and The
         Availability of Customary Land in a Later Medieval
         Community." *EcHR* 49 (1996), 250–67. [Birdbrook,
         Essex: post-plague years saw more flexibility and new-
         comers—perhaps servants—gained and held land.]

1155.   ———. "The Late Medieval View of Frankpledge and the
         Tithing System: An Essex Case Study." In item 79.
         Pp. 408–49. [To about 1412: what pledging reveals about
         networks, land turnovers, and village activity.]

1156.   Sherlock, David. "Wisbech Barton's Farm Buildings in
         1412–13." *CAS* 80 (1991), 21–29. [An account roll
         analyzed; a bishop of Ely's estate.]

1157.   Smith, Richard M. "Coping with Uncertainty: Women's
         Tenure of Customary Land in England, c. 1370–1430."
         In item 59. Pp. 43–67. [How manorial accounts dealt
         with women and land transfers in which they had a role.]

1158.   ———. "The Manorial Court and the Elderly Tenant in
         Late Medieval England." See item 1370. Pp. 39–61. [The
         courts played a role in family and life adjustments
         centering around "retirement."]

1159.   Stone, David. "The Productivity of Hired and Customary
         Labour: Evidence from Wisbech Barton in the Fourteenth
         Century." *EcHR* 50 (1997), 640–56. [Hired labor was
         productive.]

1160. Swanson, Robert N. "Economic Change and Spiritual Profits: Receipts from the Peculiar Jurisdiction of the Peak District in the 14th Century." In item 80. Pp. 171–95. [Changes hit hard, though tithe levels held fairly well after the plague.]

1161. Thompson, John S., ed., with introduction by Patricia Bell. *Hundreds, Manors, Parishes and the Church: A Selection of Early Documents from Bedfordshire.* Bedfordshire Historical Record Society 69 (1990). [Pp. 64–123 for an account roll from Higham Gobion and Sheatley, 1379–1382; documents calendared and in English.]

1162. Titow, Jan. "Lost Rents, Vacant Holdings and the Contraction of Peasant Cultivation after the Black Death." *AgHR* 42 (1994), 97–114. [Winchester estates, with data in tabular form.]

1163. Tonkinson, A. M. *Macclesfield in the Later Fourteenth Century: Communities of Town and Forest.* Chetham Society, 3rd series, 42 (1999). [Detailed community study, covering economics, court appearances, and family histories and biographies.]

1164. Tuck, Anthony. "The Northern Borders." In item 65. Pp. 34–42, 175–82, and 587–96.

1165. Watkins, Andrew. "Maxstoke Priory in the Fifteenth Century: The Development of an Estate Economy in the Forest of Arden." *Warwickshire Historian* 10/1 (1996), 3–18. [Crops and livestock for the house; sales and the cash economy.]

1165A. ———. "Peasants in Arden." In item 18. Pp. 83–101. [Community control of individual enterprise, but much diversity.]

1166. Workman, Katherine J. "Manorial Estate Officials and Opportunities in Late Medieval English Society." *Viator* 26 (1995), 223–40. [New opportunities after the plague for haywards and the like, with Norfolk the data base.]

1167. Yates, Margaret. "Change and Continuities in Rural Society from the Later Middle Ages to the Sixteenth Century: The Contribution of West Berkshire." *EcHR* 523 (1999), 617–37. [Regional peculiarities, population, and the distribution of wealth.]

IX. The Church and Religion

1168.   Abbot, Christopher. "Piety and Egoism in Julian of
Norwich: A Reading of Long Text Chapters 2 and 3." *DR*
114 (1996), 267–82. [With attention to and a comparison
with her "pre-visionary" outlook.]

1169.   ———. "His Body, The Church: Julian of Norwich's
Vision of Christ Crucified." *DR* 115 (1997), 1–22. [As
seen from an internalized and an externalized view.]

1170.   ———. *Julian of Norwich: Autobiography and Theology.*
Woodbridge, 1999. [In Brewer's "Studies in Medieval
Mysticism," and working with her long text.]

1171.   Aers, David. "The Humanity of Christ: Representations
in Wycliffite Texts and *Piers Plowman*." In item 1.
Pp. 43–76.

1172.   ———. "The Humanity of Christ: Reflections on Julian
of Norwich's *Revelation of Love*." In item 1. Pp. 77–104.

1173.   Armstrong, Elizabeth P. "Motives of Charity in the
Writing of Julian of Norwich and St. Teresa of Avila."
Mystics Quarterly 16 (1990), 9–26. [The comparison sets
women into the tradition of mystical writing.]

1174.   Ashdown-Hill, John. "Walsingham in 1469: The Pilgrimage of Edward IV and Richard, Duke of Gloucester."
Ricardian 11/136 (March 1997), 2–16. [The journey they
made and what they would have seen upon arrival.]

1175.   Aston, Margaret. "Corpus Christi and Corpus Regni:
         Heresy and the Peasants' Revolt." *Past and Present* 143
         (May 1994), 3–47. [What Corpus Christi meant to dif-
         ferent sensibilities; popular identification with rituals
         and feasts.]

1176.   ———. "Segregation in Church." In item 87. Pp. 237–94.
         [Major study of the "sociology" of religion from the view
         of those who worshiped within the church itself.]

1177.   ———. "Were the Lollards a Sect?" In item 13. Pp. 163–
         91. [A hostile label, but there seems no better term.]

1178.   Baker, Denise N. *Julian of Norwich's "Showings": From
         Vision to Book*. Princeton, 1994. [In the context of
         women and mysticism.]

1179.   ———. "The Image of God: Contrasting Configurations
         in Julian of Norwich's *Showings* and Walter of Hilton's
         Scale of Perfection." In item 61. Pp. 35–60.

1180.   Baldwin, Anna P. "The Triumph of Patience in Julian of
         Norwich and Langland." In item 75. Pp. 71–83. [For her,
         it meant strength through suffering.]

1181.   Ball, R. M. "The Opponents of Bishop Pecock." *J Eccl H*
         48 (1997), 230–62. [Who they were (beside Gascoigne):
         the background and scholarship of the issues and the
         points of dispute.]

1182.   Barratt, Alexandra, ed. *The Seven Psalms: A Com-
         mentary on the Penitential Psalms Translated from
         French into English by Dame Eleanor Hull*. EETS, 307
         (1995). [Rare work from a woman of letters.]

1183.   ———. "How Many Children Had Julian of Norwich?
         Editions, Translations and Versions of Her Revelation."
         In *Vox Mystica: Essays on Medieval Mysticism in Honor
         of Professor Valerie M. Lagorio*. Edited by Anne C.
         Bartlett, Thomas H. Bestul, Janet Joebel, and William F.

Pollard. Cambridge, 1995. Pp. 27–39. [A survey of modern editions (since 1610), an attempt to straighten out all the "modernizations," and a call for more work on the Middle English manuscripts.]

1184. ———. "'In the Lowest Part of Our Need': Julian and Medieval Gynecological Writing." In item 62. Pp. 239–56.

1185. Bauerschmidt, Frederick C. "Seeing Jesus: Julian of Norwich and the Text of Christ's Body." *JM & EMS* 27/2 (Spring, 1997), 189–214. [Analyzing the vision of May 1373: what did she "really" see?]

1186. ———. *Julian of Norwich and the Mystical Body Politic of Christ*. Notre Dame, Ind., 1999. [Notre Dame's Studies in Spirituality and Theology, 5; reading Julian as imagining the political working outward from theology and metaphysics.]

1187. Beckwith, Sarah. *Christ's Body: Identity, Culture and Society in Late Medieval Writings*. London and New York, 1993. [English vernacular writers, with some attention to Margery Kempe.]

1188. Beer, Frances. *Women and Mystical Experience in the Middle Ages*. Woodbridge, 1993. [For Julian of Norwich, pp. 130–57: an exposition of her revelation.]

1189. ———. *Julian of Norwich: Revelations of Divine Love: The Brotherhood of God: An Excerpt*. Woodbridge, 1998. [In the "Library of Medieval Women"; translated from BL Add Ms 37790 and BL Sloane Ms 2477, with introduction.]

1190. Blamires, Alcuin, and C. W. Marx. "Woman Not to Preach: A Disputation in British Library Ms Harley 31." *Journal of Medieval Latin* 3 (1993), 34–63. [Walter Brut's dangerous views of the 1390s, with a refutation.]

1191.   Bowker, Margaret. "Historical Survey, 1450–1750." In item 71. Pp. 164–209. [Pp. 164–72 cover 1450 to 1530.]

1192.   Bradley, Ritamary. "The Goodness of God: A Julian Study." In item 75. Pp. 85–95. [The existence of evil was always a problem.]

1193.   ———. *Julian's Way*. San Francisco, 1992.

1194.   ———. "Julian of Norwich: Everyone's Mystic." In item 78. Pp. 139–58. [Criticisms of the Colledge & Walsh edition of the text, plus some comments on Julian's theology of atonement.]

1195.   Brown, Andrew D. *Popular Piety in Late Medieval England: The Diocese of Salisbury, 1250–1550.* Oxford, 1995. [A survey: regulars, parochial religion, guilds and fraternities, charities, etc.]

1196.   Burgess, Clive. "Late Medieval Wills and Pious Convention: Testamentary Evidence Reconsidered." In item 54. Pp. 14–33. [Good discussion of the use of wills as a source; Bristol data to support the generalizations.]

1197.   ———, ed. *The Pre-Reformation Records of All Saints, Bristol, Part I.* Bristol Record Society, 46 (1995). [Fifteenth-century accounts, gifts, inventories; the text is in English.]

1198.   ———. "Shaping the Parish: St. Mary at Hill, London, in the Fifteenth Century." In item 14. Pp. 246–86. [A very close study: chantries, parish hierarchy, clerks, rentals, wills, wardens, and more.]

1199.   Burgess, Clive, and Beat Kümin. "Penitential Bequests and Parish Regimen in Late Medieval England." *J Eccl H* 44 (1993), 610–30. [The sources of revenues for parish churches.]

1200.   Burton, Janet. "Priory and Parish: Kirkham and Its Practitioners, 1496–97." In item 93. Pp. 329–47.

[Monastic rights over the Church and a quarrel over who had it in gift.]

1201. Catto, Jeremy. "Sir William Beauchamp between Chivalry and Lollardy." In *The Ideals and Practice of Medieval Knighthood, III (Papers from the Fourth Strawberry Hill Conference, 1988)*. Edited by Christopher Harper-Bill and Ruth Harvey. Woodbridge, 1990. Pp. 39–48. [Maybe he ran with Clanvowe and the Lollard Knights.]

1202. ———. "Wycliffe and Wycliffism at Oxford, 1356–1430." In item 24. Pp. 175–261. [Tracing the course of Wycliffe's writing and thinking, and how much of later Lollard thought rested on Oxford scholarship.]

1203. ———. "Theology after Wycliffism." In item 24. Pp. 263–80. [With a discussion of Pecock's views.]

1204. ———. "Fellows and Helpers: The Religious Identities of Followers of Wyclif." In item 13. Pp. 141–61. [Perverse beliefs, early defections, some men at Queen's College, and how far Wycliffe's ideas spread beyond his direct followers.]

1205. ———. "The King's Government and the Fall of Pecock, 1457–58." In item 3. Pp. 201–22. [Complaints led to the proceedings and how Pecock exacerbated a bad situation: appendix gives letters of complaint and the king's response.]

1206. Catto, Jeremy, and Linne Mooney, eds. *The Chronicle of John Somer, OFM*. Camden Miscellany: Camden Society, 5th series, 10 (1997), 201–85. [Introduction, pp. 203–19; chronicle runs from 1001–1532, mostly in short entries, one-liners, and comments about kings and weather; see item 1579.]

1207.   Clark, John P. H. "Time and Eternity in Julian of Nor-
        wich." *DR* 109 (1991), 259–76. [Pauline and Augustinian
        influences, though she rarely cited her authorities.]

1208.   ———. "Late Fourteenth-Century Cambridge Theology
        and the English Contemplative Tradition." In item 39.
        Pp. 1–16. [The theology taught at Cambridge, how it was
        transmitted, and possible links with Lynn and Norwich
        (and Julian).]

1209.   Cocks, Terence Y. "The Archdeacons of Leicester, 1092–
        1992." *Leicester* 67 (1993), 27–46. [Pp. 31–32 list the men
        from our years.]

1210.   Connolly, Margaret. " A London Widow's Psalter:
        Beatrice Cornburgh and Alexander Turnbull Library MS
        MSR–01." In *Sources, Exemplars, and Copy-Texts:
        Influence and Transmissions*. Edited by William Marx.
        [A paper from the 1997 Lampeter Conference of the
        Early Book Society.]

1211.   Copeland, Rita. "William Thorpe and His Lollard Com-
        munity: Intellectual Labor and the Representation of
        Dissent." In item 50. Pp. 199–221. [The meanings of
        "representation" and Thorpe's interrogation by Arundel
        in 1407.]

1212.   Courtenay, William J. "Theology and Theologians from
        Ockham to Wyclif." In item 24. Pp. 1–34. [Largely
        dealing with how well Ockham's ideas held up.]

1213.   Crampton, Georgia R., ed. *The Shewings of Julian of
        Norwich*. TEAMS Middle English Texts series.
        Kalamazoo, Mich., 1993. [For students: glosses, good
        introduction, extensive bibliography of a growth field.]

1214.   Cross, Claire. *Church and People: England, 1450–1660*.
        2nd ed. Oxford, 1999. [Excellent survey, first published
        in 1976.]

1215.　Cullum, Patricia H. "'For Pore People Hurbles': What Was the Function of the Maisondieu?" In item 26. Pp. 36–54. [Foundations of wealthy individuals, with female founders; not so different from chantries.]

1216.　———. "Vowesses and Female Lay Piety in the Province of York, 1300–1530." *Northern* 32 (1996), 21–41. [Licenses to veil and a survey of women's (few) alternatives.]

1217.　Daffern, Adrian. *The Cross and Julian.* Nottingham, 1993. [A pamphlet in the Grove Spirituality series, no. 46; useful clarifications in a mere eighteen pages.]

1218.　Davies, Oliver. "Transformational Processes in the Work of Julian of Norwich and Mechtild of Magdeburg." In item 39. Pp. 39–52. [A one-shot vision as against one bit by bit over the years.]

1219.　Davies, Richard G. "Lollardy and Locality." *TRHS*, 6th series, 1 (1991), 191–212. [Its geographical and social composition: the "substantial local self-sufficiency" of the cells.]

1220.　———. "The Church and the Wars of the Roses." In item 76. Pp. 134–61. [The political ties of the bishops and the Church's limited role in the time of troubles.]

1221.　———. "Richard II and the Church." In item 43. Pp. 83–106. [Easy to make too much of Richard's piety, as against a Church policy of pragmatism and caution.]

1222.　Davis, Virginia. "Medieval English Clergy Database." *History and Computing* 2 (1990), 75–87. [Some questions we can put to a database of ordinations.]

1223.　———. "Episcopal Ordination Lists as a Source for Clerical Mobility in England in the 14th Century." In item 80. Pp. 152–70. [A lot of moving around from dioceses of origin, though much of the movement and mobility was for short intervals and casual purposes.]

1224.   ———. *William Waynflete: Bishop and Educationalist.*
             Woodbridge and Rochester, N.Y., 1993. [A detailed biog-
             raphy of an important but relatively neglected figure.]

1225.   ———. "Medieval Longevity: The Experience of
             Members of Religious Orders in Late Medieval England."
             Med Pros 19 (1998), 111–24. [Ordination lists used for
             demography; the age structure of some regular houses.]

1226.   Delany, Sheila. *Impolitic Bodies: Poetry, Saints, and
             Society in Fifteenth-Century England: The Work of
             Osbern Bokenham.* New York and Oxford, 1998. [The
             social and intellectual background of writing
             hagiography.]

1227.   del Maestro, M. L., trans. *Julian of Norwich: The
             Revelation of Divine Love in Sixteen Showings.* Liguori,
             Mo., 1994. [An accessible version of a text of surprising
             current popularity.]

1228.   Dobson, Richard Barrie. "The English Monastic Cathe-
             drals in the Fifteenth Century." *TRHS*, 6th series, 1
             (1991), 151–72. [The sources; personnel, jurisdictional
             disputes with bishops; the role of higher education.]

1229.   ———. "Citizens and Chantries in Late Medieval York."
             In *Church and City, 1000–1500: Essays in Honour of
             Christopher Brooke* (see item 31). Pp. 311–32. [How the
             chantries were founded, and by whom; a test case of
             "popular" and private religion.]

1230.   ———. "The Church of Durham and the Scottish Border,
             1378–88." In item 42. Pp. 124–54. [Bishop Fordham's
             weak role and assaults on Church lands; where was
             Cuthbert when they needed him?]

1231.   ———. "The Religious Orders, 1370–1540." In item 24.
             Pp. 539–79. [Nearby abbeys did not get into the
             university groove, though forty Benedictine houses sent
             men to study.]

1232.　　———. "The Monks of Canterbury in the Later Middle Ages." In item 27. Pp. 69–153. [Especially pp. 99–115, monastic learning at the universities and in the cloister; pp. 115–135, on the Christ Church monks after the Black Death.]

1233.　　———. "English and Welsh Monastic Bishops: The Final Count, 1433–1533." In item 93. Pp. 349–67. [Nineteen men, many of little note; these positions were not highly coveted or prized.]

1234.　　———. "The Monastic Orders in Late Medieval Cambridge." In item 13. Pp. 239–64. [Much less important than Oxford, though the number of men was rising after 1450, with some serious intellectual contributions.]

1235.　　Dodwell, Barbara. "The Monastic Community." In item 6. Pp. 231–54. [Mainly an internal study of monastic life: numbers, education, buildings.]

1236.　　Dohar, William J. "Medieval Ordination Lists: The Origin of a Record." *Archives* 20/4 (1992), 17–35. [A general view, with some fourteenth- and fifteenth-century examples.]

1237.　　Dolnikowski, Edith W., "The Encouragement of Lay Preaching as an Ecclesiastical Critique in Wyclif's Latin Sermons." In *Models of Holiness in Medieval Sermons: Proceedings of the International Symposium (Kalamazoo, Mich., 4–7 May 1995).* Edited by Beverly M. Kienzle et al. Textes et Études du Moyen Âge, 5. Louvain-la-Neuve: Fédération Internationale des Instituts d'Études Médiévales, 1996. Pp. 193–209. [Wycliffe placed great emphasis on lay preaching, as expounded in his *De veritate sacrae scripturae* and other works.]

1238.　　Downs, Kevin. "The Administration of the Diocese of Worcester under the Italian Bishops, 1497–1535." *Midland* 20 (1995), 1–20. [Four permanent absentees, and how episcopal duties were actually covered.]

1239.   Duffy, Eamon. "Holy Maydens, Holy Wyfes: The Cult of
         Women Saints in Fifteenth- and Sixteenth-Century
         England." In item 87. Pp. 175–96. [Based on East
         Anglian and Devonshire screens, and arguing for the
         homogeneity of "popular religion."]

1240.   ———. *The Stripping of the Altars: Traditional Religion
         in England, c. 1400–1580.* New Haven and London,
         1992. [A massive treatment of popular religion from a
         "conservative" perspective, drawing largely on East
         Anglian records and iconography. Reviewed by David
         Aers, *Literature and History*, 3rd series, 3/1 (1994),
         90–105; for Duffy's response, ibid., 4/1 (1995), pp. 86–89;
         also, R. B. Dobson, *EHR* 109 (1994), 111–14.]

1241.   Dymond, David, ed., *The Register of Thetford Priory,
         Part I: 1482–1517.* Norfolk Record Society, 59 (1994),
         and "Records of Social and Economic History," British
         Academy, n.s. 24 (1995). [Largely devoted to expendi-
         ture, with a general introduction and then the
         transcription. Part II (1996) covers 1518–40.]

1242.   Edden, Valerie. "Marian Devotions in a Carmelite
         Sermon Collection of the Late Middle Ages." *Mediaeval
         Studies* 57 (1995), 101–29. [Explication of a Worcester
         manuscript, now in the Bodleian.]

1243.   Ellis, Roger, "Further Thoughts on the Spirituality of
         Syon Abbey." In item 78. Pp. 219–43. [Their books and
         manuscripts, though largely those of the early sixteenth
         century.]

1244.   Erler, Mary C. "English Vowed Women at the End of the
         Middle Ages." *Mediaeval Studies* 57 (1995), 155–203.
         [Appendix of 254 vowed women, pp. 183–201; a "provi-
         sional list" to open up the topic.]

1245.   ———. "Exchange of Books between Nuns and Lay-
         women: Three Surviving Examples." In item 11.

Pp. 360–73. [Fifteenth- and early sixteenth-century examples; the plates depict some women's signatures.]

1246.   ———. "A London Anchorite, Simon Appulby: His *Fruyte of Redempcyon* and Its Milieu." *Viator* 29 (1998), 227–39. [Text first published in 1514, as translation of anonymous fifteenth-century work; also, Appulby's will.]

1247.   ———. "Devotional Literature." In item 53. Pp. 495–525. ["Popular" devotion, books of hours, some special manuscripts, private prayers, key texts.]

1248.   Farnhill, Ken. "A Late Medieval Parish Gild: The Gild of St Thomas the Martyr in Cratfield, c. 1470–1542." *Suffolk* 38/3 (1995), 261–67. [A look at guild activity, but a thin record.]

1249.   Fletcher, Alan J. "'Magnus Predicator et Deuotus': A Profile of the Life, Work, and Influence of the Fifteenth-Century Oxford Preacher, John Felton." *Mediaeval Studies* 53 (1991), 125–75. [Some biography, but mostly a look at extant manuscripts and an edition of three long sermons (one partially in English).]

1250.   ———. "A Hive of Industry or a Hornets' Nest? Ms. Sidney Sussex 74 and Its Scribes." In item 66. Pp. 131–55. [Who wrote this collection of Lollard material; plates, and a search for the scriptorium.]

1251.   ———. "Performing the Seven Deadly Sins: How One Late-Medieval English Preacher Did It." *Leeds* n.s. 29 (1998), 89–108. [A sermon of the 1420s, designed for the fifth Sunday after Trinity.]

1252.   ———. *Preaching, Politics and Poetry in Late Medieval England.* Dublin, 1998. [Some sermons published, with running commentary; codicology, manuscripts, estate sermons, and a look at Langland and Chaucer in this collection of Fletcher's papers.]

1253.   Flight, Colin. "Parish Churches in the Diocese of
          Rochester, c. 1320–c. 1520." *Arch Cant* 119 (1999),
          285–310. [A list with maps; changes in status and
          patronage are noted.]

1254.   Forde, Simon N. "Social Outlook and Preaching in a
          Wycliffite 'Sermones Dominicales' Collection." In item
          99. Pp. 179–91 [Repyngdon's sources traced here.]

1255.   ———. "Lay Preaching and the Lollards of Norwich Dio-
          cese, 1428–1431." *Leeds* n.s. 29 (1998), 109–26. [How
          much the records tell about "what was really going on,"
          plus an official view of what constituted preaching.]

1256.   Gibson, Gail McMurray. "Saint Anne and the Religion of
          Childbed: Some East Anglian Texts and Talismans." In
          *Interpreting Cultural Symbols: St Anne in Late Medieval
          Society.* Edited by Kathleen Ashley and Pamela Shein-
          gorn. Athens, Ga., and London, 1990. Pp. 95–110. [As
          depicted in art and told in literature; tombs, windows
          and Osbern Bokenham.]

1257.   Gilchrist, Roberta, and Marilyn Oliva. *Religious Women
          in Medieval East Anglia: History and Archaeology,
          c. 1100–1540.* Studies in East Anglian History, 1
          (University of East Anglia, 1993). [A survey of women's
          regular life and some pertinent physical sites.]

1258.   Gillespie, Vincent. "Dial M for Mystic: Mystical Texts in
          the Library of Syon Abbey and the Spirituality of the
          Syon Brethren." In item 40. Pp. 241–68. [Books and
          manuscripts in that tradition, though the house did not
          produce its own mystical thinkers.]

1259.   Gillespie, Vincent, and Maggie Ross. "The Apophatic
          Image: The Poetics of Effacement in Julian of Norwich."
          In item 39. Pp. 53–77. [Tension between absence and
          presence, in mystical thinking.]

1260.   Glasscoe, Marion. "Time of Passion: Latent Relation-
         ships between Liturgy and Mediation in Two Middle
         English Mystics." In item 75. Pp. 141–60. [The primer
         and the liturgy served as guides toward mystical
         contemplation.]

1261.   ———. *English Medieval Mystics: Games of Faith.*
         London and New York, 1993. ["Julian of Norwich,
         'Endless knowyng in God'" (pp. 215–67) and "Margery
         Kempe: The Form of Her Living" (pp. 268–319) are
         relevant.]

1262.   ———. "Changing *Chere* and Changing Text in the
         Eighth Revelation of Julian of Norwich." *Medium Aevum*
         66 (1997), 115–21. [A critique of Colledge and Walsh's
         editorial policy on the eighth and ninth revelations.]

1263.   Goodrich, Margaret. "Westwood, A Rural English Nun-
         nery with its Local and French Connections." In item 45.
         Pp. 43–57. [Not badly treated, though a French house;
         local recruiting and many long-lived nuns.]

1264.   Gradon, Pamela, and Anne Hudson, eds. *English
         Wycliffite Sermons, 4–5.* Oxford, 1996. [The completion of
         a major project: vol. 4 covers the production of the
         sermons, and vol. 5 comments on some of them, with
         indices. Basic to a study of Wycliffe's learning and the
         relevant Middle English texts. Vol. 1 was reprinted, with
         corrections, in 1990; see also item 1304.]

1265.   Gransden, Antonia. "Letters of Recommendation from
         John Whethamstede for a Poor Pilgrim, 1453/4." *EHR*
         106 (1991), 932–39. [From a Bury Register, now a
         Harleian manuscript—to encourage the faithful to give
         alms to pilgrims.]

1266.   Gray, Douglas. "Popular Religion in Late Medieval
         English Literature." In *Religion and the Poetry and
         Drama of the Late Middle Ages in England: The J. A. W.*

Bennett Memorial Lecture. Edited by Pietro Boitani and Anna Torti. Cambridge, 1990. Pp. 1–28. [What is popular religion? Much attention is given to Margery Kempe's contribution to this assessment. See item 1385.]

1267.   ———. "Medieval English Mystical Lyrics." In item 78. Pp. 203–18. [How the mystical tradition infused literary composition, with some illustrations.]

1268.   Greatrex, Joan. "The English Cathedral Priories and the Pursuit of Learning in the Later Middle Ages." *J Eccl H* 45 (1994), 396–411. [The institutional structure encouraged learning; rising university attendance and intellectual life.]

1269.   ———. "Prosopography of English Benedictine Cathedral Chapters: Some Monastic *Curriculum Vitae.*" *Med Pros* 16/1 (1995), 1–26. [Some trends and patterns.]

1270.   ———. "Prosopographical Perspectives, or What Can Be Done with Five Thousand Monastic Biographies." *Med Pros* 20 (1999), 129–45. [Career spans, transfers, apostasy, and books; lots of tabular data.]

1271.   Greenway, Diana E. "The Medieval Cathedral." In *Chichester Cathedral: An Historical Survey.* Edited by Mary Hobbs. Chichester, 1994. Pp. 11–24. [Bishops, liturgy, town-gown relations; also, item 1805.]

1272.   Gribbin, Joseph A. "Aspects of Carthusian Liturgical Practice in Later Medieval England." *Analecta Cartusiana* 99/33 (1995). [Four manuscripts reveal the extent of English deviation and variation from the common Carthusian usage.]

1273.   Hagen, Susan K. "St. Cecilia and St. John of Beverly: Julian of Norwich's Early Model and Late Affirmation." In item 62. Pp. 91–114.

1274. Haines, Roy M. "Three Worcester Entries in a Formulary Preserved among the Ely Diocesan Records." *Worcestershire*, 3rd series, 14 (1994), 235–38. [Miscellaneous documents of bishops Peverel and Wakefield, transcribed.]

1275. ———. "Patronage and Appropriation in the Ely Diocese: The Share of the Benedictines." *Revue Bénédictine* 108 (1998), 298–314. [Colleges and collegiate churches appropriated far more than the regulars.]

1276. Hammond, Gerald. "What was the Influence of the Medieval English Bible upon the Renaissance Bible?" *BJRUL* 77/3 (1995), 87–95. [The legacy of Wycliffite translations was not as great for Tyndale as for some of his contemporaries.]

1277. Hanna, Ralph III. "'Vox octuplex': Lollard Socio-Textual ideology and Ricardian-Lancastrian Prose Translation." In *Criticism and Dissent in the Middle Ages.* Edited by Rita Copeland. Cambridge, 1996. Pp. 244–63. [The Lollard reading and translation strategy; an odd mix of themes and styles. See item 1316.]

1278. Harding, Wendy. "Body in Text: *The Book of Margery Kempe.*" In *Feminist Approaches to the Body in Medieval Literature.* Edited by Linda Lomperis and Sarah Stanbury. Philadelphia, 1993. Pp. 168–87. [The power of orality and Margery's emphasis on her corporeality; see also items 1395 and 1609.]

1279. Harper-Bill, Christopher. "The Medieval Church and the Wider World." In item 6. Pp. 287–313. [Town-gown problems and the "foreign policy" of Norwich and of the cathedral.]

1280. Harris, Barbara J. "A New Look at the Reformation: Aristocratic Women and Nunneries, 1450–1540." *JBS* 32 (1993), 89–113. [A survey of the links; numbers, the calling, shifting emphases and changing interest.]

1281.   Harris, Jonathan. "Publicising the Crusade: English
         Bishops and the Jubilee Indulgence of 1455." *J Eccl H* 50
         (1999), 23–37. [Some interest fanned by the fall of
         Constantinople, some money raised, some Greek clerics
         wandered through the realm.]

1282.   Harvey, Margaret. "Martin V and the English, 1422–
         1431." In item 52. Pp. 59–86. [Limited English zeal for
         reform and for ecclesiastical freedom from secular
         oversight.]

1283.   ———. "An Englishman at the Roman Curia during the
         Council of Basle: Andrew Holes, His Sermon of 1433 and
         His Books." *J Eccl H* 42 (1991), 19–38. [A canon lawyer
         at the papal court, and his sermon was for the feast of
         Becket's translation.]

1284.   ———. "The Diffusion of the Doctrinale of Thomas
         Netter in the Fifteenth and Sixteenth Centuries. In
         *Intellectual Life in the Middle Ages: Essays Presented to
         Margaret Gibson*. Edited by Lesley Smith and Benedicta
         Ward. London, 1992. Pp. 281–94. [Polemics against
         Wycliffe by the prior of the Carmelites; they were also
         used against early Protestants.]

1285.   ———. *England, Rome and the Papacy, 1417–1464: The
         Study of A Relationship*. Manchester, 1993. [As much on
         Anglo-Papal diplomatic relations as on ecclesiastical
         interaction.]

1286.   ———. "Unity and Diversity: Perceptions of the Papacy
         in the Later Middle Ages." In *Unity and Diversity in the
         Church: Papers Read at the 1994 Summer Meeting, and
         the 1995 Winter Meeting of the Ecclesiastical History
         Society*. Studies in Church History, 32. Cambridge,
         Mass., 1996. Edited by R. N. Swanson. Pp. 145–69.
         [Mostly looking at English views; Richard Ullerston, as
         imperial formulator.]

1287.   ———. "Adam Easton and the Condemnation of John
        Wyclif, 1377." *EHR* 113 (1998), 321–34. [With proposi-
        tions of the condemnation, from Sudbury's register:
        Easton wrote a *Defensiorum Ecclesiastice Potestatis*.]

1288.   Hayes, Rosemary C. E. "The Jurisdiction of the Dean
        and Chapter of the Cathedral Church of St. Peter in the
        City of York." In item 89. Pp. 87–96. [From a book
        covering 1387–1494, on the canons' authority over
        parish churches.]

1289.   ———. "The 'Private Life' of a Late Medieval Bishop:
        William Alnwick, Bishop of Norwich and Lincoln." In
        item 81. Pp. 1–18. [Career, household, will, books, and
        educational benefaction.]

1290.   Heale, Nicholas. "John Lydgate, Monk of Bury St
        Edmunds, as Spiritual Director." In item 45. Pp. 59–71.
        [Links themes in his poems to the monastic experience,
        with some spiritual guidance.]

1291.   Hicks, Michael. "Four Studies in Conventional Piety."
        Southern 13 (1991), 1–21. [Hungerford chantries: books,
        prayers, wills, and a high level of lay interest in the
        liturgy.]

1292.   Hilles, Carroll. "The Sacred Image and the Healing
        Touch: The Veronica in Julian of Norwich's Revelation of
        Love." *JM & EMS* 28/3 (Fall, 1998), 552–80. [Visions of
        Christ's bleeding hand; no end to Julian's joy in
        suffering.]

1293.   Hodapp, William F. "Sacred Time and Space Within:
        Drama and Ritual in Late Medieval Affective Passion
        Meditations." *DR* 115 (1997), 235–48. [Much on Julian
        and Margery Kempe; seeing the Passion as a current
        event.]

1294.   Hope, Andrew. "The Lady and the Bailiff: Lollardy among the Gentry in Yorkist and Early Tudor England." In item 5. Pp. 250–77. [Pervasive if odd opinions; some Colchester case studies.]

1295.   Horner, Patrick J. "'The King Taught Us the Lesson': Benedictine Support for Henry V's Suppression of the Lollards." *Mediaeval Studies* 52 (1996), 196–220. [Especially as in a Benedictine sermon c. 1410 (Bodl. ms. 649).]

1296.   Horrall, Sarah. "Middle English Texts in a Carthusian Commonplace Book: Westminster Cathedral, Diocesan Archives, MS H 38." *Medium Aevum* 59 (1990), 214–27. [Mixed theological texts; seven short works of the fourteenth and fifteenth century transcribed.]

1297.   Hoskin, Philippa. "Some Late Fourteenth-Century Gild and Fabric Wardens' Accounts from the Church of St Margaret's, Walmgate, York." In item 89. Pp. 75–86. [Covering the keepers of the fabric, 1394, and the St Anne guild, 1397.]

1298.   Hudson, Anne. "John Wyclif." In *The English Religious Tradition and the Genius of Anglicanism*. Edited by Geoffrey Rowell. Wantage, 1992. Pp. 65–78. [Good introduction, from the perspective of "would he have been an Anglican?" Also see item 1447.]

1299.   ———, ed. *Two Wycliffite Texts*. EETS, o.s. 301 (1993). [A sermon of William Taylor, 1406, and the testimony of William Thorpe, 1407.]

1300.   ———. "Aspects of the 'Publication' of Wyclif's Latin Sermons." In item 66. Pp. 121–29. [Cross references to the sermons in the manuscript, but who wrote them is unknown.]

1301.   ———. "'Laicus litteratus': The Paradox of Lollardy." In *Heresy and Literacy, 1000–1530*. Edited by Peter Biller and Anne Hudson. Cambridge, 1994. Pp. 222–36. [Literate heretics (like Walter Brute in the 1390s) terrified the authorities.]

1302.   ———. "William Taylor's 1406 Sermon: A Postscript." *Medium Aevum* 64 (1995), 100–06. [A Latin copy (from Prague), to go with the English version that Hudson published in 1993.]

1303.   ———. "Trial and Error: Wyclif's Works in Cambridge Trinity College MS B. 16.2." In item 11. Pp. 53–80. [The major manuscript, taken apart to compare what we have now and how it was put together and worked over; six plates.]

1304.   ———, ed. *English Wycliffite Sermons, 3.* Oxford and New York, 1996. [120 sermons published here as part of this major project; see item 1264.]

1305.   ———. "Hermofodrita or Ambidexter: Wycliffite Views on Clerks in Secular Office." In item 5. Pp. 41–51. [You did not have to be a heretic to wonder about this.]

1306.   ———. "Cross-Referencing in Wyclif's Latin Works." In item 13. Pp. 193–215. [By Wycliffe or a scribe? The loss of many works is highlighted by this approach.]

1307.   ———. "Wyclif and the North: The Evidence from Durham." In item 98. Pp. 87–103. [Northern interest and northern Wycliffite manuscripts.]

1308.   Hughes, Jonathan. "'True Ornaments to know a Holy Man': Northern Religious Life and the Piety of Richard III." In item 77. Pp. 149–90. [Family piety, links with university men, and other ways of assessing the data.]

1309.   Hughes, Jonathan, and with a foreword by Jeremy Catto. *The Religious Life of Richard III: Piety and Prayer in the North of England.* Stroud, 1997. [A lot of psychology brought into play.]

1310.   James, Josephine M. "The Norman Benedictine Alien Priory of St George, Modbury, A.D. c. 1135–1480." *Devon* 131 (1999), 81–103. [A twelfth-century foundation and late medieval decline; a survey of 1378 published.]

1311.   Jones, Edward A. "Jesus College Oxford, Ms. 39: Signs of a Medieval Compiler at Work." *English Manuscript Studies* 7 (1998), 236–48. [A fifteenth-century compendium: a guide to religious life for vowesses or a female recluse.]

1312.   ———. "The Hermits and Anchorites of Oxfordshire." *Oxon* 63 (1998), 51–77. [Updating Rotha Clay's list, though the numbers become thin by the fifteenth century.]

1313.   Jones, Malcolm. "The Parodic Sermon in Medieval and Early Modern England." *Medium Aevum* 66 (1997), 94–114. [A long-neglected source, focusing on a sermon of c. 1478.]

1314.   Jurkowski, Maureen. "New Light on John Purvey." *EHR* 110 (1995), 1180–90. [An inventory of goods, c. 1413, including some books.]

1315.   ———. "Lawyers and Lollardy in the Early Fifteenth Century." In item 5. Pp. 155–82. [Some case studies of men who brushed up against heresy.]

1316.   Justice, Steven. "Inquisition, Speech, and Writing: A Case from Late Medieval Norwich." See item 1277. Pp. 289–322. [John Burrell, summoned before Bishop Alnwick in 1429, and what followed in the context of lay Lollardy.]

1317.   ———. "Lollardy." In item 96. Pp. 662–89. [Doctrine, the movement, its suppression, and the types of works it produced.]

1318. Kelly, Henry Ansgar. "Sacraments, Sacramentals, and Lay Piety in Chaucer's England." *Chaucer Review* 28/1 (1993), 5–22. [Survey of lay piety and popular religion.]

1319. Kempster, Hugh. "A Question of Audience: The Westminster Text and Fifteenth-Century Reception of Julian of Norwich." In item 62. Pp. 257–89.

1320. Krantz, M. Diane F. *The Life and Text of Julian of Norwich: The Poetics of Enclosure.* New York, 1997. [Manuscripts, aural-oral issues, the psychology of enclosure, and an emphasis on "kynd" in the long text.]

1321. Kuczynski, Michael P. "Rolle among the Reformers: Orthodoxy and Heterodoxy in Wycliffite Copies of Richard Rolle's *English Psalter*." In item 78. Pp. 177–202. [How a Wycliffite writer came to identify with Rolle's works on the Psalms.]

1322. Lee, Paul. "Orthodox Parish Religion and Chapels of Ease in Late Medieval England: The Case of St George's Chapel in Gravesend." *Arch Cant* 119 (1999), 55–70. [History of the chapel, its endowments, and its benefactors; founded around 1438.]

1323. Le Faye, D. G. "Selborne Priory and the Vicarage of Basingstoke." *Hampshire* 46 (1990), 91–99. [Difficult town-cloister relations, 1233–1484.]

1324. Lepine, David N. "The Origins and Careers of the Canons of Exeter Cathedral, 1300–1455." In item 52. Pp. 87–120. [Mostly from the southwest, some with university training.]

1325. ———. "'My Beloved Sons in Christ': The Chapter of Lincoln Cathedral, 1300–1541." *Med Pros* 16/1 (1995), 89–113. [Geographical origins, social origins, and other basic issues on the prosopographical agenda.]

1326.   ———. *A Brotherhood of Canons Serving God: English Secular Cathedrals in the Later Middle Ages.* Woodbridge and Rochester, N.Y., 1995. [The nine secular communities; prosopography, education, service.]

1327.   Lewis, Katherine J. "The Life of St Margaret of Antioch in Late Medieval England: A Gendered Reading." In *Gender and Christian Religion: Papers Read at the 1996 Summer Meeting and the 1997 Winter Meeting of the Ecclesiastical History Society.* Studies in Church History, 34. Edited by Robert N. Swanson. Woodbridge and Rochester, N.Y., 1998. Pp. 129–42. [Lydgate and Bokenham and artistic depiction; a role model for young women.]

1328.   Leyser, Henriette. "Piety, Religion, and the Church." In item 84. Pp. 174–206.

1329.   Lichtmann, Maria R. "'I desyrede a bodylye syght': Julian of Norwich and the Body." *Mystics Quarterly* 17 (1991), 12–19. [Looking for the roots of her "sensualyte."]

1330.   Lindberg, Conrad, ed. *John Wyclif, English Wycliffite Tracts, 1–3.* Oslo, 1991. [Editions of three polemical tracts, previously only available in a nineteenth-century edition.]

1331.   ———. "Literary Aspects of the Wyclif Bible." *BJRUL* 77/3 (1995), 79–85. [Translator's techniques; comments on changes and choices Wycliffe made as he worked.]

1332.   ———, ed. *The Earlier Version of the Wycliffite Bible, 8: The Epistles, Etc.—Edited from MS Christ Church 145.* Acta Universitatis Stockholmiensis, Stockholm Studies in English, 87. Stockholm, 1997. [Nicholas Hereford was the probable translator of this text; this project goes back to 1959.]

1333.   ———, ed. *King Henry's Bible: MS Bodley 277: The Revised Version of the Wyclif Bible, Vol. I: Genesis–Ruth.* Acta Universitatis Stockholmiensis: Stockholm Studies in English, 89. Stockholm, 1999. [Introduction covers manuscripts; text with notes on vocabulary.]

1334. Logan, F. Donald. "The Cambridge Canon Law Faculty: Sermons and Addresses." In item 36. Pp. 151–64. [A Queen's College Ms. of 1480. Twenty-one sermons covered: themes, sources, discussion of manuscripts, and a positive view of canon law.]

1335. ———. *Runaway Religious in Medieval England, c. 1240–1540.* Cambridge, 1996. [The basic study of an intriguing subject.]

1336. Lomas, Richard. "A Priory and Its Tenants." In item 18. Pp. 103–24. [Durham Priory: the bursar's manors, appropriated parishes, and some accounts.]

1337. Lucas, Peter J. "A Bequest to the Austin Friars in the Will of John Spycer, 1435–40; John Capgrave, O.S.A. (1393–1469); William Wellys, O.S.A. (fl. 1434–40), and Augustinian Learning at Lynn in the Fifteenth Century." *Norfolk* 41/4 (1993), 482–89. [Wills, background on the order, and a look at Capgrave's life and writings.]

1338. Lutton, Robert. "Connections between Lollards, Townsfolk and Gentry in Tenterden in the Late Fifteenth and Early Sixteenth Centuries." In item 5. Pp. 199–228. [Local families (especially the Castelyns): their wills and the Jesus mass.]

1339. Marcombe, David. "Thomas de Aston: The Chantries and Charities of a Fourteenth-Century Archdeacon." In *Thomas de Aston and the Diocese of Lincoln: Two Studies in the Fourteenth-Century Church.* Lincoln Cathedral Publications. Lincoln, 1998. Pp. 32–55. [Life, career, and bequests.]

1340. Martin, Geoffrey. "Knighton's Lollards." In item 5. Pp. 28–40. [The value of this chronicle was undervalued by K. B. McFarlane; Repingdon's role is of considerable importance.]

1341.   Masson, Cynthea. "The Point of Coincidence: Rhetoric and Apophatic in Julian of Norwich's *Showings*." In item 62. Pp. 153–81.

1342.   McDermid, Richard T. W., ed. *Beverley Minster Fasti*. Yorkshire Archaeological Society, Yorkshire Record Series 149 (1993). [Provosts and canons, c. 1100–1546, with a (colored) map of Beverley's Thraves and biographical notes.]

1343.   McEntire, Sandra J. "The Likeness of God and the Restoration of Humanity in Julian of Norwich's *Showings*." In item 62. Pp. 3–33.

1344.   McHardy, Alison. "Church Courts and Criminous Clerks in the Later Middle Ages." In item 36. Pp. 165–83. [The procedure by the late fourteenth century; clerical privileges and purgation procedures.]

1345.   ———. "The Churchmen of Chaucer's London: The Seculars." *Med Pros* 16/1 (1995), 57–87. [The groups and types; numbers and mobility.]

1346.   ———, ed. *Royal Writs Addressed to John Buckingham, Bishop of Lincoln, 1363–1398*. Canterbury and York Society, 86, and Lincoln Record Society, 86 (1997). [Long introduction and calendared items on a wide range of topics, both secular and ecclesiastical.]

1347.   ———. "The Loss of Archbishop Stratford's Register." *HR* 70 (1997), 337–341. [A fourteenth-century register, lost in a highway robbery in Sussex in 1402.]

1348.   ———. "De Heretico Comburendo, 1401." In item 5. Pp. 112–26. [The politics behind putting the statute together.]

1349.   McHardy, Alison, and Nicholas Orme. "The Defence of
         an Alien Priory: Modbury (Devon) in the 1450s." *J Eccl
         H* 50 (1999), 303–12. [A long-lived alien priory; corre-
         spondence over who was to say mass.]

1350.   McInerny, Maud B. "*In the Meydens Womb*: Julian of
         Norwich and the Poetics of Enclosure." In item 74.
         Pp. 157–82. [Mothering and the procreative body, from a
         reclusive virgin mystic.]

1351.   McSheffrey, Shannon. *Gender and Heresy: Women and
         Men in Lollard Communities, 1420–1530.* Philadelphia,
         1995. [Careful examination of the role of women and
         gender relations among the Lollards: less role for women
         than we might have hoped.]

1352.   McVeigh, Terrence A., trans. *John Wyclif, On Simony.*
         New York, 1992. [Long introduction to open the doors to
         a dense, argumentative, and erudite text.]

1353.   Morgan, D. A. L. "The Cult of St George, c. 1500:
         National and International Connotations." In *L'Angle-
         terre et les pays bourguignons: Relations et comparisons
         (xv^e–xv^{ie} s.).* Neuchatel, 1995. [Considerable Burgundian
         interest in St. George even while he was becoming the
         emblem of English nationalism.]

1354.   Morgan, Philip. "Adbaston Churchwarden's Accounts,
         1478–1488." In item 68. Pp. 83–96. [History of Church
         and community; some (English) transcriptions.]

1355.   Morrissey, Thomas E. "Surge, Illuminnae: A Lost
         Address by Richard Fleming at the Council of
         Constance." *Anuarium Historiae Conciliorum* 22 (1990),
         86–130. [Sermon of January 1471, in a Munich
         manuscript, published and annotated here.]

1356.   Nederman, Cary J., and Kate L. Forhan, eds. *Medieval
         Political Theory: A Reader: The Quest for the Body*

Politic, 1100–1400. London and New York, 1993. [Selections from Wycliffe's "On the Duty of the King," pp. 221–30; translated by Nederman.]

1357.   Nilson, Ben, and Ruth H. Frost. "The Archiepiscopal Indulgences for the City of York, 1450–1500." In item 89. Pp. 112–22. [Mostly granted on behalf of institutions by William Booth, George Neville, and Thomas Rotherham.]

1358.   Noble, Claire, ed. *Norwich Cathedral Priory Gardener's Accounts, 1329–1530.* Norfolk Record Society 61 (1997). [Introduction on monastic gardens and priory accounting (pp. 1–30), accounts (pp. 31–84); in English, with a glossary.]

1359.   Northeast, Peter. "The Chantry at Brundish." *Suffolk* 38/2 (1994), 138–48. [Founded by Sir John Pyshall, executor of Robert de Ufford, Earl of Suffolk (in 7 Richard II) and followed through to the dissolution.]

1360.   Nuth, Joan M. *Wisdom's Daughter: The Theology of Julian of Norwich.* New York, 1991.

1361.   Oakley, Anne. "Rochester Priory, 1185–1540." In *Faith and Fabric: A History of Rochester Cathedral.* Edited by Nigel Yates. Rochester, 1996. Pp. 29–55. [Covers the estates, priors' relations with bishops and others, and priory personnel to the Dissolution. Published by "Friends of Rochester Cathedral."]

1362.   Obbard, Elizabeth Ruth. *Introducing Julian, Woman of Norwich.* Hyde Park, N.Y., 1996. [An introduction and then selections; a volume for spiritual guidance, not for scholarly reading.]

1363.   Oliva, Marilyn. "Aristocracy or Meritocracy? Office-Holding Patterns in Late Medieval English Nunneries." In item 87. Pp. 197–208. [Many women from middling and lower social ranks.]

1364.   ———. "Counting Nuns: A Prosopography of Late Medi-
         eval English Nuns in the Diocese of Norwich." *Med Pros*
         16/1 (1995), 27–55. [Covers 1350–1540: identities, size of
         houses, and their reliance on local women of mixed social
         origins.]

1365.   ———. *The Convent and the Community in Late Medieval
         England: Female Monasteries in the Diocese of Norwich,
         1350–1540*. Woodbridge, 1998. [Setting women's houses
         into the context of community and the local economy:
         spirituality, personnel, and links with the local laity.]

1366.   ———. "All in the Family? Monastic and Clerical
         Careers among Family Members in the Late Middle
         Ages." *Med Pros* 20 (1999), 161–80. [Many Norfolk nuns
         had kin in the local church; tabular data.]

1367.   Olsen, Ulla Sander. "Work and Work Ethics in the Nun-
         nery of Syon Abbey in the Fifteenth Century." In item
         39. Pp. 129–43. [Women's work in light of Benedict's
         views about manual labor.]

1368.   O'Mara, Veronica M. "Saints' Plays and Preaching:
         Theory and Practice in Late Middle English Sanctorale
         Sermons." *Leeds* n.s. 29 (1998), 257–74. [Sermons for
         saints' days: how many, how important?]

1369.   Orme, Nicholas, ed. *Unity and Variety: A History of the
         Church in Devon and Cornwall*. Exeter Studies in
         History, 29 (1991). [The only relevant paper is by Orme,
         "The Later Middle Ages and the Reformation," pp. 53–80.]

1370.   ———. "Sufferings of the Clergy: Illness and Old Age in
         Exeter Diocese, 1300–1540." In *Life, Death and the
         Elderly: Historical Perspective*. Edited by Margaret
         Pelling and Richard M. Smith. London and New York,
         1991. Pp. 62–73. [Statistics on pensions and related
         issues.]

1371.   ———. "A letter of Saint Roche." *D & C NQ* 36 (1992), 153–59. [A late medieval cult around Exeter.]

1372.   ———. "Indulgences in Medieval Cornwall." *Cornwall* n.s. 1, part 2 (1992), 149–70. [Not all that many granted; list of some indulgences and some manuscript sources.]

1373.   ———. "Warland Hospital, Totnes, and the Trinitarian Friars in Devon." *D & C NQ* 36 (1/1987–12/1992), 41–48. [Institutional history, bequests, a list of wardens, and the charter of 1275–80 that transferred the house to the Trinitarian Friars.]

1374.   ———. "The Clergy of Clyst Gabriel, Devon, 1312–1508." *Devon* 126 (1994), 107–21. [Hospital and alms house, with analysis of chantry priests; data on longevity and seasonal mortality rates.]

1375.   ———. "Church and Chapel in Medieval England." *TRHS*, 6th series, 6 (1996), 75–102. [Numbers, role, distribution, and relations with parish churches and clergy.]

1376.   Owen, Dorothy. "Historical Survey, 1091–1450." In item 71. Pp. 112–63. [Pp. 136–52 are the most relevant for these years.]

1377.   ———. "Accounts for the Rectory of Wainfleet St Mary for the Year 2 February 1475 to 1 February 1476." *Lincoln* 30 (1995), 53–54. [The vicar received £10 per annum.]

1378.   Page, Mark, ed. *The Pipe Rolls of the Bishopric of Winchester, 1409–10.* Hampshire Record Series 16 (1999). [In translation; Winchester Cathedral was big business, as its records indicate.]

1379.   Palliser, Margaret Ann. *Christ, our Mother of Mercy: Divine Mercy and Compassion in the Theology of the "Shewings" of Julian of Norwich.* Berlin and New York, 1992.

1380.   Park, Tarjei. "Reflecting Christ: The Role of Flesh in
          Walter Hilton and Julian of Norwich." In item 39.
          Pp. 17–37. [Links Hilton with Julian's first visionary
          sequence.]

1381.   ———. "'Whom clepist the þou trewe pilgrimes?' Lollard
          Discourse on Pilgrimages in *The Testimony of William
          Thorpe*." In *Essayes and Explorations: A "Freundschrift"
          for Liisa Dahl*. Edited by M. Gustafsson. Anglicana
          Turkuensia 15, University of Turku. Turku, Finland,
          1996. Pp. 73–84. [Lollards and pilgrimages were an
          unhappy combination, as Lollards were eager to tell one
          and all.]

1382.   Pelphrey, Brant, "Leaving the Womb of Christ: Love,
          Domesday, and Space/Time in Julian of Norwich and
          Eastern Orthodox Mysticism." In item 62. Pp. 291–320.

1383.   Peters, Brad. "Julian of Norwich and her Conceptual
          Development of Evil." *Mystics Quarterly* 17 (1991),
          181–88. [Using Lev Bygotsky's theories of language (or
          so we are told).]

1384.   ———. "A Genre Approach to Julian of Norwich's Epis-
          temology." In item 62. Pp. 115–52.

1385.   Pezzini, Domenico. "The Theme of the Passion in
          Richard Rolle and Julian of Norwich." See item 1266.
          Pp. 29–66. [How the two major thinkers dealt with pain,
          death, and spirituality.]

1386.   Phillips, Heather. "John Wyclif and the Religion of the
          People." In item 21. Pp. 561–90. [What people knew and
          thought about the Eucharist, plus Wycliffe's views and
          comments on this major issue.]

1387.   Powell, Susan. "Lollards and Lombards: Late Medieval
          Bogeymen." *Medium Aevum* 59 (1990), 133–39. [Mirk's
          worries about Lollards and the date of the *Festial*.]

1388. ———. "John Mirk's *Festial* and the Pastoral Pro-
       gramme." *Leeds* ns. 22 (1991), 85–102. [The evolution of
       the text, from the 1380s onwards, through printed
       versions of the 1530s.]

1389. ———. "The Transmission and Circulation of the *Lay
       Folks' Catechism*." In item 66. Pp. 67–84. [John
       Gaytryge, et al., englishing Thoresby's injunctions, and
       later changes in the popular text.]

1390. Rawcliffe, Carole. "'Gret criynge and joly chauntynge':
       Life, Death and Liturgy at St Giles's Hospital, Norwich,
       in the Thirteenth and Fourteenth Centuries." In *Counties
       and Communities: Essays on East Anglian History, Pre-
       sented to Hassell Smith*. Edited by Carole Rawcliffe,
       Roger Virgoe, and Richard Wilson. Norwich, 1996.
       Pp. 37–55. [The hospital's liturgy; performance and piety.]

1391. Reeves, A. Compton. "Lawrence Booth: Bishop of
       Durham (1457–76), Archbishop of York (1476–80)." In
       item 64. Pp. 64–88. [Climbing and careerism for self and
       family, traced here with care and detail.]

1392. Richmond, Colin F. "Religion." In item 57. Pp. 183–201.
       [A survey, and a verdict of lukewarm spirituality.]

1393. ———. "Margins and Marginality: English Devotion in
       the Later Middle Ages." In item 81. Pp. 242–53. [Miscel-
       laneous marginalia, leading to a tale of devotion and
       some authorial comments about late medieval
       spirituality.]

1394. Riddy, Felicity. "Julian of Norwich and Self-Textuali-
       zation." In *Editing Women*. Edited by Ann M. Hutchison.
       Toronto, 1998. Pp. 101–24. [The development of the two
       texts and Julian's efforts to turn visions into texts.]

1395. Robertson, Elizabeth. "Medieval Medical Views of
       Women and Female Spirituality in the *Ancrene Wisse*
       and Julian of Norwich's *Showings*." See item 1278.

Pp. 142–67. [Julian's references to blood, fluids, and sensuality.]

1396. Robson, Michael. *The Franciscans in the Medieval Custody of York.* Borthwick Papers, 93. University of York, 1997. [A survey, strong on fifteenth-century relations between friars and the town.]

1397. Rohrkaster, Jens. "Londoners and London Mendicants in the Late Middle Ages." *J Eccl H* 47 (1996), 446–77. [Wills, signs of crisis in the friaries, some decline in lay support.]

1398. Rollason, Lynda. "The *Liber Vitae* of Durham and Lay Association with Durham Cathedral in the Later Middle Ages." In item 93. Pp. 276–95. [The geographical range and many different links that enabled people to have ties with the cathedral.]

1399. Rosenthal, Joel T. "Lancastrian Episcopal Wills: Directing and Distributing." *Med Pros* 11/1 (1990), 35–84. [A survey of bequests in the extant wills.]

1400. ———. "The Northern Clergy: Clerical Wills and Family Ties." *Med Pros* 20 (1999), 147–59. [The power of family; 60 percent of the wills refer to at least one relative.]

1401. Ross, Ellen, "'She Wept and Cried Right Loud for Sorrow and for Pain': Suffering, the Spiritual Journey, and Women's Experience in Late Medieval Mysticism." In *Maps of Flesh and Light: The Religious Experience of Medieval Women Mystics.* Edited by Ulrike Wiethaus. Syracuse, 1993. Pp. 45–59. [Margery Kempe and Julian had to suffer with Jesus to know his love.]

1402. Rosser, Gervase. "Parochial Conformity and Voluntary Religion in Late-Medieval England." *TRHS*, 6th series, 1 (1991), 173–89. [Quest for "religious freedom," chapels, the absence of close supervision, and "sub-parochial" localism.]

1403.   Ruud, Jay. "'I wolde for thy loue dye': Julian, Romance
         Discourse, and the Masculine." In item 62. Pp. 183–205.

1404.   Sargent, Michael G., ed., with introduction and glossary.
         *Nicholas Love's "Mirror of the Blessed Life of Jesus
         Christ": A Critical Edition Based on Cambridge Univer-
         sity Library Add MSS 6578 and 6686*. London and New
         York, 1992. [A fifteenth-century translation of a treatise
         once attributed to Bonaventure; a text of great popu-
         larity, arranged for contemplation by days of the week.]

1405.   ———. "The Problem of Uniformity in Carthusian Book
         Production from the *Opus Pacis* to the *Tertio Compilatio
         Statutorum*." In item 11. Pp. 122–41. [Problems within
         the Carthusian order are reflected in the editing and
         arranging of their basic texts.]

1406.   Sharman, Ian. *Thomas Langley—England's First Spin
         Doctor*. Foreword by Colin Richmond. London, 1999. [A
         dim view of episcopal service.]

1407.   Shinner, John, and William J. Dohar. *Pastors and the
         Care of Souls in Medieval England*. Notre Dame, Ind.,
         1998. [A book of primary sources, in translation:
         examples from sermons, literary depictions, and other
         sources.]

1408.   Simonetta, S. "The Concept of the Two Churches in the
         Religious Philosophy of the English Reformer John
         Wyclife." *Studi Medievali* 40 (1999), 37–119. [Not quite a
         separation of church and state, but a way to purify the
         Church.]

1409.   Smith, David M. "The Exercise of Probate Jurisdiction of
         the Medieval Archbishops of York." In item 98. Pp. 123–
         44. [Survey of sources, jurisdictions, and the administra-
         tive apparatus.]

1410. Smith, Jennifer. "Shaving, Circumcision, Blood and Sin: Gendering the Audience in John Mirk's Sermons." In *Venus and Mars: Engendering Love and War in Medieval and Early Modern Europe*. Edited by Andrew Lynch and Philippa Maddern. Nedlands, Western Australia, 1995. Pp. 106–18. [The possibilities of purification.]

1411. Somerset, Fiona E. "Vernacular Argumentation in *The Testimony* of William Thorpe." *Mediaeval Studies* 58 (1996), 207–41. [Thorpe's brand of anti-clericalism and his high level of learning.]

1412. ———. "Answering the Twelve *Conclusions*: Dymmock's Halfhearted Gestures towards Publication." In item 5. Pp. 52–76. [Responding to the Lollards and pushing his own credentials (to a courtly audience?).]

1413. Spencer, H. Leith. *English Preaching in the Later Middle Ages*. Oxford, 1993. [Sermon literature, c. 1370–1500; Middle English sermons and the two-way links between preaching and Lollardy.]

1414. Sprung, Andrew. "The Invented Metaphor: Earthly Mothering as *Figura* of Divine Love in Julian of Norwich's *Book of Showings*." In item 74. Pp. 183–99. [More on mother Jesus.]

1415. Staley, Lynn. "Julian of Norwich and the Late Fourteenth-Century Crisis of Authority." In item 1. Pp. 107–78.

1416. Storey, Robin L. "Papal Provisions in English Monasteries." *Nottingham* 35 (1991), 77–91. [Very strong limits on papal intervention.]

1417. ———. "Malicious Indictment of Clergy in the Fifteenth Century. In item 36. Pp. 221–40. [As seen by convocation and supported by records of proceedings and trials.]

1418.   Sutcliffe, Sebastian. "The Cult of St. Sitha in England:
          An Introduction." *Nottingham* 37 (1993), 84–89. [Much
          evidence for fifteenth-century interest, centering in
          Lincolnshire.]

1419.   Swanson, Heather. "Building Accounts from St Martin's,
          Coney Street, York, 1447–1452." In item 89. Pp. 97–104.
          [Bequests and fund raising, an indenture of 1445, ac-
          counts of 1447 and 1449.]

1420.   Swanson, Robert N. "Sede Vacante Administration in
          the Medieval Diocese of Carlisle: The Accounts of the
          Vacancy of December 1395 to March, 1396." *Cumberland*
          90 (1990), 183–94. [Calendared appendix of documents
          from the register, now in the Borthwick Institute.]

1421.   ———. "Problems of the Priesthood in Pre-Reformation
          England." *EHR* 105 (1990), 845–69. [Personnel, adminis-
          tration, theology, and pre-figurings of reformation.]

1422.   ———, ed. *The Register of John Catterick, Bishop of
          Coventry and Lichfield, 1415–1419*. Canterbury and
          York Society 77 (1990). [Introduction, calendared
          entries, ordinations, etc.]

1423.   ———. "Standards of Living: Parochial Revenue in Pre-
          Reformation England." In item 52. Pp. 151–96. [An in-
          secure and uncertain world, as shown by a wealth of
          statistics.]

1424.   ———. "Chaucer's Parson and Other Priests." *Studies in
          the Age of Chaucer* 13 (1991), 41–50. [The kinds and
          levels of clerics, and the usual career course.]

1425.   ———. "Medieval Liturgy as Theatre: The Props." In
          *The Church and the Arts: Papers Read at the 1990
          Summer Meeting and the 1991 Winter Meeting of the
          Ecclesiastical History Society*. Studies in Church
          History, 28. Oxford and Cambridge, Mass., 1992. Edited

by Diana Wood. Pp. 239–53. [Lichfield Cathedral
inventories as the guide, with a look at vestments and
other treasures.]

1426.   ———. "Devotional Offerings at Hereford Cathedral in
the Later Middle Ages." *Analecta Bollandiana* 111
(1993), 83–99. [A gauge of Cantilupe's waning popularity
as a focus of pilgrimage.]

1427.   ———. "Economic Change and Spiritual Profits:
Receipts from the Peculiar Jurisdiction of the Peak
District in the Fourteenth Century." In item 80. Pp. 171–
95. [Revenues for the dean and chapter of Lichfield;
falling, though lead and wool were paying well.]

1428.   ———, trans. and annotator. *Catholic England: Faith,
Religion, and Observance before the Reformation.* Manchester, 1993. [A source book, with introduction and
commentary, covering both "theory" and practice of
religion.]

1429.   ———. "The Priory in the Later Middle Ages." In
*Coventry's First Cathedral: The Cathedral and Priory of
St. Mary: Papers from the 1993 Anniversary Symposium.*
Edited by George Demidowicz. Stamford, 1994. Pp. 139–
57. [Building demolished at the Reformation.]

1430.   ———. "Parochialism and Particularism: The Dispute
over the Status of Ditchford Friary, Warwicksire, in the
Early Fifteenth Century." In item 36. Pp. 241–57.
[Where should parishioners worship? Merton College vs.
the Bishop of Worcester.]

1431.   ———. "The 'Mendicant Problem' in the Later Middle
Ages." In item 13. Pp. 217–38. [Much English material
in a general discussion of the friars, and the attacks on
them, across Europe.]

1432.   ———. "An Appropriate Anomaly: Topcliffe Parish and
the Fabric Fund of York Minster in the Later Middle

Ages." In item 98. Pp. 105–21. [Links between an appropriated church and the minster, mainly based on accounts and finances.]

1433.   Tate, Robert B. "Robert Langton, Pilgrim (1470–1524)." *Nottingham* 39 (1995), 182–91. [Late medieval pilgrimage, especially to Santiago.]

1434.   Thompson, Benjamin. "The Laity, the Alien Priories, and the Redistribution of Ecclesiastical Property." In item 81. Pp. 19–41. [Royal policy, fourteenth-century precedents and background, and the Commons' views of the alien houses tempore Henry IV.]

1435.   Thompson, John T. "Another Look at the Religious Texts in Lincoln Cathedral Library, Ms 91." In item 66. Pp. 169–87. [Scribe was Robert Thornton, and the manuscript gives a good idea of lay tastes for religious materials.]

1436.   Thomson, John A. F. *The Early Tudor Church and Society, 1485–1529.* London and New York, 1993. [Events of Tudor England, but set against the late medieval background.]

1437.   ———. "Knightly Piety and the Margins of Lollardy." In item 5. Pp. 95–111. [A reexamination of McFarlane's Lollard knights: flirting with heresy became more dangerous than it was worth.]

1438.   Timmins, T. C. B., ed. *The Register of John Waltham, Bishop of Salisbury, 1388–1395.* Canterbury and York Society, 80 (1994). [In English, with some light on Lollardy, plus Waltham's will and a visitation of the city.]

1439.   Tinsley, David F. "Julian's Diabology." In item 62. Pp. 207–37.

1440.   Turville-Petre, Thorlac. "A Middle English Life of St Zita." *Nottingham* 35 (1991), 102–05. [The forty-one-line fifteenth-century life is the only one from England.]

1441.   van Engen, John. "Anticlericalism among the Lollards."
         In *Anticlericalism in Late Medieval and Early Modern
         Europe.* Edited by Peter Dykema and Heiko Oberman.
         Leiden and New York, 1993. Pp. 53–63. [Compared to
         the New Devout in the Low Countries, Lollards jumped,
         early on, into serious heresies.]

1442.   [No entry.]

1443.   Vickers, Noreen. "The Social Class of Yorkshire
         Medieval Nuns." *YAJ* 67 (1995), 127–32. [The few we
         can trace are of good birth.]

1444.   von Nolcken, Christine. "A 'Certain Sameness' and Our
         Response to It in English Wycliffite Texts." In *Literature
         and Religion in the Later Middle Ages: Philological
         Studies in Honor of Siegfried Wenzel.* Edited by Richard
         G. Newhauser and John A. Alford. Binghamton, N.Y.,
         1995. Pp. 191–208. [On their common interest in
         generalizing and a common style of elucidation.]

1445.   ———. "Richard Wyche, A Certain Knight, and the
         Beginning of the End." In item 5. Pp. 127–52. [His
         examination by Arundel and his version of the issues.]

1446.   ———. "The Democratization of God's Law and the
         Lollards." In *The Bible as Book: The Manuscript
         Tradition.* Edited by K. Van Kemper and John L.
         Sharpe, III. London, 1998. Pp. 177–95. [A fifteenth-
         century manuscript and the traditions and themes of
         Lollard biblical translation.]

1447.   Ward, Benedicta. "Lady Julian of Norwich and Her
         Audience: 'mine even Christian'." See item 1298.
         Pp. 47–73.

1448.   Watson, Nicholas. "The Trinitarian Hermeneutic in
         Julian of Norwich's *Revelation of Love.*" In item 39.
         Pp. 79–100. [To be read as a literal text; not easy to
         describe a revelation.]

1449.   ———. "The Composition of Julian of Norwich's *Revela-tion of Love.*" *Speculum* 68 (1993), 637–83. [Argues for a long, slow, choppy process of composition; her isolation as an author.]

1450.   ———. "Censorship and Cultural Change in Late-Medi-eval England: Vernacular Theology, the Oxford Transla-tion Debate, and Arundel's Constitutions of 1409." *Speculum* 70 (1995), 822–864. [1390–1410 as a golden age of vernacular work of much diversity; then the clamp-down.]

1451.   ———. "The Trinitarian Hermeneutic in Julian of Norwich's *Revelation of Love.* In item 62. Pp. 61–90.

1452.   ———. "The Middle English Mystics." In item 96. Pp. 539–65. [The usual suspects: Rolle, Hilton, Julian of Norwich, *The Cloud*, and Margery Kempe.]

1453.   Wenzel, Siegfried. *Macaronic Sermons: Bilingualism and Preaching in Late Medieval England.* Ann Arbor, Mich., 1994. [Latin, Anglo-Norman, and Middle English, and how linguistic use was linked to the message.]

1454.   ———. "A Sermon Repertory from Cambridge Univer-sity." *History of Universities* 14 (1995–96), 43–67. [A Caius and Gonville manuscript of the early fifteenth century, when 156 sermons were preached, over a three-year span.]

1455.   Wilks, Michael. "Wyclif and the Wheel of Time." In *The Church Retrospective: Papers Read at the 1995 Summer Meeting and the 1996 Winter Meeting of the Ecclesi-astical History Society.* Studies in Church History, 33 (Woodbridge and Rochester, N.Y., 1997). Edited by Robert N. Swanson. Pp. 177–93. [Stages of Church history: were we ready for reform?]

1456.   ———. "Thomas Arundel of York, The Appellant Arch-
         bishop." In item 98. Pp. 57–86. [Richard II stood between
         Arundel and the war on Lollardy, as Arundel became a
         major political player in Church and state.]

1457.   Williams, Barrie. "Richard III's Other Palatinate: John
         Shirwood, Bishop of Durham." *Ricardian* 9/115
         (December 1991), 166–69. [Primarily a biographical
         study.]

1458.   Winstead, Karen A. "Piety, Politics, and Social Commit-
         ment in Capgrave's *Life of St Katherine*." *Medievalia et
         Humanistica*, n.s. 17 (1991), 59–80. [A model of lay piety,
         written c. 1415.]

X. Intellectual History: Science and Technology, Schools and Education, Medicine and Hospitals

1459. Acker, Paul, and Eriko Amino. "The Book of Palmistry." In item 60. Pp. 141–83. [With illustrations of palms; everyone seems to have been right-handed.]

1460. Allmand, Christopher. "The Fifteenth-Century English Versions of Vegetius' *De Re Militari*." In item 91. Pp. 30–45. [Its enduring popularity and influence; prose and verse translations.]

1461. Ashworth, E. J. "Text-books: A Case Study—Logic." In item 53. Pp. 380–86. [Many older texts still being used in the fifteenth century.]

1462. Ashworth, E. J., and P. V. Spode. "Logic in Late Medieval Oxford." In item 24. Pp. 35–64. [The men who taught, and their subjects; Wycliffe is included in the survey.]

1463. Backhouse, Janet. "The Royal Library from Edward IV to Henry VII." In item 53. Pp. 267–73. [Edward IV is the founder; his manuscripts and family tradition.]

1464. Barron, Caroline M. "The Education and Training of Girls in 15th-Century London." In item 33. Pp. 139–53. [A sanguine view of opportunities and achievements.]

1465. Bell, David N. "Monastic Libraries, 1400–1557." In item 53. Pp. 229–54. [The book trade, monastic acquisitions before and after printing, with an analysis of some libraries.]

1466. Bennett, Michael J. "The Court of Richard II and the Promotion of Literature." In item 48. Pp. 3–20. [The court's role in culture; a positive assessment.]

1467. ———. "Education and Advancement." In item 57. Pp. 79–96. [A survey of schooling and career training.]

1468. Boffey, Julia. "Women Authors and Women's Literacy in Fourteenth and Fifteenth-Century England." In item 63. Pp. 158–82. [Hard to be too certain about numbers and levels attained, though we can trace networks and some authors.]

1469. Boffey, Julia, and Anthony S. G. Edwards. "Literary Texts." In item 53. Pp. 555–75. [Secular material; the popularity of French work, in translation.]

1470. Bowers, Roger. "The Almonry Schools of the English Monasteries, c. 1265–1540." In item 93. Pp. 177–222. [A wide sweep, with a tentative list of schools, mostly from late in the period.]

1471. Briggs, Charles F. "Manuscripts of Giles of Rome's *De Regimine Principum* in England, 1300–1500: A Handlist." *Scriptorium* 47 (1993), 60–73. [Fifty-three manuscripts cited and described.]

1472. ———. "Ms. Digby 233 and the Patronage of John Trevissa's *De Regimine Principum*." *English Manuscript Studies* 7 (1998), 249–63. [In the Bodleian, and probably done for the Berkeleys by a scribe working from a Trevissa autographed copy.]

1473. ———. *Giles of Rome's "De Regimine Principum": Reading and Writing Politics at Court and University, c. 1275–c. 1525.* Cambridge, 1999. [Its dissemination: many copies, widely read; with plates and an appendix on the manuscripts.]

1474.   Brown, Peter. "The Seven Planets." In item 60. Pp. 3–21.
        [Sloane MS 1315, showing how each planet governed a
        different day of the week.]

1475.   Butterfield, Ardis. "French Culture and the Ricardian
        Court." In item 67. Pp. 82–120. [Scholarship exalts the
        English, though French influences and literary models
        were still pervasive.]

1476.   Camargo, Martin. "Beyond the *Libri Castoniani*: Models
        of Latin Prose Style at Oxford University, ca. 1400."
        Mediaeval Studies 56 (1994), 165–87. [Some formulaic
        manuscripts used for teaching and reference; a table
        gives mss. and texts.]

1477.   Carey, H. M. *Courting Disaster: Astrology at the English
        Court and Universities in the Later Middle Ages.* New
        York, 1992. [From the elite to the popular, touching
        astrology's friends and foes plus the court's role;
        appendix of mss. and horoscopes.]

1478.   Carlson, David R. *English Humanist Books: Writers and
        Patrons, Manuscript and Print, 1475–1525.* Toronto,
        1993. [Really gets into gear with Henry VII.]

1479.   ———. "The Civic Poetry of Abbot John Whethamstede
        of St Albans (d. 1465)." *Mediaeval Studies* 61 (1999),
        205–42. [Classed as "mere doggerel"; Latin poetry, some
        "civil war poems"; a eulogy of Henry V published.]

1480.   Cattermole, Paul. "Schools in Medieval and Early Tudor
        Norwich." In *A History of Norwich School: King Edward
        VI's Grammar School at Norwich.* Edited by Richard
        Harries, Paul Cattermole, and Peter Mackintosh.
        Norwich, 1991. [An active civic tradition, not awaiting
        Edward VI and the Reformation.]

1481.   Catto, Jeremy. "Conclusion: Scholars and Studies in
        Renaissance Oxford." In item 24. Pp. 769–83. [Changing
        times: how, when, and why.]

1482.   Christianson, C. Paul. *A Directory of London Stationers
           and Book Artisans, 1300–1500*. Bibliographical Society of
           America, New York, 1990. [Introduction covers the
           London book trade, and then mostly a biographical
           register or dictionary.]

1482A.   Clark, James. "Monachi and Magistri: The Context and
           Culture of Learning at Late Medieval St. Albans." In
           item 45. Pp. 1–25. [Continues the rehabilitation of late
           medieval intellectual life: graduates, books, teaching,
           some "new learning."]

1483.   Cobban, Alan B. "Pembroke College: Its Educational Sig-
           nificance in Late Medieval Cambridge." *Cambridge
           Bibliographical Society* 10/1 (1991), 1–16. [Prominent
           men and early lectureships, with a lot of training in
           theology.]

1484.   ———. "Colleges and Halls, 1380–1500." In item 24.
           Pp. 581–633. [New College (1379) and other foundations;
           seven secular colleges in 1400.]

1485.   ———. "John Arundel, The Tutorial System, and the
           Cost of Undergraduate Living in the Medieval English
           Universities." *BJRUL* 77, 1 (1995), 143–59. [Arundel's
           accounts of the 1420s for Mildred Hall or Black Hall are
           our best glimpse into life under the tutorial system.]

1486.   ———. *English University Life in the Middle Ages*. Lon-
           don, 1999. [General treatment: undergraduates, gradu-
           ates, teaching, town-gown relations, university govern-
           ance, etc.]

1487.   Coleman, Joyce. *Public Reading and the Reading Public
           in Late Medieval England and France*. Cambridge, 1996.
           [A strong argument for the continuing importance of
           aural history, and against a simple or one-way transition
           from orality to literacy.]

1488.   Connolly, Margaret. *John Shirley: Book Production and the Noble Household in Fifteenth-Century England.* Aldershot, 1998. [Shirley's career as a scribe, with a look at his manuscripts.]

1489.   ———. "A London Widow's Psalter: Beatrice Cornburgh and Alexander Turnbull Library's Ms MSR-01 [Wellington, New Zealand.]" In *Sources, Exemplars, and Copy Texts: Influences and Transmissions.* Edited by William Marx. *Trivium* 31 (1999), 101–16.

1490.   Cox, A. D. M., transcriber; R. H. Darwell-Smith, ed. *Account Rolls of University College, Oxford: Vol. I: 1381/2–1470/1.* Oxford Historical Society, n.s. 39 (1999). [Accounts, by bursaries, for the college's estates, halls, etc.]

1491.   Cullum, P. H. *Cremets and Corrodies: Care of the Poor and Sick at St Leonard's Hospital, York.* Borthwick Papers, 79. University of York, 1991. [Mostly on an earlier period, but some fifteenth-century activity (including a new maisondieu).]

1492.   Cylkowski, David G. "A Middle English Treatise on Horticulture: *Godfridus Super Palladium.*" In item 60. Pp. 301–29. [An unusual text, clearly explicated.]

1493.   Davis, Virginia. "The Making of English Collegiate Statutes in the Later Middle Ages." *History of Universities* 12 (1993), 1–23. [Founders took this seriously: basic guidelines and with Gonville College as the main case study.]

1493A.   de Hamel, Christopher. "The Dispersal of the Library of Christ Church Canterbury, from the Fourteenth to the Sixteenth Century." In item 22. Pp. 263–79. [Begins with the founding of Canterbury College, Oxford, 1331, and runs to unreturned loans at the Reformation.]

1494.   Denley, Marie. "Elementary Teaching Techniques and
         Middle English Religious Didactic Writing." In item 75.
         Pp. 223–41. [Their base in preaching and teaching man-
         uals: questions and answers, rhymes, etc.]

1495.   Diekstra, F. N. M., ed. *Books for a Simple and Devout
         Woman: A Late Middle English Adaptation of Peraldus's
         Summa de Vitiis et Virtutibus and Friar Laurent's
         Somme le Roi, Edited from B.L. Ms. Harley 6571 and
         Addl. 309044*. Medievalia Groningana, 24 (1998).

1496.   Dobson, Richard Barrie. "The Educational Patronage of
         Archbishop Thomas Rotherham of York." *Northern* 31
         (1995), 65–85. [His background disposed him toward
         generosity; patron of Lincoln College as well as Jesus
         College (and Rotherham College).]

1497.   Doyle, A. I. "Book Production by the Monastic Orders in
         England (c. 1375–1530): Assessing the Evidence." In
         *Medieval Book Production: Assessing the Evidence: Pro-
         ceedings of the 2nd Conference—Seminar in the History
         of the Book to 1500, Oxford, July, 1988*. Edited by Linda
         L. Brownrigg. Los Altos Hills, Calif., 1990. Pp. 1–19.
         [The Carthusians score well; plates depict hands and
         page layouts. See also item 1543.]

1498.   ———. "Stephen Dodesham of Witham and Sheen." In
         *Of the Making of Books: Medieval Manuscripts, Their
         Scribes and Readers: Essays Presented to M. B. Parkes*.
         Edited by P. R. Robinson and Rivkah Zim. Aldershot,
         1997. Pp. 94–115. [Tracing a mid-fifteenth-century
         scribe, with twenty of his manuscripts. The volume has a
         Parkes bibliography, pp. 300–06. See also item 1550.]

1499.   Eberle, Patricia J. "Richard II and the Literary Arts." In
         item 43. Pp. 231–53. [Hard to assess the king's active
         patronage; a close look at some historical, legal, and
         chivalric manuscripts presented to him.]

1500. Edwards, A. S. G. "The Transmission and Audience of Osbern Bokenham's *Legendys of Hooly Wummen*." In item 66. Pp. 157–67. [Aristocratic patronage and prominent East Anglian families.]

1501. ———. "John Shirley and the Emulation of Courtly Culture." In *The Court and Culture and Diversity*. Edited by Evelyn Mullally and John Thompson. Woodbridge, 1997. [An active career: copyist, collector, translator, and some commercial motivation as well; see also item 1827.]

1502. ———. "Decorated Caxton." In *Incunabula: Studies in Fifteenth-Century Printed Books Presented to Lotte Hellinga*. Edited by Martin Davies. British Library, London, 1999. Pp. 483–506. [The addition of color and/or illuminations. There is a Hellinga bibliography, 1960–98, pp. 629–38; see also item 1580.]

1503. Edwards, A. S. G., and Carol M. Meale. "The Marketing of Printed Books in Late Medieval England." *The Library*, 6th series, 15/2 (1993), 95–124. [A complicated business, mostly unraveled by following De Worde's activities.]

1504. Eldredge, L. M., Karianne R. Schmidt, and M. A. Smith. "Four Medieval Manuscripts with Mathematical Games." *Medium Aevum* 68 (1999), 209–17. [Fifteenth-century treatises, printed so readers can go and play.]

1505. Erler, Mary C. "Pasted-in Embellishments in English Manuscripts and Printed Books, c. 1480–1533." *The Library*, 6th series, 14/3 (1992), 185–206. [Examples shown and described.]

1506. Evans, T. A. R. "The Number, Origin, and Careers of Scholars." In item 24. Pp. 485–538. [Historiographical controversies, the dominance of law, career opportunities, and men's social origins.]

1507.   Evans, T. A. R., and Rosamund J. Faith. "College Estates
         and University Finances." In item 24. Pp. 635–707.
         [Financial administration, quarrels over taxation, em-
         ployees, leasing, and strategies for improvement and
         more revenue.]

1508.   Fischer, Andreas. "'Sumer is icumen in': The Seasons of
         the Year in Middle English and Early Modern English."
         In item 1082. Pp. 79–95. [The many terms used to mark
         the divisions of the four-season year.]

1509.   Fisher, Celia. "A Study of the Plants and Flowers in the
         Wilton Diptych." In item 44. Pp. 155–63. [Symbolism
         and botany.]

1510.   Fletcher, J. M. "Developments in the Faculty of Arts,
         1370–1520." In item 24. Pp. 315–45. [A powerful faculty
         group: their set texts, bachelors' duties, and the
         emphasis on "linguistic logic."]

1511.   Fletcher, J. M., and Christopher A. Lipton, eds. *The
         Domestic Accounts of Merton College, Oxford, 1 August
         1482–1 August 1494*. Oxford Historical Society, n.s. 34
         (1996, for 1992–93). [With a long biographical index and
         glossary; verbatim transcription for the first full version
         of such accounts.]

1512.   Foot, M. M. "Bookbinding." In item 53. Pp. 109–27.
         [Where it was done, owner's commissions, and the craft
         and trade.]

1513.   Ford, Margaret Lane. "Importation of Printed Books into
         England and Scotland." In item 53. Pp. 179–201. [Picks
         up in 1470; the trail is warmest when it comes from
         Venice, Cologne, and Paris.]

1514.   ———. "Private Ownership of Printed Books." In item
         53. Pp. 205–228. [Universities, high clerics, fancy
         patrons, lesser folk; England and Scotland compared.]

1515.   Forde, Simon. "The Educational Organization of the
         Augustinian Canons in England and Wales and Their
         University Life at Oxford, 1325–1448." *History of Univer-
         sities* 13 (1994), 21–60. [Affluent houses sent men to the
         universities; some careers, scholarship, libraries, writers.]

1516.   Foster, Meryl R. "Durham Monks of Oxford, c. 1286–1381:
         A House of Studies and Its Inmates." *Oxon* 55 (1990),
         99–114. [An old and small house, refounded by Hatfield
         in 1381 as Durham College.]

1517.   Fowler, David C. *The Life and Times of John Trevisa,
         Medieval Scholar.* Seattle, Wash., 1995. [With much on
         late medieval Oxford.]

1518.   ———. *John Trevisa.* Aldershot, 1996. [A pamphlet in
         the Authors of the Middle Ages series, edited by C.
         Seymour. Covers biography, some documents, and a
         good bibliography.]

1519.   Fowler, David C., Charles Briggs, and Paul Remley, eds.
         *The Governance of Kings and Princes: John Trevisa's
         Middle English Translations of the "De Regimine
         Principum" of Aegidius Romanus.* London and New
         York, 1997. [Text and a few plates; little by way of
         introduction.]

1520.   Friedman, John B. "Cluster Analysis and the Manuscript
         Chronology of William du Staphel, a Fourteenth-
         Century Scribe at Durham." *History and Computing* 4
         (1992), 75–97. [Tracing his handwriting by means of a
         fine-tooth cluster analysis.]

1521.   ———. *Northern English Books: Owners and Makers in
         the Late Middle Ages.* Syracuse, N.Y., 1995. [Case
         studies in regional culture and patronage.]

1522.   Getz, Faye. "Medical Practitioners in Medieval England."
         Social History of Medicine 3 (1990), 245–83. [A supple-
         ment with corrections to Charles H. Talbot and E. A.

Hammond, *Medieval Practitioners: A Biographical Register* (1965).]

1523.   ———. *Healing and Society in Medieval England: A Middle English Translation of the Pharmaceutical Writings of Gilbertus Anglicus*. Wisconsin Publications in the History of Science and Medicine, 8 (1991). [Introduction on medical care as per this edition of Wellcome MS 537; later additions to the thirteenth-century text make this an independent contribution.]

1524.   ———. "To Prolong Life and Promote Health: Baconian Alchemy and Pharmacy in the English Learned Tradition." In *Health, Disease and Healing in Medieval Culture*. Edited by Sheila Campbell, Bert Hall, and David Klausner. London and New York, 1992. Pp. 141–51. [Looks at fifteenth-century interest in alchemy. See item 1638.]

1525.   ———. "The Faculty of Medicine before 1500." In item 24. Pp. 373–405. [A university discipline, like theology and law; how physicians fought for control of their field.]

1526.   ———. "Medical Education in Late Medieval England. In *The History of Medical Education in Britain*. Edited by V. Nutton and Roy Porter. Amsterdam, 1995. Pp. 76–93. [As taught at the universities, often to clerics who would double as doctors.]

1527.   Gardner, Elizabeth J. "The English Nobility and Monastic Education, c. 1100–1500." In item 14. Pp. 80–94. [Most of the records used are prior to 1377.]

1528.   Gilchrist, Roberta. "Christian Bodies and Souls: The Archaeology of Life and Death in Later Medieval Hospitals." In item 9. Pp. 101–18. [Linking the physical layout with duties and functions of the institution.]

1529.   Greatrex, Joan. "Monk Students from Norwich Cathedral
           Priory at Oxford and Cambridge, c. 1300 to 1530." *EHR*
           106 (1991), 555–83. [Statistics on careers and educa-
           tional activities after university days; biographical
           appendices cover some of the men.]

1530.   ———. "Rabbits and Eels at High Table: Monks of Ely at
           the University of Cambridge, c. 1337–1539." In item 93.
           Pp. 312–28. [About 10 percent of Ely monks went to
           university and then returned to hold office, with contri-
           butions more intellectual than administrative; appendix
           gives details for thirty-seven men.]

1531.   Green, Monica H. "Obstetrical and Gynecological Texts
           in Middle English." *Studies in the Age of Chaucer* 14
           (1992), 53–88. [Thirty manuscripts and eleven different
           treatises enlarging on the work of Rossell Hope Robbins
           and Beryl Rowland.]

1532.   Griffiths, Jeremy. "A Mid-Fifteenth-Century Book-List
           and Inventory from East Dereham, Norfolk, Ms Bought
           by Schøyen Collection, 1992." *Norfolk* 42/3 (1996),
           332–37. [Books, ecclesiastical paraphernalia, relics of
           Sts. Withburga and Nicholas.]

1533.   Hanna, Ralph, III. "Two Lollard Codices and Lollard
           Book-Production." *Studies in Bibliography* 43 (1990),
           49–62. [Codicological problems caused confusion when
           the texts were edited.]

1534.   ———. "Henry Daniel's *Liber Uricrisiarum*." In item 60.
           Pp. 185–218. [Daniel proclaimed his translation as a
           contribution to a discussion of health and healing.]

1535.   ———. "Some Norfolk Women and their Books, ca.
           1390–1440." In *The Cultural Patronage of Medieval
           Women*. Edited by June Hall McCash. Athens, Ga., 1996.
           Pp. 288–305. [With an overview of the topic, by McCash,
           pp. 1–49. Also see item 1541.]

1536.   Harper-Bill, Christopher, ed. *Charters of the Medieval Hospital of Bury St. Edmund*. Suffolk Record Society: Suffolk Charters, 14 (1994). [Four hospitals, with English calendars; most material prior to 1377.]

1537.   Hellinga, Lotte. "Importation of Books Printed on the Continent into England and Scotland before c. 1520. In *Printing the Written Word: The Social History of Books, circa 1450–1520*. Edited by Sandra Hindman. Ithaca, 1991. Pp. 205–24. [Based on an analysis of some large libraries and collections: Oxford, the Royal Library, etc.]

1538.   ———. "Printing." In item 53. Pp. 65–108. [Physical aspects of printing: supplies, business problems, how to illustrate, etc.]

1539.   Hughes, Jonathan. "Stephen Scrope and the Circle of Sir John Fastolf: Moral and Intellectual Outlook." See item 1201. Pp. 109–46. [The personalities of the men involved, the culture of Fastolf's circle, and Stephen's hard life and circumstances.]

1540.   Hutchison, Ann M. "What the Nuns Read: Literary Evidence from the English Bridgettine House, Syon Abbey." *Mediaeval Studies* 57 (1995), 205–22. [Identifying books they owned, and what links enable us to do this.]

1541.   Jambeck, Karen K. "Pattern of Women's Literary Patronage: England, 1200–ca. 1475." Pp. 228–65. [Wide ranging treatment and a list of dedications (pp. 246–48). See item 1535.]

1542.   Jensen, Kristian. "Text-books in the Universities: The Evidence from the Book." In item 53. Pp. 354–79. [Mostly looking at grammar, theology, and classical texts.]

1543.   Jones, Peter M. "British Library ms Sloane 76: A Translator's Holograph." See item 1497. Pp. 21–39. [Late medieval translation of John of Arderne and others, within a clouded textual tradition.]

1544. ———. "Information Science." In item 57. Pp. 97–111.
[Development and writing in the universities in an
"information age."]

1545. ———. "Thomas Fayreford: An English Fifteenth-
Century Practitioner." In *Medicine from the Black Death
to the French Disease*. Edited by Roger French, Jon
Arrizabalaga, Andrew Cunningham, and Luis García-
Ballester. Aldershot, 1998. Pp. 156–83. [An academic
west country general practitioner whose writings
touched colic, suffocation of the womb, the efficacy of
charms, and still more.]

1546. ———. "Medicine and Science." In item 53. Pp. 433–48.
[What was around before and after printing entered the
scene.]

1547. Jurkowski, Maureen. "Heresy and Factionalism at
Merton College in the Early 15th Century." *J Eccl H* 48
(1997), 658–81. [Merton's role and personnel in preserv-
ing Wycliffe's tradition, and its northern manors and
centers of dissent.]

1548. Keiser, George R. "Epilepsy: The Falling Evil." In item
60. Pp. 219–44. [Two manuscripts, with some suggested
remedies; excerpts from *Liber de Diversis Medicinis*.]

1549. Kibbee, Douglas A. *For to Speke Frenche Trewely: The
French Language in England, 1000–1600: Its Status,
Description and Instruction*. Amsterdam and Philadelphia, 1991. Pp. 58–93. [From the statute of 1362 to
the Age of Printing (1470).]

1550. Krochalis, Jeanne E. "History and Legend at Kirkstall in
the Fifteenth Century." See item 1498. Pp. 230–56.
[Adding five manuscripts to Ker's list, including the
abbey's chronicle.]

1551. Kuuskin, William. "Caxton's Worthies Series: The Production of Literary Culture." *ELH* 66 (1999), 511–51.

[The choices from and the reconstruction of historical material.]

1552.   Landman, James H. "'The Doom of Resoun': Accommodating Lay Interpretation in Late Medieval England." In item 51. Pp. 90–123. [Pecock and Fortescue on human reason and the role of law.]

1553.   Lawton, David. "Englishing the Bible, 1066–1549." In item 96. Pp. 454–482. [Wycliffe and the long discourse on setting the text and determining its accessibility.]

1554.   Leader, Damien R. "Cauis Auberinus: Cambridge's First Professor." In item 21. Pp. 322–27. ["Poet Laureate" and early classicist, tempore Edward IV.]

1555.   Leedham-Green, Elisabeth. "University Libraries and Book-Sellers." In item 53. Pp. 316–53. [College libraries, loan policies, size of trade and demand, and the entry of humanism and printing.]

1556.   Le Pard, Gordon. "Medieval Sundials in Dorset." *Dorset* 119 (1997), 65–86. [Many from the fourteenth and fifteenth centuries, and how they worked.]

1557.   Lovatt, Roger. "The Library of John Blacman and Contemporary Carthusian Spirituality." *J Eccl H* 43 (1992), 195–230. [Largest such library of devotional and mystical literature; a gift to the house at Witham.]

1558.   ———. "The Triumph of Colleges in Late Medieval Oxford and Cambridge: The Case of Peterhouse." *History of Universities* 14 (1995–96), 95–142. [Tale of internal feuds and checks, with case studies and Peterhouse as the prime example.]

1559.   Marshall, John. "'good in-to Bernysdale': The trail of the Paston Robin Hood Play." *Leeds* n.s. 29 (1998), 183–217. [The play and John Paston's ownership of the manuscript.]

1560.   Martin, Geoffrey H., and John Roger L. Highfield. *A History of Merton College, Oxford*. Oxford, 1997. [Chapters 1–6 run up to the Reformation, being Wycliffe's college was a mixed blessing, at best.]

1560A. Matheson, Lister M., and Ann Shannon. "A Treatise on the Elections of Times." In item 60. Pp. 23–59. [Go with the flow.]

1561.   Maxfield, David. "A Fifteenth-Century Lawsuit: The Case of St Anthony's Hospital, London." *J Eccl H* 44 (1993), 199–223. [The hospital as John Macclesfield's pet project.]

1562.   ———. "St Mary Rouncivale, Charing Cross: The Hospital of Chaucer's Pardoner." *Chaucer Review* 28/2 (1993), 148–63. [The irony of tying the Pardoner to a pilgrim hospital.]

1563.   ———. "St Anthony's Hospital, London: A Pardoner-Supported Alien Priory, 1219–1461." In item 37. Pp. 225–47. [Austin canonry, bestowed in 1389 on John Macclesfield, a secular priest—and the problems that ensued.]

1564.   McKendrick, Scot. "The *Romuléon* and the Manuscripts of Edward IV." In item 81. Pp. 149–69. [Tracing Edward's manuscripts and comparing them with some continental versions of the same texts.]

1565.   McKinley, Kathryn L. "Manuscripts of Ovid in England, 1100 to 1500." *English Manuscript Studies* 7 (1998), 41–85. [By place, date, and the known details, with institutional and individual owners (some being men of note).]

1566.   Meale, Carole M. "Caxton, de Worde, and the Publication of Romance in Late Medieval England." *The Library*, 6th series, 14/4 (1992), 283–98. [The course of such publishing after Caxton's death, and how de Worde reissued Caxton's works.]

1567.   ———. "'oft siþis with Grete deuotion I þought what I
         migt do pleysyng to god': The Early Ownership and
         Readership of Love's *Mirror*, with Special Reference to
         Its Female Audience." In *Nicholas Love at Waseda:
         Proceedings of a Conference, 20–22 July, 1995*. Edited by
         Shoichi Oguro, Richard Beadle, and Michael J. Sargent.
         Cambridge, 1997. Pp. 19–46. [Extremely popular work,
         manuscripts owned by men and women; had influence in
         the feminization of Christ. Also see item 1791.]

1568.   ———. "' . . . alle the bokes that I haue of latyn, englisch,
         and frensch': Laywomen and Their Books in Late Medi-
         eval England." In item 63. Pp. 128–58. [Ownership, collec-
         tions, bequests, and women's networks and family ties.]

1569.   Meale, Carole M., and Julia Boffey. "Gentlewomen's
         Reading." In item 53. Pp. 526–40. [Women of different
         ranks, and the reading of religious communities.]

1570.   Means, Laurel. "A Translation of Martin of Spain's *De
         Germancia*." In item 60. Pp. 61–121. [Good and evil
         figures, fighting it out.]

1571.   Meek, Edward L. "Printing and the English Parish
         Clergy in the Later Middle Ages." *Cambridge Biblio-
         graphic Society* 11/2 (1997), 112–26. [Ely and York wills
         show the turn to printed books, but with little distinc-
         tion in choice or taste.]

1572.   Michalove, Sharon D. "The Education of Aristocratic
         Women in Fifteenth-Century England." In item 64.
         Pp. 117–39. [A survey; women's opportunities and
         achievements.]

1573.   Middleton-Stewart, Judith. "The Provision of Books for
         Church use in the Deanery of Dunwich, 1370–1547."
         Suffolk 38/2 (1994), 148–63. [Survey of books in wills
         and inventories.]

1574. Minnis, Alastair J. "Looking for a Sign: The Quest for Nominalism in Chaucer and Langland." In item 67. Pp. 142–78. [Be cautious about finding philosophical doctrines and clarity in major (creative) writers.]

1575. Mitchell, Shelagh. "Richard II: Kingship and the Cult of Saints." In item 44. Pp. 115–24. [Richard's devotion to the three saints depicted, which argues that the work was his own commission.]

1576. Mooney, Linne R. "A Middle English Text on the Seven Liberal Arts." *Speculum* 68 (1993), 1027–52. [A Trinity College, Cambridge, manuscript; gramer, logik, retorik, arsmetrik, etc.]

1577. ———. "The Cock and the Clock: Telling Time in Chaucer's Day." *Studies in the Age of Chaucer* 15 (1993), 91–109. [Time keeping was a matter of great confusion, though clocks were beginning to play a role.]

1578. ———. "Diet and Bloodletting: A Monthly Regimen." In item 60. Pp. 245–61. [Difficult manuscript with a difficult schedule of good and bad days for this exciting activity.]

1579. ———, ed. *The Kalendarium of John Somer*. For The Chaucer Library, Athens, Ga., 1998. [Also see item 1206.]

1580. Needham, Paul. "Continental Printed Books Sold in Oxford, c. 1480–3: Two Trade Records." See item 1502. Pp. 243–70. [Two early lists and inventories: eighty-nine books covered in the two inventories.]

1581. Nissé, Ruth. "'Oure Fadres Olde and Modres': Gender, Heresy, and Hoccleve's Literary Politics." *Studies in the Age of Chaucer* 21 (1999), 275–99. [Enemies, including Lollards, were feminized, and they threatened to feminize others.]

1582. Norri, Juhani. *Names of Sicknesses in English, 1440–1550: An Explication of the Lexical Fields*. Dissertationes

Humanorum Litterarum, 63. Helsinki, 1992. [An odd mix of linguistic analysis and medical history; diagnosis depends on identification.]

1583.   ———. *Names of Body Parts in English, 1400–1550.* Annales Academiae Scientiarum Fenicae, Humaniora, 291: Helsinki, 1998. [Reviewed by M. T. Tavormina, *Speculum* (July 2001), 772–74.]

1584.   North, John D. "Natural Philosophy in Late Medieval Oxford." In item 24. Pp. 65–102. [Math, optics, physics and motion, prime matter, and kinematics.]

1585.   ———. "Astronomy and Mathematics." In item 24. Pp. 103–75. [The great names: Scotus, Bradwardine, plus astrology, the calendar, some algebra and explorations of infinity.]

1586.   O'Mara, V. M. "Female Scribal Ability and Scribal Activity in Late Medieval England: The Evidence." *Leeds* n.s. 27 (1996), 87–130. [A strong and important case against women doing much actual writing, even when it was in their name.]

1587.   Orme, Nicholas. "Two Early Prayer Books from North Devon." *D&C NQ* 36 (1992), 345–50. [Fifteenth-century volumes; later owners made notes that explicate their piety.]

1588.   ———. "Children and the Church in Medieval England." *J Eccl H* 45 (1994), 563–87. [Methods of education; introducing children to the world of literacy-based Christianity.]

1589.   ———. "John Holt (d. 1504), Tudor Schoolmaster and Grammarian." *The Library*, 6th series, 18/4 (1996), 283–305. [His career and his grammar text (*Lac Puerorum*); some of its diagrams reproduced.]

1590.   ———. "Schools and School-Books." In item 53.
Pp. 449–69. [What schools were likely to own, both
before and after the advent of printing.]

1591.   ———. *Education in Early Tudor England: Magdalen
College, Oxford, and Its School, 1480–1540*. Magdalen
College Occasional Papers, 4. Oxford, 1998.

1592.   Orme, Nicholas, and Margaret Webster. *The English
Hospitals, 1070–1570*. New Haven and London, 1995.
[Lavish illustrations in a general survey, with a close
look at Devon and Cornwall and with more focus on
institutions than on medical history.]

1593.   Parkes, Malcolm B. "The Provision of Books." In item 24.
Pp. 407–83. [Inventories and material on scribes, book
sellers, mendicant libraries, donors, and Duke
Humphrey.]

1594.   Pearsall, Derek. *John Lydgate (1371–1449): A Bio-
Biography*. Victoria, B.C., 1997. [A survey of manuscripts
and basic background and biography.]

1595.   ———. "Language and Literature." In item 84.
Pp. 245–76. [The development of Middle English and of
vernacular literature.]

1596.   Pereira, Michela. "*Mater Medicinarum*: English Physicians and the Alchemical Elixir in the Fifteenth
Century." See item 1543. Pp. 26–52. [Despite a royal
ban, considerable interest in alchemy and the "pseudo-
Lullian *Testamentum*."]

1597.   Pickett, Joseph P. "A Translation of the 'Canutus' Plague
Treaties." In item 60. Pp. 263–82. [French treatise, pre-
1384, taken from Sloane Ms. 404.]

1598.   Powell, Susan. "Lady Margaret Beaufort and her Books."
The Library, 6th series, 20/3 (1998), 197–240. [Her
library, book bequests, reading habits, and patronage.]

1599.   Ramsey, Nigel. "The Cathedral Archives and Library."
         In item 27. Pp. 341–407. [The later Middle Ages,
         c. 1340–1540 are covered, pp. 362–73.]

1600.   Rawcliffe, Carole, selected, introduced, and translated.
         *Sources for the History of Medicine in Late Medieval
         England.* TEAMS Documents of Practice series.
         Kalamazoo, Mich., 1995. [A source book of documents
         with introduction, succinctly covering a broad field and
         intended for classroom use; see also item 905.]

1601.   ———. *The Hospitals of Medieval Norwich.* University of
         East Anglia: Studies in East Anglian History, 2, Norwich,
         1995. [A survey of numerous institutions, with maps,
         plates, and tables on size and foundation (and photos by
         the author).

1602.   ———. *Medicine and Society in Later Medieval England.*
         Stroud, 1995. [A well illustrated survey of medical his-
         tory and its institutions.]

1603.   [No entry.]

1604.   ———. "Hospital Nurses and Their Work." In item 18.
         Pp. 43–64. [Sin and punishment and the role of the good
         ladies.]

1605.   ———. *Medicine for the Soul: The Life, Death and Resur-
         rection of an English Hospital: St Giles, Norwich, c.
         1249–1550.* Stroud, 1999. [Happy 750th birthday for St
         Giles: major study of a major East Anglian institution.]

1606.   Richmond, Colin F. "A Letter of 19 April 1483 from John
         Gigur to William Wainfleet." *HR* 65 (1992), 112–16.
         [Concerning the endowment of Magdalen.]

1607.   Riddy, Felicity. "'Women talking about things of God': A
         Late Medieval Sub-Culture." In item 63. Pp. 104–27.
         [Women as readers, book owners, and participants in a
         feminist discourse.]

1608.   Riggs, A. G. "Anglo-Latin in the Ricardian Age." In item
        67. Pp. 121–41. [With political events as the main area
        of focus.]

1609.   Robertson, Elizabeth. "Medieval Medical Views of Women
        and Female Spirituality in the *Ancrene Wisse* and Julian
        of Norwich's *Showings*." See item 1278. Pp. 142–67.
        [How medical ideology shaped literary presentation—
        surmounted by Julian by feminizing Jesus.]

1610.   Rothwell, W. "The Trilingual England of Geoffrey
        Chaucer." *Studies in the Age of Chaucer* 16 (1994),
        45–67. [Especially revealing at the seams: new words,
        mixed words and language, composite phrases.]

1611.   Rundle, David. "On the Difference between Virtue and
        Weiss: Humanist Texts in England during the Fifteenth
        Century." In item 33. Pp. 181–203. [Humanist activity
        earlier than we once thought.]

1612.   ———. "Two Unnoticed Manuscripts from the Collection
        of Humfrey, Duke of Gloucester: Part I." *Bodleian
        Library Record* 16 (1997–99), 211–24; "Part II" Ibid.,
        299–313. [The first is a humanist debate, the second a
        manuscript of Seneca.]

1613.   Scase, Wendy. "Reginald Pecock, John Carpenter, and
        John Colop's 'Common-Profit' Books: Aspects of Book
        Ownership and Circulation in Fifteenth-Century
        London." *Medium Aevum* 61 (1992), 261–74. [Common
        profit books and post mortem charity: Pecock and
        Carpenter both advocated easier access to books.]

1613A. Shinner, John. "Parish Libraries in Medieval England."
        In item 21. Pp. 207–30. [Donors and books.]

1614.   Sims, Tony. "Aspects of Heraldry and Patronage." In
        item 6. Pp. 451–66.

1615.   Stell, Philip M. *Medical Practice in Medieval York.*
         Borthwick Papers, 90. University of York, 1996. [A
         pamphlet, covering practitioners (1100–1500), disease,
         personnel, and methods of treatment.]

1616.   ———. "The Apothecaries of Medieval York." *York
         Historian* 14 (1997), 26–31. [Some of the men, a little on
         their work.]

1617.   Stocker, Margarita. "Apocryphal Entries: Judith and the
         Politics of Caxton's *Golden Legend.*" In item 90. Pp. 167–
         81. [Did Caxton have a political agenda? The political
         nuances of the Judith tale.]

1618.   Storey, Robin L. "University and Government, 1430–
         1500." In item 24. Pp. 709–746. [The chancellors and
         links with central government figures; problems posed
         by great patrons such as George Neville.]

1619.   Stouck, Mary-Ann. "A Poet in the Household of the
         Beauchamp Earls of Warwick, c. 1393–1427." *Warwick-
         shire* 9/3 (1994), 113–17. [William Parys, author and
         translator of a life of St Christina, as he also got into
         quarrels and legal problems.]

1620.   Stratford, Jenny. "The Royal Library in England before
         the Reign of Edward IV." In item 81. Pp. 187–97. [Prior
         acquisitions and the loss of many identifiable items.]

1621.   ———. "The Early Royal Collections and the Royal
         Library to 1461." In item 53. Pp. 255–66. [Back to the
         fourteenth century and the role of the House of
         Lancaster.]

1622.   Summerson, Henry. "An English Bible and Other Books
         Belonging to Henry IV." *BJRUL* 79/1 (1997), 109–15. [A
         volume recovered in 1419, plus general comments on
         Henry's learning, piety, and books.]

1623.   Summit, Jennifer. "William Caxton, Margaret Beaufort
          and the Romance of Female Patronage." In item 90.
          Pp. 151–65. [Caxton's prologues and his search for
          women to back him.]

1624.   Sutton, Anne F., and Livia Visser-Fuchs. "Richard III's
          Books." *Ricardian* 8/108 (March 1990), 351–62; 8/109
          (June 1990), 403–13; 8/111 (December 1990), 494–514,
          with Lynda Dennison on the Illuminations of Royal 20 c
          vii; 9/112 (March 1991), 23–37; 9/114 (September 1991),
          110–29; 9/115 (December 1991), 154–65; 9/116 (March
          1992), 190–205; 9/118 (September 1982), 303–10, on
          "Mistaken Attribution"; 9/119 (December 1992), 343–58;
          9/129 (March 1993), 374–88; 10/132 (March 1996),
          346–86. [The whole study is brought together in item
          1626. By only covering the 1990s this lists pick up with
          the eighth Ricardian paper.]

1625.   ———. "Choosing a Book in Late Fifteenth-Century
          England and Burgundy." In item 8. Pp. 61–98. [Libraries,
          the book trade, Caxton's choice of texts, and English and
          Burgundian taste and sophistication; appendix on
          Edward IV's books.]

1626.   ———. *Richard III's Books: Ideas and Reality in the Life
          and Library of a Medieval Prince.* Stroud, 1997. [A
          thorough treatment (based on many papers in *The
          Ricardian*, as in item 1624 and earlier articles): books by
          type and category, with a catalogue and discussion of
          many individual items.]

1627.   Taavitsainen, Irma. "A Zodiacal Lunary for Medical
          Professionals." In item 60. Pp. 283–300. [From the Guild
          Book of the Barber Surgeons of York, Egerton 2572.]

1628.   Tarvers, Josephine K. "'Thys ys my mystrys boks':
          English Women as Readers and Writers in Late
          Medieval England." In *The Uses of Manuscripts in*

*Literary Studies: Essays in Memory of Judson Boyce
Allen.* Edited by Charlotte C. Morse, Penelope R. Doob,
and Marjorie C. Ward. Studies in Medieval Culture 31.
Kalamazoo, Mich., 1992. Pp. 305–27.

1629.   Taylor, Andrew. "Anne of Bohemia and the Making of
Chaucer." *Studies in the Age of Chaucer* 19 (1997),
95–119. [Assessing Anne's role as a patron and her role
in court culture.]

1630.   Theilmann, John M. "The Regulation of Public Health in
Late Medieval England." In item 37. Pp. 205–23. [Role of
medical professionals and other groups who were involved.]

1631.   Trapp, Joseph B. "Literacy, Books and Readers." In item
53. Pp. 31–43. [A survey; literacy in various languages.]

1632.   ———. "The Humanist Book." In item 53. Pp. 285–315.
[A survey of early humanism and humanists; Duke
Humphrey and pertinent books at Oxford and
Cambridge.]

1633.   Vickerstaff, J. J. "Profession and Preferment amongst
Durham County Schoolmasters, 1400–1550." *History of
Education* 19 (1990), 173–83. [The pull of a teaching
career: preferment, some careers, fees, geographical
origins of the teachers.]

1634.   Visser-Fuchs, Livia. "Edward IV's Only Romance?
Cambridge CCC MS 91, *L'Histoire des Seigneurs de
Gavre.*" *Ricardian* 11/141 (June 1998), 278–87. [Maybe it
belonged to Edward IV.]

1635.   Voigts, Linda E. "The 'Sloane Group': Related Scientific
and Medical Manuscripts from the Fifteenth Century in
the Sloane Collection." *British Library Journal* 16
(1990), 26–57. [Associated with a mysterious John
Kirkeby and an English workshop of the 1450s: plates
and a full description of each manuscript.]

1636.   ———. "The Golden Table of Pythagoras." In item 60.
          Pp. 123–39. [Spheres, numbers, and prognostication.]

1637.   ———. "What's the Word? Bilingualism in Late-Medieval
          England." *Speculum* 71 (1996), 813–26. [Examples (and
          manuscripts) of cultural-linguistic transition.]

1638.   Voigts, Linda E., and Robert P. Hudson. "'A drynke þat
          men callen dwale to make a man to slepe whyle men
          kerven him': A Surgical Anesthetic from Late Medieval
          England." See item 1524. Pp. 34–56. [The early search
          for an anaesthetic.]

1639.   Warner, Lyndan. "Fellows, Students, and Their Gifts to
          Jesus College Library, 1496–1610." *Cambridge Biblio-
          graphical Society* 11/1 (1996), 1–48. [Only one detailed
          bequest (and of but eleven books) before 1506.]

1640.   Webber, Teresa. "Latin Devotional Texts and the Books
          of the Augustinian Canons of Thurgarten Priory and
          Leicester Abbey in the Late Middle Ages." In item 22.
          Pp. 27–41. [Hilton's house; a fifteenth-century list of
          books; catalogue shows nine hundred items, mostly
          devotional.]

1641.   Wenzel, Siegfried. "Academic Sermons at Oxford in the
          Early Fifteenth Century." *Speculum* 70 (1995), 305–21.
          [To introduce students to the *Sentences*: sermon in a
          Worcester Cathedral manuscript printed.]

1642.   Woods, Marjorie C. "Shared Books: Primers, Psalters,
          and the Adult Acquisition of Literacy among Devout
          Laywomen and Women in Orders in Late Medieval
          England." In *New Trends in Feminine Spirituality: The
          Holy Women of Liège and Their Impact*. Edited by
          Juliette Dor, Lesley Johnson, and Jocelyn Wogan-Brown.
          Medieval Women: Texts and Contexts, 2. Turnhout,
          1999. Pp. 177–93. [Women's limited access to some basic
          books, and efforts to surmount the obstacles.]

1643.   Wray, Alison. "The Sound of Latin in England before and after the Reformation." See item 1662. Pp. 74–89. [We cannot be sure of the right answer to this question.]

1644.   Wright, Laura. *Sources of London English: Medieval Thames Vocabulary*. Oxford, 1996. [Reconstructing London English, 1270–1500, with an eye on the vocabulary for tools and the London trades.]

XI. The Fine Arts: Painting and Illumination, Sculpture, Architecture and Building, Music

1645. Alexander, Jonathan J. G. "The Pulpit with the Four Doctors at St James's, Castle Acre, Norfolk." In item 81. Pp. 198–206. [Augustine, Jerome, Gregory, and Ambrose; an unusual mix.]

1646. ———. "The Portrait of Richard II in Westminster Abbey." In item 44. Pp. 196–206. [Probably done late in the king's life; compared to his depiction on the great seal.]

1647. ———. "Foreign Illuminators and Illuminated Manuscripts." In item 53. Pp. 47–64. [The general currents of cultural movement, trade, and patronage, and a close look at some manuscripts.]

1648. Arnold, Janet. "The Jupon or Coat-Armour of the Black Prince in Canterbury Cathedral." *Church Monuments* 8 (1993), 12–24. [A close examination of the cloth.]

1649. Ashley, Steven, and Andrew Rogerson. "A Norfolk Hundred Seal Matrix Recently Found in Kent." *Norfolk* 43/1 (1998), 180–81. [From the Hundred of South Greenhoe, after 1388; used to enforce the Statute of Labourers.]

1650. Ayers, Brian S., and Robert Smith, with a documentary report by Paul Rutledge and a report of 1976 excavations by David Bullock. "Twelfth and Fifteenth-Century

Undercrofts at Howard Street, Great Yarmouth." *Norfolk* 41/3 (1992), 338–55. [Vaults under a nineteenth-century terrace; a major medieval structure, hitherto unknown.]

1651.   Backhouse, Janet. *The Bedford Hours.* British Library, London, 1990. [A souvenir of Bedford's marriage of 1423: BL Add Ms 18850, with thirty colored plates.]

1652.   ———. *The Sherborne Missal.* London, 1999. [Elegant short book on an elegant manuscript.]

1653.   Bertram, Jerome. "The tomb beneath the Loft." *Oxon* 63 (1998), 79–89. [In Christ Church Cathedral, c. 1462, built for Sir Robert and Katherine Daners.]

1654.   Bicknell, Stephen. *The History of the English Organ.* Cambridge, 1996. [Chapter I, pp. 11–25, covers early times; c. 900–1500.]

1655.   Binski, Paul. "The *Liber Regalis*: Its Date and European Context." In item 44. Pp. 232–46. [Probably from the 1390s, and possible signs of Bohemian influence.]

1656.   ———. "Hierarchies and Orders in English Royal Images of Power." In item 29. Pp. 74–93, 182–84. [Mostly earlier, but some discussion of Richard II's portrait.]

1657.   Blockley, Kevin, Margaret Sparks, and Tim Tatton-Brown. *The Archaeology of Canterbury: n.s. Vol. I: Canterbury Cathedral Nave: Archaeology, History, and Architecture.* Canterbury, 1997. [Pp. 35–37, 124–26, cover the late fourteenth and most of the fifteenth century.]

1658.   Bott, A. J., and J. R. L. Highfield. "The Sculpture over the Gatehouse at Merton College, Oxford, 1464–65." *Oxon* 58 (1993), 233–40. [Sculpture and bosses; a closer look than from the ground.]

1659.   Bowers, Roger. "The Musicians of the Lady Chapel of Winchester Cathedral Priory, 1402–1532." *J Eccl H* 45

(1994), 210–37. [For the Lady Mass, based on B.L. Add Ms 57950.]

1660. ————. "The Liturgy of the Cathedral and Its Music, c. 1075–1642." In item 27. Pp. 408–50. [Especially pp. 418–26: "The Cultivation of Auxiliary Repertories, c. 1350–1540."]

1661. ————. "Music and Worship to 1640." In item 71. Pp. 47–76. [Especially pp. 54–72; with a table of organists and masters of choristers.]

1662. ————. "To Chorus from Quartet: The Performing Resources for English Church Polyphony, ca. 1390–1559." In *English Choral Practice, 1400–1650.* Edited by John Morehen. Cambridge, 1996. Pp. 1–47. [Also see item 1643.]

1663. Bradham, Sally F. "London Standardisation and Provincial Idiosyncracy: The Organisation and Working Practices of Brass-Engraving Workshops in Pre-Reformation England." *Church Monuments* 5 (1990), 3–25. [Styles compared, as the title indicates.]

1664. Brighton, Trevor, and Brian Speakes. "Medieval and Georgian Stained Glass in Oxford and Yorkshire: The Work of Thomas of Oxford (1385–1427) and William Peckitt of York (1731–95) in New College Chapel, York Minster, and St James, High Melton." *Antiq J* 70 (1990), 380–415. [Peckitt restored and rearranged Thomas's glass, which had been disbursed.]

1665. Burkett, M. E. "Cumbrian Wall Paintings." *Cumberland* 99 (1999), 159–76. [From the prior's room, Carlisle Cathedral, and six other churches.]

1666. Caldwell, John. *The Oxford History of English Music.* 2 vols. Oxford, 1991. [Volume 1 is from the beginning to 1715; chapters 3 and 4 cover Lancastrian and Yorkist England, pp. 108–266.]

1667.   Campbell, Marian. "'White Harts and Coronets': The
        Jewellery and Plate of Richard II." In item 44. Pp. 94–114.
        [Its general style, what it cost, and how much has been
        preserved.]

1668.   Carlson, David R. "Thomas Hoccleve and the Chaucer
        Portrait." *Huntington Library Quarterly* 54 (1991),
        283–300. [Hoccleve's desire to be linked to Chaucer,
        though we should be wary about the Ellesmere portrait.]

1669.   Chainey, Graham. "The Lost Stained Glass of Cam-
        bridge." *CAS* 79 (1990), 70–81. [A survey of records of
        destruction, mostly from the Civil War: "we broke and
        pulled down 80 superstitious pictures."]

1670.   Cherry, John. *The Middleham Jewel and Ring.* York-
        shire Museum, York, 1994. [A major and expensive
        trinket of fifteenth-century England.]

1670A. Coldstream, Nicola. "The Visual Arts." In item 84.
        Pp. 207–44.

1671.   Coombs, Christopher. "Walter Hilton and Nicholas Hall,
        'Alabastermen' from Nottingham." East Midland *His-
        torian* 7 (1997), 25–28. [Alabaster carving not usually
        considered a major local industry; records of these men
        not supported by known architectural remains.]

1672.   [No entry.]

1673.   Coulson, Charles. "Some Analysis of the Castle of
        Bodiam, East Sussex." See item 1201. Pp. 51–107. [What
        Dallingridge learned in France and from contemporary
        English examples; many illustrations.]

1674.   Courtenay, Lynn J. "The Westminster Hall Roof: A New
        Architectural Source." *JBAA* 143 (1990), 95–111. [Work
        of the 1390s; drawings made in 1913–22 reveal coopera-
        tion between the medieval masons and carpenters.]

1675.   Crossan, C., and P. Christie, with contributions by D. D.
         Andrews, D. F. Steening, H. Major, and H. Walker. "A
         Detached Kitchen at Great Yeldham: Excavation and
         Building Study at Old Post Office Cottage, 1988–89."
         Essex 26 (1995), 174–91. [A three-bay kitchen, c. 1500.]

1676.   Deighton, Alan. "The Literary Context of the Wall Paint-
         ing at Idsworth, Hampshire." *Antiq J* 73 (1993), 69–75.
         [A "hairy anchorite" of the late fourteenth century de-
         picted; perhaps St John of Beverley.]

1677.   Dixon, Philip, and Beryl Lott. "The Courtyard and the
         Tower: Content and Symbols in the Development of Late
         Medieval Great Houses." *JBAA* 146 (1993), 93–101. [Not
         so much the decline of the castle, but new developments
         in the free standing aristocratic mansion.]

1678.   Downing, Mark. "Lions of the Middle Ages: A Prelimi-
         nary Survey of Lions of Medieval Military Effigies."
         Church Monuments 13 (1998), 17–34. [Still a popular
         motif in the fifteenth century, though most were earlier.]

1679.   Düll, Siegred, Anthony Luttrell, and Maurice Keen.
         "Faithful unto Death: The Tomb-Slab of Sir William
         Neville and Sir John Clanvowe, Constantinople, 1391."
         Antiq J 71 (1991), 174–90. [Düll on the tomb slab,
         Luttrell on the men, Keen on their coats of arms; English-
         men who wandered far from home and then died.]

1680.   Easton, Timothy, and Stephen Bicknell. "Two Pre-
         Reformation Organ Soundboards: Towards an Under-
         standing of the Form of Early Organs and Their Position
         within some Suffolk Churches." *Suffolk* 38/3 (1995), 268–
         95. [One at Westeringsett, the other at Walberswick.]

1681.   Edwards, John. "New Light on Christ of the Trades and
         Other Medieval Wall-Paintings at St Mary's, Purton."
         Wiltshire 83 (1990), 105–17. [Probably late fourteenth
         century; an odd scene, perhaps showing the consecration
         of labor.]

1682. ———. "Some Lost Medieval Wall-Paintings." *Oxon* 55
       (1990), 81–98. [Some fourteenth- and fifteenth-century
       material as some fraction of what we know to have been
       lost.]

1683. Emery, Anthony. *Greater Medieval Houses of England
       and Wales, 1300–1500: I. Northern England.* Cambridge,
       1996. [The first of three projected volumes: house by
       house: architecture, chronology, later changes, covering
       Lancashire, Yorkshire, and the Lake District.]

1684. Emmerson, Robin. "Design for Mass Production: Monu-
       mental Brasses made in London, c. 1420–85." In *Artistes,
       Artisans et Production artistique au Moyen Âge.* Edited
       by Xavier Barral Altet. Paris, 1990. Pp. 133–71.

1685. Evans, Jean-Marc. "A Unique Cantus Firmus Usage in a
       15th-Century English Mass Movement." *Early Music*
       26/3 (1998), 469–77. [An anonymous credo.]

1686. Falvey, Heather. "The More: Archbishop George Neville's
       Palace in Ricksmanworth, Hertfordshire." *Ricardian*
       9/118 (September 1992), 290–302. [The king seized it;
       also its subsequent history.]

1687. Farmer, David L. "Millstones from Medieval Manors."
       AgHR 40 (1992), 97–111. [Where they came from, the
       cost of good French and cheaper domestic varieties;
       appendix of places where purchased.]

1688. Fawcett, Richard. "The Influence of the Gothic Parts of
       the Cathedral on Church Building in Norfolk. In item 6.
       Pp. 210–27. [The Cathedral's seminal role as *the* local
       model.]

1689. ———. "The Master Masons of Later Medieval Norfolk."
       In *A Festival of Norfolk Archaeology.* Edited by Sue
       Margeson, Brian Ayers, and Stephen Heywood. Norwich
       and Norfolk Archaeological Society, Norwich, 1996.

Pp. 101–26. [Styles as they became diffused from major buildings to set the style for regional taste and building.]

1690. Fernie, Eric. *An Architectural History of Norwich Cathedral*. Oxford, 1993. [A close look at separate features and characteristics of the great building.]

1691. Foot, Mirjam M. "A Binding by the Scales Binder, circa 1456–65." *British Library Journal* 16 (1990), 103–07. [An original binding—depicted back and front—binding a book of assizes.]

1692. Ford, Judy Ann. "Art and Identity in the Parish Communities of Late Medieval Kent." In *The Church and the Arts*. Edited by Diana Wood. See item 1425. Pp. 225–37. [Patronage, mostly as tracked through wills.]

1693. French, Thomas W. "The Dating of York Minster Choir." *YAJ* 64 (1992), 123–33. [Probably 1393–1413, taking heraldry, building accounts, and secular events into consideration.]

1694. ———. *York Minster: The Great East Window*. Corpus Vitrearum Medii Aevi series: Great Britain, Summary Catalogue, 2 (1995). Oxford and New York. [Detailed coverage of 1680 square feet of glass.]

1695. ———. *York Minster: The St William Window*. British Academy and Oxford University Press, 1999, for the Corpus Vitrearum Medii Aevi series. [A lavish study and a proposed scheme for arrangement and interpretation; see also item 1763.]

1696. Gaimster, David R. M., and Beverley Nenk. "A Late Medieval Hispano-Moresque Vase from the City of London." *Med Arch* 35 (1991), 118–21. [From around 1480; an import found near Cannon Street.]

1697. Geddes, Jane. "The Medieval Decorative Ironwork." In item 6. Pp. 431–42. [Hinges and ornaments, a large chest, and a mechanical clock; some of the work from local workshops.]

1698.   ———. "The End of the Middle Ages." In *Medieval Decorative Ironwork in England*. Society of Antiquaries, London, 1999. Pp. 271–76. [Doors and chest fittings, tomb railings, grills, and other decorative work; a catalogue of the sites, pp. 297–392.]

1699.   Gill, Miriam. "A Saint with a Scythe: A Previously Unidentified Wall Painting in the Church of St Andrew, Cavenham." *Suffolk* 38/3 (1995), 245–54. [Uncovered in 1967; probably St Walstan, painted c. 1465–85.]

1700.   ———. "'Kenelm Cunebearn . . . Haudes Bereafed': A Reconstructed Cycle of Wall Paintings from St Kenelm's Chapel, Ramsley." *JBAA* 149 (1996), 23–36. [Late fourteenth-century depiction of a local cult not revealed by literary records.]

1701.   Goodall, John A. "Heraldry in the Decoration of English Medieval Manuscripts." *Antiq J* 77 (1997), 179–220. [Mostly looking at psalters and books of hours, with some interest in cartularies.]

1702.   Gordon, Dillian. *Making and Meaning: The Wilton Diptych*. London, National Gallery, 1993. [Item 190, pp. 13–19, "Image and Reality," plus contributions by Ashok Roy, Martin Wyld, and Gordon on technique (pp. 74–81) and Wyld on "recent treatment" (pp. 86–87). This book whets the appetite for the feast found in item 44.]

1703.   ———. "The Wilton Diptych: An Introduction." In item 44. Pp. 19–26. [A survey of historiography, major themes, and scholarly problems.]

1704.   Grössinger, Christa. "The Unicorn on English Misericords." In *Medieval Art: Recent Perspectives: A Memorial Tribute to C. R. Dodwell*. Edited by Gale R. Owen-Crocker

and Timothy Graham. Manchester, 1998. Pp. 142–58.
[The enduring fascination of this particular fantasy.]

1705.   Grundy, Thirlie. "The Misericords of Carlisle Cathedral:
        Their Carver and His Psyche, ca. 1400." *Cumberland* 94
        (1994), 91–103. [Two men—perhaps master and appren-
        tice, at the turn of the fifteenth century; a list of miseri-
        cords but no indication of local themes or allusions.]

1706.   Gwynne, Paul. "The Frontispiece of an Illuminated
        Panegyric of Henry VII: A Note on the Sources." *JWCI*
        55 (1992), 266–70. [First English monarch depicted
        riding in a triumphal procession; in a York Minster
        manuscript.]

1707.   Hamburger, Jeffrey. "The Casanatense and the Carmelite
        Missals: Continental Sources for English Ms. Illumina-
        tion of the Early 15th Century." In *Masters and
        Miniatures: Proceedings of the Congress on Medieval
        Manuscript Illumination in the Northern Netherlands.*
        Edited by Koert van der Horst and Johann Christian
        Klant. Doornspijk, 1991. Pp. 161–73.

1708.   Harf-Lancner, Laurence. "Image and Property: The
        Illustrations in Book 1 of Froissart's *Chroniques.*" In
        Froissart across the Genres. Edited by Donald Maddox
        and Sara Sturm-Maddox. Gainesville, Fla., 1998.
        Pp. 220–50. [How illustrations mesh with Froissart's
        biases and his audience's reception and interpretation;
        see also item 1080.]

1709.   Harris, Jonathan. "Two Byzantine Craftsmen in Fif-
        teenth-Century London." *JMH* 21 (1995), 387–403.
        [Experts in drawing gold thread; they may have brought
        the technique with them, 1441–85.]

1710.   Harrison, Frank Ll. "Plainsong into Polyphony: Reper-
        tories and Structure *circa* 1270–*circa* 1420." In *Music in
        the Medieval English Liturgy: Plainsong and Mediaeval*

Music Society Centennial Essays. Edited by Susan
Rankin and David Hiley. Oxford, 1993. Pp. 303–53. [Also
see item 1727.]

1711.   ———. "Music at Oxford before 1500." In item 24.
Pp. 347–71. [Music as a liberal art, with theories of
Boethius and Roger Bacon; an appendix of music degrees
granted before 1535.]

1712.   Harvey, Anthony, and Richard Mortimer. *The Funeral
Effigies of Westminster Abbey.* London, 1994. [Intro-
duction by Harvey; "The Funeral Effigy: Its Function
and Purpose" by Julian Liften (pp. 3–19); "The History of
the Collection" by Mortimer (pp. 21–28); looking at the
effigies of Anne of Bohemia, pp. 37–39; Katherine of
Valois, pp. 41–43; and Elizabeth of York, pp. 44–49.]

1713.   Harvey, John H. "Architecture in Oxford, 1350–1500." In
item 24. Pp. 747–68.

1714.   Hebgin-Barnes, Penny. "A Triumphant Image: Henry
Scrope's Window in Heydour Church." *Medieval Life* 4
(190), 26–28. [Regional pride and family patronage from
a major northern clan.]

1715.   ———. *The Medieval Stained Glass of the County of
Lincolnshire.* Corpus Vitrearum, Summary Catalogue 3.
London, 1996. [By sites, alphabetically; parish churches
but not the cathedral; black and white illustrations.]

1716.   Henry, Avril. "Lichfield Cathedral Ms. 16: Its Illuminated Borders and Original Order." *Scriptorium* 48
(1994), 39–61. [A religious and didactic miscellany, with
the "Prick of Conscience" and other texts.]

1717.   Hepburn, Frederick. "The Portraiture of Lady Margaret
Beaufort." *Antiq J* 72 (1992), 118–40. [Oft-portrayed, on
her tomb and elsewhere, though all seven portraits are
posthumous.]

1718.   ————. "The Portraiture of Arthur, Prince of Wales." *JBAA* 148 (1995), 148–68. [One from his lifetime, though not realistic, all others later; appendix of representations supposedly of Arthur.]

1719.   Heslop, David, and Barbara Harbottle. "Chillingham Church, Northumberland: The South Chapel and the Grey Tomb." *Arch Ael*, 5th series, 27 (1999), 123–34. [Grey of Wark, in a fifteenth-century tomb, with modern conservation described, plus a colored plate.]

1720.   Hirst, Susan M., David A. Walsh, and Susan M. Wright. "A Grotesque Corbel Head from Bordley Abbey." *Antiq J* 76 (1996), 248–54. [Around 1400: a double-tongued head and an allusion by Lydgate to double-tongued deception.]

1720A.   Hislop, Malcolm J. B. "The Date of the Warkworth Donjon." *Arch Ael*, 5th series, 19 (1991), 79–92. [From the turn of the fifteenth century.]

1721.   ————. "John of Gaunt's Building Works at Dunstan-burgh Castle." *Arch Ael*, 5th series, 23 (1995), 139–44. [Exceptionally good documentation from when the castle was strengthened and made more liveable.]

1722.   ————. "Lumley Castle, Its Antecedents and Its Architec-ture." *Arch Ael*, 5th series, 24 (1996), 83–98. [Unusually regular design for a fifteenth-century castle; ecclesias-tical influences, some Neville projects, and Scrope's castle at Wensley. John Leuyn was the architect?]

1723.   ————, with appendix by Anne Hislop. "Bolton Castle and the Practice of Architecture in the Middle Ages." *JBAA* 149 (1996), 10–22. [An indenture of the 1380s reveals the world of master masons (indenture in Latin and English, ed. and trans. Anne Hislop).]

1724.   ————. "John Lewyn of Durham: A North Country Master Mason of the Fourteenth Century." *JBAA* 151 (1998), 170–89. [An influential figure, with a hand in many buildings—some of dissimilar style: Raby Castle, Bolton Castle, etc.]

1725. Hlavackova, Hana. "The Bible of Wenceslaus IV in the Context of Court Culture." In item 44. Pp. 223–31. [If we move the date up it may be a work with considerable influence on English work.]

1726. Homer, Ronald F. "Exeter Pewterers from the Fourteenth Century to about 1750." *Devon* 127 (1995), 57–79. [To p. 61, to cover pre-sixteenth-century production; pp. 74–75 for a list of early pewterers.]

1727. Hughes, Andrew. "British Rhymed Offices: A Catalogue and Commentary." See item 1710. Pp. 239–84.

1728. Hutchinson, Michael. "Edward IV's Bulwark: Excavation at Tower Hill, London, 1985." *London and Middlesex* 47 (1996), 103–44. [Finds of the dig reported by Helen Rees, vessels by R. Sewart and Michael Heyworth, building material by Susan Degnan, waste material by R. Sewart, and ivory and bone artifacts by Lyn Blackmore.]

1729. James, Susan E. "Parr Memorials in Kendal Parish Church." *Cumberland* 92 (1992), 99–103. [Tomb now gone, windows broken by Roundheads.]

1730. Jones, Malcolm, and Charles Tracy. "A Medieval Choir-stall Desk-End at Haddon Hall: The Fox-Bishop and the Geese-Hangman." *JBAA* 144 (1991), 107–15. [Probably mid-fourteenth century; early example of a fox as a bishop, with an uncertain vernacular inscription.]

1731. Jones-Baker, Doris. "Makers' Marks Engraved in Graffito on English Medieval and Post-Medieval Tombs and Other Funeral Monuments." *Antiq J* 76 (1996), 254–57. [Not many; some fifteenth- and sixteenth-century examples of a topic worthy of further study.]

1732. Keen, Laurence, and Thomas Cocke, eds. *Medieval Art and Architecture at Salisbury*. BAA, Conference

Transaction 19 (1997). [See item 954 for more about these volumes.]

1733. Kelly, Francis, ed. *Medieval Art and Architecture at Exeter Cathedral*. BAA, Conference Transaction 11 (1991). [See item 954.]

1734. Kemp, Brian. "English Church Monuments during the Period of the Hundred Years War." In item 28. Pp. 195–211. [Monuments to the dead; effigies, styles, heraldry, a few cadavers.]

1735. Keyte, Hugh, and Andrew Barratt, eds., with Clifford Bartlett, associate editor. *The New Oxford Book of Carols*. Oxford 1992 (repr. 1994, with corrections). [Pp. 2–70 on the Middle Ages; pp. 71–150 on English carols, 1400–1700.]

1736. King, Donald. "Types of Silk Cloth Used in England, 1200–1500." In *La Seta in Europe, secc. xiii–xx, atti della 'Ventiquattresimo Settimana di Studi, 1992*. Prato, 1993. Pp. 457–64.

1737. Leedy, Walter. "King's College, Cambridge: Observations on its Context and Foundation." In item 35. Pp. 209–17. [Growth, why choices about building and style were made, some contemporary comments; the chosen site posed difficulties from the start.]

1738. Liddy, Christian. "The Palmer's Guild Window, St Lawrence's Church, Ludlow: A Study of the Construction of Guild Identity in Medieval Stained Glass." *Shropshire* 72 (1997), 26–27. [The guild depicted Edward the Confessor as a palmer in a fifteenth-century window.]

1739. Lindley, Phillip. "'Una grande opera al mio se': Gilt-Bronze Effigies in England from the Middle Ages to the Renaissance." *JBAA* 143 (1990), 112–30. [Especially Margaret Beaufort, Henry VII, and Richard, Earl of Warwick; Torrigiano's innovation.]

1740.   ———. *Gothic to Renaissance: Essays on Sculpture in England*. Stamford, 1995. [Essays on "The English Sculpture in the Middle Ages" (pp. 1–30) and "Two Late-Medieval Statues at Eton College" (pp. 156–69) are relevant among Lindley's collected papers.]

1741.   ———. "Absolutism and Regal Image in Ricardian Sculpture." In item 44. Pp. 60–83. [Reflecting a unified view of exalted kingship; styles, materials, comparisons with Westminster Hall.]

1742.   Mahoney, Dhira B. "Courtly Presentation and Authorial Self-Fashioning: Frontispiece Miniatures in Late Medieval French and English Manuscripts." *Mediaevalia* 21/1 (1996), 97–160. [Depicted events may have been fictitious but were stock expressions of humility and inadequacy.]

1743.   Marcombe, David. "The Bishop's Works: The Building Schemes of John Russell, Bishop of Lincoln, 1480–94." *East Midland Historian* 5 (1995), 14–26. [His palace at Buckden, Hunts., and his chantry at Lincoln Cathedral.]

1744.   Marks, Richard. *Stained Glass in England during the Middle Ages*. London and Toronto (and Buffalo), 1993. [Covers donors, techniques, and iconography (pp. 3–102), the international style between 1350–1450 (pp. 166–89), and "The End of the Middle Ages" (pp. 190–204).]

1745.   ———. "Two Illuminated Guild Registers from Bedfordshire." In *Illuminating the Book: Makers and Interpreters: Essays in Honour of Janet Backhouse*. Edited by Michelle P. Brown and Scot McKendrick. London and Toronto, 1998. Pp. 120–41. [Luton Holy Trinity in 1475 and a Dunstable cartulary of the early sixteenth century. A Backhouse bibliography, pp. 299–305. See also item 1814.]

1746.   ———. *The Medieval Stained Glass of Northampton*. British Academy: Corpus Vitrearum Medii Aevi of Great Britain, Summary Catalogue 4 (1998). [Alphabetically by churches; general introduction on themes: the biggest church is Stamford on Avon (95 pages of coverage).]

1747.   Martindale, Andrew. "The Wall-Paintings in the Chapel of Eton College." In item 8. Pp. 133–52. [Tale of an empress and the Virgin, compared with Flemish work.]

1748.   Marx, C. W. "British Library Harley Ms 1740 and Popular Decoration." In item 81. Pp. 207–22. [A manual of private/popular devotion with an English text.]

1749.   McKendrick, Scot. "Tapestries from the Low Countries in England during the Fifteenth Century." In item 8. Pp. 43–60. [Used and new goods, though many are hard to trace and identify.]

1750.   Milner, Lesley. "Warkworth Keep, Northumberland: A Reassessment of Its Plan and Date." In item 35. Pp. 219–28. [Probably much of the work was from the 1470s and 1480s, and a good deal was new work, not just additions piled atop the old.]

1751.   Milsom, John. "Music." In item 53. Pp. 541–54. [Polyphony and plainchant, both foreign and domestic.]

1752.   Mitchell, M. A. "English Illumination, c. 1190–1450: A Survey from Documentary Sources." *English Manuscript Studies* 4 (1993), 62–113. [Who and when, from which manuscripts do we draw conclusions; with a list of illuminations and documents (and their location).]

1753.   Monks, Peter R. "The Bedford Master's Chief Associate Illustrates Gerson." *Parergon*, n.s. 8/1 (June 1990), 47–56. [Individual touches on conventional themes; mainly French work.]

1754.   Monnas, Lisa. "Opus Anglicanum and Renaissance Velvet: The Whalley Abbey Vestments." *Textile History* 25/1 (Spring, 1994), 3–27. [Vestments probably 1415–30; compared with Italian work, with a look at velvet weaving techniques.]

1755.   ———. "Fit for a King: Figured Silks Shown in the
        Wilton Diptych." In item 44. Pp. 164–77. [Cloth of gold,
        Italian silk, etc.; clothes depicted conform to what
        royalty really wore.]

1756.   Moore, Bruce. "Wild Men in the Misericords of St Mary's
        Church, Beverley." *YAJ* 64 (1992), 135–43. [Twenty-
        three misericords, c. 1445; was the wild man a "positive"
        or "negative" creature?]

1757.   Morgan, Nigel. "The Significance of the Banner in the
        Wilton Diptych." In item 44. Pp. 178–88. [The banner
        signifies the king and "his" nation.]

1758.   ———. "The Coronation of the Virgin by the Trinity and
        Other Texts and Images of Glorification of Mary in
        Fifteenth-Century England." In item 81. Pp. 223–41.
        [Traces the scene through various depictions.]

1759.   Munby, Julian. "Manorial Building in Timber in Central
        and Southern England, 1200–1550." In *Manorial
        Domestic Buildings in England and Northern France.*
        Edited by Gwyn Meirion-Jones and Michael Jones.
        Society of Antiquaries, Occasional Papers 15. London,
        1993. Pp. 49–64. [The different styles, with an eye on
        geographical diversity or variation.]

1760.   Murray, Hugh. "The Scrope Tapestries." *YAJ* 64 (1992),
        145–56. [Some fifteenth-century heraldry and iconog-
        raphy in tapestries that probably hung for centuries.]

1761.   Newman, John. "A Late Medieval Jewellery and Coin
        Hoard from Holbrook." *Suffolk* 38/2 (1994), 193–95.
        [Unusual to find coins (half angles of Edward IV), and
        jewels (silver ring brooches) buried together.]

1762.   Nichols, Ann E. *Seeable Signs: The Iconography of the
        Seven Sacraments, 1350–1544.* Woodbridge, 1994.
        [Drawing largely on the evidence of East Anglian fonts.]

1763.   Nilson, Ben. "A Reinterpretation of the St William
         Window in York Minster." *YAJ* 68 (1996), 157–79.
         [Reconstruction of the original (and proper) order, with a
         more logical color pattern, resulting in a clarification of
         the narrative and the iconography; see also item 1695.]

1764.   Norris, Malcolm. "The Analysis of Style in Monumental
         Brasses." In item 12. Pp. 103–31. [Types, between 1273
         and 1630, by places and series.]

1765.   Oosterwijk, Sophie. "Lost, Found, and Lost Again? The
         Continuing Enigma of the Gisborough Priory Effigies."
         JBAA 151 (1998), 190–202. [Of William, IV Lord
         Latimer? New excavations help untangle the tale of
         important but fragmentary figures.]

1766.   Orr, Michael T. "Illustration as Preface and Postscript in
         the Hours of the Virgin of Trinity College Ms. B. 11.7."
         Gesta 34/2 (1995), 162–76. [Mixing the Virgin and the
         Passion.]

1767.   Page-Phillips, John. "Palimpsests—Re-Used Brasses." In
         item 12. Pp. 132–45. [How, why, and to what end.]

1768.   Pearson, Sarah. *The Medieval Houses of Kent: An His-
         torical Analysis.* HMSO and RCHM, 1994. [Chapter 6:
         distribution maps, construction techniques, "demise of
         the open hall" and a list of houses.]

1769.   Pearson, Sarah, and A. T. Adams. *A Gazetteer of
         Medieval Houses in Kent.* HMSO: RCHM, 1994. [Town
         by town, with diagrams and floor plans.]

1770.   Penoyre, Jane. "Medieval Somerset Roofs." *Vernacular
         Architecture* 29 (1998), pp. 22–32. [Progressive develop-
         ment, with many fourteenth- or fifteenth-century
         examples.]

1771.   Peters, Christine. "A Sacred or Royal Marriage? The
         Identification of Fifteenth-Century Stained Glass from
         Great Rollright." *Oxon* 57 (1992), 354–58. [Now in the

Bodleian; maybe it depicts Henry VI and Margaret of Anjou at their wedding.]

1772.   Platt, Colin. *The Architecture of Medieval Britain: A Social History.* New Haven and London, 1990. [Architecture as a window into social values, with many photographs (by Anthony Kersting) and attention to late medieval contributions.]

1773.   Rehm, Ulrich. "'Ascende lumen sensibus:' Illustrations of the Sherborne Missal Interpreting Pentecost." *Word and Image* 10/3 (1994), 230–61. [How to depict the mystical when combined with the ceremonial.]

1774.   Reilly, Lisa A. *An Architectural History of Peterborough Cathedral.* Oxford, 1997. [Chapter 6 covers "Later Medieval Additions," pp. 112–25.]

1775.   Reynolds, Catherine. "English Patrons and French Artists in Fifteenth-Century Normandy." In item 10. Pp. 299–313. [With reference to a Reading University manuscript and the attractions of the English art market.]

1776.   Richmond, Colin F. "The Visual Culture of Fifteenth-Century England." In item 76. Pp. 186–209. [The contemporary interest in acquiring art in many forms.]

1777.   ———. "A Drawing of a 15th-Century Rector of Halesworth." *Suffolk* 38/4 (1996), 455–56. [Walter of Halesworth, d. 1465, as sketched in Nicholas Greenhagh's account book.]

1778.   Roberts, Edward. "A Fifteenth-Century Inn at Andover." *Hampshire* 47 (1991), 153–70. [Contract to build for Winchester College, 1455; contract published, building's history traced.]

1779.   ———. "William of Wykeham's House at East Meon, Hants." *Arch J* 150 (1993), 456–81. [Not completed until Henry Beaufort, 1430s.]

1780. Robinson, Paul. "A Medieval Heraldic Roundel from Potterne." *Wiltshire* 89 (1996), 136–38. [Arms of bishop Hallum.]

1781. Rodwell, K. A. "A Structural Analysis of the Chantry, Bridport, Dorset." *Med Arch* 34 (1990), 122–43. [An earlier municipal building converted to a chantry priest's house: originally, two rooms per floor, three stories.]

1782. Rogers, Nicholas. "The Artist of Trinity B. 11.7 and his Patrons." In item 81. Pp. 170–86. [Descriptions of the manuscript's contents and iconography.]

1783. ———. "Brasses in their Art-historical Context." In item 12. Pp. 146–59. [A survey of styles and of the medium's potential for depiction and craftwork.]

1784. ———. "Monuments to Monks and Monastic Servants." In item 93. Pp. 262–76. [Who, and where in the church.]

1785. Routh, Pauline S. "Lionel, Lord Welles and His Methley Monument." *YAJ* 63 (1991), 77–83. [Alabaster monument from a midland workshop, with wife's effigy well done but now badly mutilated.]

1786. Routh, Pauline S., and Richard Knowles. "The Markenfield Collar." *YAJ* 62 (1990), 133–40. [Worn by Sir Thomas Markenfield, in Ripon; a park paling, with stag couchant and with similarities to a Neville collar depicted in a book of hours.]

1787. Roy, Ashok. "The Technique of the Wilton Diptych." In item 44. Pp. 125–35. [How it was painted; the paints and pigments.]

1788. Ryder, Peter, with photography by Paul Gwilliams. *Medieval Churches in West Yorkshire.* West Yorkshire Archaeological Service, Wakefield, 1993. [Chapters 6 and 7 (pp. 47–78) cover our years.]

1789.   Sandler, Lucy Freeman. "The Wilton Diptych and Images of Devotion in Illuminated Manuscripts." In item 44. Pp. 136–54. [Models and precedents for the depiction of worshiped and worshipers.]

1790.   Scheifele, Eleanore. "Richard II and the Visual Arts." In item 43. Pp. 255–71. [Richard's predilection for personal symbolism.]

1791.   Scott, Kathleen L. "The Illustrations and Decoration of Manuscripts of Nicholas Love's *Mirror of the Blessed Life of Jesus Christ.*" See item 1566. Pp. 61–80. [Fifty-six manuscripts—half of them illuminated—together with two illuminated miniatures, all in a distinctively English style; with ten black-and-white plates.

1792.   ———. "Two Sequences of Dated Illuminated Manuscripts Made in Oxford, 1450–64." In item 22. Pp. 43–69. [Merton and Balliol manuscripts, with datable hands and limners.]

1793.   ———. "Limning and Book-Production in Terms of Signs *in situ* in Late-Medieval English Manuscripts: A First Listing." In item 11. Pp. 142–88. [A look at and discussion of signs, terms, etc., with seventeen plates.]

1794.   ———. *Later Gothic Manuscripts, 1390–1460.* 2 vols. London, 1996. [Volume 6 of "A Survey of Illuminated Manuscripts in the British Isles, general editor J. J. G. Alexander. Vol. 1, Text and Illustrations (in line with Eric Millar's 1928 *English Illuminated Manuscripts*), with 505 black-and-white illustrations: vol. 2, Catalogue and Indexes, with a description of 140 manuscripts, scholarly literature, glossary, table of subjects depicted in Psalter cycles, 1400–1500, etc.]

1795.   Sekules, Veronica. "The Gothic Sculpture." In item 6. Pp. 197–209.

1796.   Smith, J. T. *English Houses, 1200–1800: The Hertfordshire Evidence.* HMSO, London, 1992. [Pp. 12–45 cover the medieval manor house and late medieval vernacular houses in the countryside.]

1797.   Smith, Julie A. "An Image of a Preaching Bishop in Late Medieval England: The 1498 Woodcut Portrait of Bishop John Alcock." *Viator* 21 (1990), 301–22. [With seventeen illustrations; Pynson published the sermon with illustrations chosen to magnify Alcock's role.]

1798.   Stocker, David. "'A Very goodly House Longging to sutton . . .': A Reconstruction of 'John of Gaunt's Palace', Lincoln." *Lincolnshire* 34 (1999), 5–15. [Probably a late fourteenth-century merchant's house; medieval features still evident.]

1799.   Stopford, John, and Susan M. Wright. "A Group of Late Medieval Inscribed Tiles from Bordesley Abbey." *Antiq J* 78 (1998), 307–22. [Locally made in the sgraffiato technique.]

1800.   Stratford, Jenny. *The Bedford Inventories: The Worldly Goods of John, Duke of Bedford, Regent of France (1389–1435)*. Society of Antiquaries, London, 1993. [Lavish scholarly book; items treated by genre, looking at Bedford as a patron; three inventories from the PRO; biographical appendices.]

1801.   Sullivan, R. W. "The Wilton Diptych: Mysteries, Majesty and A Complex Exchange of Faith and Power." *Gazette des Beaux-Arts* 129 (1997). [Royal iconography merging with religious as well as political symbolism.]

1802.   Sutton, Anne F., and Livia Visser-Fuchs. *The Hours of Richard III*. Stroud, 1990, for the Richard III and Yorkist History Trust. [Books, manuscripts, lay piety, and patronage.]

1803.   ———. "The Cult of Angels in Late Fifteenth-Century England: An Hours of the Guardian Angel Presented to

Queen Elizabeth Woodville." In *Women and the Book: Assessing the Visual Evidence*. Edited by Lesley Smith and Jane H. M. Taylor. London and Toronto, 1996. Pp. 230–65. [A presentation scene to Elizabeth; text of "Hours of the Guardian Angel" described and explained.]

1804.   ———. "Richard III and the Knave of Cards: An Illuminator's Model in Manuscript and Print, 1440s to 1990s." *Antiq J* 79 (1999), 257–99. [A "Richard III portrait" in a manuscript of Edward IV, and the tradition of a royal depiction. An eighteenth-century yarn, traced and debunked.]

1805.   Tatton-Brown, Tim. "The Medieval Fabric." See item 1271. Pp. 25–46. [Most building completed by 1377.]

1806.   ———. "The Church of St. Thomas of Canterbury, Salisbury." *Wiltshire* 90 (1997), 101–09. [Present building began in fifteenth century; the tower replaces one that fell in 1448.]

1807.   Taylour, C., P. Everson, and R. Wilson-North. "Bodiam Castle, Sussex." *Medieval Archaeology* 34 (1990), 155–57. [A survey of earthworks.]

1809.   Thompson, Michael. *The Medieval Hall: The Basis of Secular Domestic Life, 600–1600*. Aldershot, 1995. [A general survey; pp. 99–175 look at late medieval developments; well illustrated to show changes, variations in size and grandeur.]

1810.   Tracy, Charles. *English Gothic Choir Stalls, 1400–1540*. Woodbridge, 1990. [A collection of essays, mostly of case studies: Norwich, Bristol, Sefton, etc., with more than two hundred illustrations.]

1811.   ———. "The St. Albans Abbey Watching Chamber: A Reassessment." *JBAA* 145 (1992), 104–11. [Built c. 1400, of wood.]

1812.   ———. "Choir Stalls from the 14th century: Whitefriars
         Church in Coventry." *JBAA* 150 (1997), 76–95. [Late
         fourteenth century. Some good misericords, some
         heraldry. Appendix on misericords, with notes on the
         heraldry by John A. Goodall.]

1813.   Tudor Craig, Pamela. "The Wilton Diptych in the Con-
         text of Contemporary English Panel and Wall Painting."
         In item 44. Pp. 207–22. [Mostly with church painting, a
         few with manuscripts]

1814.   ———. "The 'Large Letters' of the Litlington Missal and
         Westminster Abbey in 1383–84." See item 1745. Pp. 102–
         19. [Linking the illuminations to the abbey's architecture
         and as a guide to the objects chosen for depiction.]

1815.   Vale, Malcolm. "Cardinal Henry Beaufort and the
         'Albergati Portrait'." *EHR* 105 (1990), 337–54. [A Van
         Eyk portrait in Vienna; if not Albergati, perhaps of
         Beaufort? But no certainty.]

1816.   Walker, Helen. "Pottery from a Possible Late Medieval
         Kiln Dump at 77 High Road, Rayleigh." *Essex* 21 (1996),
         92–102. [No sign of a kiln but fourteenth- and fifteenth-
         century shards argue for its existence.]

1817.   Wathey, Andrew. "John of Gaunt, John Pycard and the
         Amiens Negotiations of 1392." In item 8. Pp. 29–42.
         [Mostly about the way a diplomat introduced new music
         into England.]

1818.   Watson, Bruce. "A Late Medieval Sword from Benge-
         worth." *Worcestershire* 14 (1994), 239–40. [Perhaps
         jettisoned in the flight from Tewkesbury.]

1819.   Wayment, Hilary. "10 Carmelite Roundels at Queens'
         College, Cambridge." *CAS* 82 (1993), 139–56. [Individ-
         ualized portraits.]

1820.   Whitehead, David, ed. *Medieval Art, Architecture and Archaeology at Hereford*. BAA, Conference Transaction 15 (1995). See item 954.

1821.   Whittick, Christopher. "Dallingridge's Bay and Bodiam Castle Millpond." *Sussex* 131 (1993), 119–23. [Medieval landscaping, with contracts of 1385; Bodiam was an ambitious project from the start.]

1822.   Wilson, Christopher. "The Medieval Monuments." In item 27. Pp. 451–510. [Many late medieval monuments: royalty, aristocracy, the priors, and the general upper class public.]

1823.   ———. "Rulers, Artificers and Shoppers: Richard II's Remodelling of Westminster Hall, 1393–99." In item 44. Pp. 33–59. [A huge project, even when just "recycled" to fit into the agenda of sacral kingship.]

1824.   Woodman, Francis. "Hundley, Norfolk, and the Re-building of Its Chancel." In *Studies in Medieval Art and Architecture Presented to Peter Lasko*. Edited by David Buckton and T. A. Heslop. British Museum, London, and Stroud, 1994. Pp. 203–10. [Fancy new fifteenth-century chancel, under patronage of the Great Hospital.]

1825.   ———. "The Gothic Campaigns." In item 6. Pp. 158–96. [From the 1250s on.]

1826.   Wright, Sylvia. "The Author Portraits in the Bedford Psalter-Hours: Gower, Chaucer and Hoccleve." *British Library Journal* 18 (1992), 190–201. [290 contemporary portraits, in the initial letters; many of Gower, some of Chaucer.]

1827.   ———. "The *Gesta Henrici Quinti* and the Bedford Psalter-Hours." See item 1501. Pp. 267–85. [Contemporary author portraits in large numbers.]

XII. BETTER LATE THAN NEVER[4]

1828.   Ainsworth, Peter. "Froissardian Perspectives on Late
         Fourteenth-Century Society." In item 29. Pp. 56–73. [ch.
         vi.]

1829.   Allen, Rosamund S. "John Gower and Southwark: The
         Paradox of 'The Social Self'." In *London and Europe in
         the Later Middle Ages.* Edited by Julia Boffey and
         Pamela King. Centre for Medieval and Renaissance
         Studies, Queen Mary and Westfield College, University
         of London, London, 1995. Pp. 111–47. [The suburb, as
         Gower knew it, and how it figures in his writing; ch. vii;
         see also items 1860 and 1867.]

1830.   Badham, Sally F. "Richard Gough's Papers Relating to
         Monumental Brasses in the Bodleian Library, Oxford."
         MBS 14, part 6 (1991), 467–512. [The author of *Sepul-
         chral Monuments* (d. 1809). His papers tell of many late

---

[4] Because of the time needed to alphabetize, cross-reference, and index there came
a day when I had to draw a line on adding entries in their proper place (i.e., in the
appropriate chapter). However, since that day of decision many items have come to
my attention: some through late discovery, some through an earlier decision to omit
that I subsequently reversed, and some simply because of the disorder that is in-
herent in this kind of work. In this chapter the entries are alphabetized, by author,
but I indicate at the end of each entry the chapter in which the entry *should* have
appeared, had I invariably been on my toes, and these references are given in lower
case roman numerals to avoid confusion with citations within the entry.

medieval monuments, with a list by places (and by
counties): ch. xi.]

1831.   ———. "Status and Salvation: The Design of Medieval
English Brasses and Incised Slabs." *MBS* 15, part 5
(1996), 413–65. [A full discussion of styles, family
traditions, individual attributes, imagery of salvation,
resurrection imagery, etc.: ch. xi.]

1832.   Badham, Sally F., and H. Martin Stuchfield, with an
appendix by Peter Northover. "A Civilian of c. 1400 in
Private Possession." *MBS* 16 (1999), 207 ff. [The style of
a small brass, with an analysis of its metallography: ch.
xi.]

1833.   Baker, Denise N. "Julian of Norwich and Anchoritic
Literature." *MQ* 19 (1993), 148–60. [Her writing, in the
context of anchoritic work, especially Hilton: ch. ix.]

1834.   Begent, Peter J. *The Most Noble Order of the Garter: Its
History and Ceremonial.* Windsor, for the Dean and
Canons of Windsor Chapel, 1990. [ch. iii; see also item
193.]

1835.   Bent, Margaret. "Pycard's Double Canon: Evidence of
Revision?" In *Sundry Sorts of Music Books: Essays on the
British Library Collection, Presented to O. W. Neighbour
on his 70th Birthday.* Edited by Chris Banks, Arthur
Searle, and Malcolm Turner. British Library, London,
1993. [Late fourteenth-century material, in the Old Hall
Ms., and trying to unravel how Pycard worked: ch. xi.]

1836.   Blamires, Alcuin, with Karen Pratt and C. W. Marx, eds.
*Woman Defamed and Woman Defended; An Anthology of
Medieval Texts.* Oxford, 1992. [Pp. 250–60 for selections
from "The Trial of Walter Brut (1391)," and pp. 260–70
from "Dives and Pauper"; both selections are in the
book's "Responses to Antifeminism" section: ch. vi.]

1837.   Bridbury, Anthony R. *The English Economy from Bede to the Reformation*. Woodbridge, 1992. [Collected papers, mostly the 1960s to the 1980s. Most relevant: "The Black Death," "The Hundred Years War: Costs and Profits," and "English Provincial Towns in the Later Middle Ages" (a reply to S. H. Rigby on the use of lay subsidies to gauge urban economic fortunes: ch. i.]

1838.   Britnell, Richard. "Rochester Bridge, 1381–1530." In *Traffic and Politics: The Construction and Management of Rochester Bridge, AD 43–1993*. Edited by Nigel Yates and James M. Gibson. Rochester Bridge Trust, as part of the Kent History Project, Woodbridge, 1994. Pp. 43–106. [Bridges, income, supplies, maintenance, profits, and administration: ch. vii.]

1839.   Brooks, Nicholas P. "The Bridge from 1066 to the 1380s." See item 1834. Pp. 35–40. [Old bridge was going and the bad winter of 1380–81 finished it: ch. vii.]

1840.   Campbell, Bruce M. S. "The Livestock of Chaucer's Reeve: Fact or Fiction?" In item 30. Pp. 271–305. [ch. viii.]

1841.   Childs, Wendy. "The English Export Trade in Cloth in the Fourteenth Century." In item 20. Pp. 121–47. [ch. v.]

1842.   Corless, Roger J. "Comparing Cataphatic Mystics: Julian of Norwich and T'an-luan." *MQ* 21 (1994), 18–27. [The local girl and a fifth-century Buddhist abbot of the Shanxi region: ch. xi.]

1843.   Craymer, Suzanne L. "Margery Kempe's Imitation of Mary Magdelene and the 'Digby Plays'." *MQ* 19 (1993), 173–81. [Parallels and some borrowing from the drama to "authorize" Margery's mysticism: ch. vi.]

1844.   Cross, Claire. "Origins and University Connections of Yorkshire Religious, 1480–1540." In item 13. Pp. 271–91. [Tracking families, places of origin, university activities, and looking at women as well as men: ch. ix.]

1845.   Dale, Judith. "'Sin Is Behovely': Art and Theodicy in the
        Julian Text." *MQ* 25 (1999), 127–46. [Arguing for two
        modes of Julian's discourse: ch. ix.]

1846.   Dixon, Philip. "Mota Aula et Turris: The Manor-Houses
        of the Anglo-Scottish Border." See item 1759. Pp. 27–38.
        [Stages of development and building: ch. xi.]

1847.   Dyer, Christopher. "How Urban Was Medieval England?"
        History Today 45 (January 1994), 34–43. [ch. vii.]

1848.   ———. "Piers Plowman and Plowmen: A Historical Per-
        spective." *Yearbook of Langland Studies* 8 (1994), 155–76.
        [Deconstructing agricultural labor and labor services, in
        both their literal and metaphorical meanings: ch. viii.]

1849.   Fernie, Eric. "The Building: An Introduction." In item 6.
        Pp. 47–58. [ch. xi.]

1850.   Giry-Deloison, Charles. "On Second Thoughts: France,
        Burgundy, and England." *History Today* 40 (August
        1990), 47–52. [The current historiographical pendulum
        on "foreign affairs": ch. iii.]

1851.   Glasscoe, Marian, ed. *Julian of Norwich's "A Revelation
        of Love."* Exeter, 1993. [To offer the text for classroom
        use as well as scholarly consumption: ch. xi.]

1852.   Goldberg, P. J. P. "Girls Growing Up in Later Medieval
        England." *History Today* 45 (June 1995), 25–32. [A quick
        look at an intriguing subject: ch. vi.]

1853.   Gordon, Dillian. "A New Discovery in the Wilton
        Diptych." *Burlington Magazine* 134 (1992), 662–67. [See
        item 44: ch. xi.]

1854.   Gorlach, Manfred. "Middle English Legends, 1220–1530."
        Hagiographies 1 (1994), 429–85. [ch. ix.]

1855.   Gross, Anthony. "Lancastrians Abroad, 1461–71."
        History Today 42 (August 1992), 31–37. [The strange
        diplomacy of exiles: ch. iii.]

1856.   Hall, David N. "Hemington and Barnwell, Northampton-
        shire: A Study of Two Manors." In item 30. Pp. 341–69.
        [Comparisons and the dynamics of village life: ch. viii.]

1857.   Hanawalt, Barbara A. "Of Good and Ill Repute": Gender
        and Social Control in Medieval England. Oxford, 1998.
        [A collection of essays: six of the eleven were previously
        published, and seven are from the 1990s: ch. v.]

1858.   Hanna, Ralph, III. Pursuing History: Middle English
        Manuscripts and Their Texts. Stanford, Calif., 1996.
        [Chapter 3, "Two Lollard Codices and Lollard Book Pro-
        duction" is pertinent among essays that mostly look at
        literary manuscripts: ch. ix.]

1859.   Harding, Vanessa. "Medieval Documentary Sources for
        London and Paris: A Comparison." See item 1829.
        Pp. 35–54. [Such comparisons are (still) fairly rare:
        ch. vii.]

1860.   Haskett, Timothy S. "Country Lawyers? The Composers
        of English Chancery Bills." In The Life of the Laws: Pro-
        ceedings of the British Legal History Conference, Oxford,
        1991. Edited by Peter Birks. London and Rio Grande,
        Ohio. Pp. 9–23. [To whom were petitions addressed?
        Who wrote them? Who set the standard form?: ch. iv.]

1861.   Hudson, Anne. "Piers Plowman and the Peasants'
        Revolt: A Problem Revisited." Yearbook of Langland
        Studies 8 (1994), 85–106. [Why the Peasants saw the
        poem as a voice on their behalf: ch. viii.]

1862.   Jones, Michael, Trevor Foulds, and Jill Hughes, eds. The
        Nottingham Borough Court Rolls: The Reign of Henry VI
        (1422–57). Transactions of the Thoroton Society of Not-
        tinghamshire, 97 (1993), pp. 74–87. [See also "Une ville
        anglaise et ses rues à la fin du moyen âge à travers ses
        archives méconnues: les Borough Court Rolls de Not-
        tingham (1303–1455), La Rue, lieu de sociabilité?

Rencontres de la Rue." In *Actes du Colloque de Rouen, 16–19 novembre, 1994.* Edited by Alain Lemenorel. Rouen: Publications de L'université de Rouen, no. 214 (1997). Pp. 179–88: ch. vii.]

1863.   Kamerick, Kathleen. "Art and Moral Vision in Angela Foligno and Margery Kempe." *MQ* 21 (1995), 148 ff. [Margery's theology and that of *De Oculo Morali*: ch vi.]

1864.   Lord, Evelyn. "The Cornwell-Leghs of High Legh: Approaches to the Inheritance Patterns of North West England." *BJRUL* 73 (1991), 21–36. [Various patterns were in operation or competition; not easy to say which was typical: ch. iv.]

1865.   MacKay, Angus, ed., with David Ditchburn. *Atlas of the Medieval World.* London and New York, 1997. [For the "Late Middle Ages," pp. 157–243. Maps of the Hundred Years' War, Burgundy, Deserted Villages, 1381 and more; some of the maps are by Michael Jones: ch: ii.]

1866.   McAvoy, Liz H. "'The Moders Service': Motherhood as Matrix in Julian of Norwich." *MQ* 24 (1998), 181–97. [ch. ix.]

1867.   Meale, Carole M. *"The Libelle of Englyshe Polycye* and Mercantile Literary Culture in Late Medieval London." See item 1829. Pp. 181–227. [What the men of this world read and wrote: ch. vii.]

1868.   ———. "Reading Women's Culture in Fifteenth-Century England: The Case of Alice Chaucer." In *Mediaevalitas: Reading the Middle Ages: The J. A. W. Bennett Memorial Lectures, Ninth Series, Perugia, 1995.* Edited by Piero Boitani and Anna Torti. Cambridge, 1996. Pp. 81–101. [With eleven plates: Alice's books, showing an interest in contemporary writing and continental intellectual life, including Christine de Pisan: ch. x.]

1869. Nightingale, Pamela. "The Growth of London in the
       Medieval English Economy." In item 20. Pp. 89–106.
       [ch. vii.]

1870. Olson, Mary. "God's Inappropriate Grace: Images of
       Courtesy in Julian of Norwich's *Showings*." *MQ* 20
       (1994), 47–59. [The importance of the idea and the virtue
       of courtesy, as Christ showed by dying for us: ch. ix.]

1871. Pearce, Judith. "Liturgy and Image: The Advent Minia-
       ture in the Salisbury Breviary." In *Medieval Texts and
       Images: Studies in Manuscripts from the Middle Ages*.
       Edited by Margaret M. Manion and Bernard J. Muir.
       Sydney, 1991. Pp. 25–42. [Early fifteenth-century French
       manuscript, but done for an English patron: ch. xi.]

1872. Peters, Brad. "Julian of Norwich and the Internalized
       Dialogue of Prayer." *MQ* 20 (1994), 122–30. [ch. ix.]

1873. Pollard, Anthony J. "Percies, Nevilles, and the Wars of
       the Roses." *History Today* 43 (September 1993) 42–48.
       [Politics in the North: ch. iii.]

1874. Richmond, Colin F. "Propaganda in the Wars of the
       Roses." *History Today* 42 (July 1991), 12–18. [Selling the
       cause was always a priority: ch. iii.]

1875. Rosser, Gervase. "Sanctuary and Social Negotiations in
       Medieval England." In item 14. Pp. 57–79. [Sacred space
       and many case studies: ch. vi.]

1876. Ruud, Jay. "Nature and Grace in Julian of Norwich."
       MQ 19 (1993), 71–81. [ch. ix.]

1877. Saul, Nigel. "The Fragments of the Golafre Brass in
       Westminster Abbey." *MBS* 15, part 1 (1992), 19–32.
       [Pieces preserved in the muniment room, biography of
       Golafre, with an analysis of the bits and some compar-
       isons of their style: ch. xi.]

1878.   ———. "The Brass of Sir Thomas le Strange at Welles-bourne, Warwickshire: Its Dating and Its Place in the 'E' Series." *MBS* 15, part 3 (1994), 236–48. [E was a fairly new series or style; compared here with other work-shops: ch. xi.]

1879.   ———. "Bodiam Castle." *History Today* 45 (January 1995), 16–21. [A builder's ego trip and/or a monument to posterity? Ch. xi.]

1880.   ———. "Richard II: Author of his Own Downfall?" *History Today* 49 (September 1999), 36–41. [ch. iii.]

1881.   Sprung, Andrew. "'We nevyr shall come out of hym': En-closure and Immanence in Julian of Norwich's Book of Showings." *MQ* 19 (1993), 47–62. [ch. ix.]

1882.   Stokes, Charity Scott. "Margery Kempe: Her Life and the Early History of Her Book." *MQ* 25 (1999), 9–67. [ch. vi.]

1883.   Szarmach, Paul E., M. Teresa Tavormina, and Joel T. Rosenthal, eds.; associate editors Catherine E. Karkov, Peter M. Lefferts, and Elizabeth Parker McLachlan. *Medieval England: An Encyclopedia.* New York and London, 1998. [A lot of information in one large volume: Rosenthal edited the "history" entries: ch. ii.]

1884.   Tamburr, Karl. "Mystic Transformation: Julian's Version of the Harrowing of Hell." *MQ* 20 (1994), 60–67. [ch. ix.]

1885.   Titterton, John E. "The Malyns Family and Their Brasses at Chinnor, Oxon." *MBS* 15, part 3 (1994), 225 ff. [Five generations of family brasses, now on the church walls: ch. xi.]

1886.   Virgoe, Roger. "Estates of Norwich Cathedral Priory, 1101–1538." In item 6. Pp. 339–59. [Keeping ahead of the wolf was never easy, even for a great ecclesiastical establishment: ch. viii.]

1887.   Wright, Laura. "Macaronic Writing in a London Archive, 1380–1480." In *History of Englishes*. Edited by Matti Rissanen, Ossi Ihalainen, Terttu Nevalainen, and Irma Taavitsainen. Berlin, 1994. Pp. 762–70. [London Bridge records, covering the accounts and a style of writing shaped by the accountants: ch. x.]

1888.   Young, Charles R. *The Making of the Neville Family, 1166–1400*. Woodbridge, 1996. [Fairly straight political-biographical: chapters 8 and 9 (pp. 125–49) cover the late fourteenth century and the kingmaker: ch. iii.]

INDEX OF AUTHORS AND EDITORS

Medieval Institute Publications is a program
of The Medieval Institute, College of Arts
and Sciences, Western Michigan University

Typeset in 10 pt. Century Schoolbook
with Century Schoolbook display
Composed by Juleen Audrey Eichinger
for Medieval Institute Publications
Manufactured by Thomson-Shore, Inc.—Dexter, Michigan

Medieval Institute Publications
College of Arts and Sciences
Western Michigan University
1903 W. Michigan Avenue
Kalamazoo, Michigan 49008-5432
www.wmich.edu/medieval/mip/

 WESTERN MICHIGAN UNIVERSITY